Motoring and the Mighty

RICHARD GARRETT

Motoring and the Mighty

STANLEY PAUL LONDON

STANLEY PAUL & CO LTD
3 Fitzroy Square, London W1

AN IMPRINT OF THE HUTCHINSON GROUP

London Melbourne Sydney Auckland
Wellington Johannesburg Cape Town
and agencies throughout the world

First published 1971

*This book has been set in Imprint type, printed in Great Britain
on antique wove paper by Anchor Press, and
bound by Wm. Brendon, both of Tiptree, Essex*

ISBN 0 09 109070 9

For Patrick Lynch
Michael Scott
Rosemary Dennington
— without whom many things would be impossible

Contents

Introduction   **xi**

  1   Requiem for Obsolescent Horses   1

  2   The Carriage Trade   12

  3   Early Royal   21

  4   The Emperor's Automobiles   34

  5   The Mysteries of Sarajevo   41

  6   The War Game   50

  7   Russian Roulette   59

  8   A Cockade of Chauffeurs   69

  9   The Indian Car Trick   81

10   Life and Death on Two Wheels   94

viii   *Contents*

11   Sporting Gentlemen   101

12   Under Tragic Circumstances   117

13   Cars for the Kings   125

14   The Assassin   133

15   The Loyal Servant   138

16   Naval and Military   152

17   Show Business on Wheels   168

18   Status Symbols   180

19   Top People   191

20   The Presidential Passenger   202

Index   215

Illustrations

Between pages 28 and 29
The Sultan of Morocco's canopy-topped Daimler
King Edward VII and Hon. John Scott Montagu in the
 latter's Daimler
Prince Henry of Prussia
The Czar of Russia—a Delaunay–Belleville enthusiast
The German Kaiser had a special vehicle equipped with a bed
King Ferdinand of Bulgaria in his Mercedes 16/45
The Panhard and Levassor used by President Fallières in 1913

Between pages 60 and 61
Archduke Franz Ferdinand of Austria and his wife
Franz Ferdinand and his wife shortly before the assassination
Queen Mary in a half-tracked Citroën.
King Alfonso XIII of Spain
The Sultan of Morocco in a 14 h.p. Panhard with his son
 Prince Moulay Hassan
The special tiger-spotters' cars of the rajahs
The swan-like car

Between pages 92 and 93
King George V's fleet of Daimlers

King George V and Queen Mary in a Daimler
Crown Prince Hirohito of Japan and his Panhard and Levassor
Crown Prince Hirohito's bullet-proof Mercedes
King George VI was a Lanchester enthusiast
Lenin's Rolls-Royce
The assassination of King Alexander of Yugoslavia in 1934

Between pages 124 and 125
Hitler in his Mercedes
Field Marshal Montgomery used a Humber, and, later, a
    Rolls-Royce during the war and later a Daimler
General Alexander's Ford
General de Gaulle's Citroën
King Hussein's very fast Mercedes
Nubar Gulbenkian's car with the chassis of a London taxi
Earl Mountbatten's former car, a Rolls-Royce

Between pages 156 and 157
Gary Cooper's 300S Mercedes
Errol Flynn's Mercedes 300 Cabriolet
Pope Pius XI owned this Mercedes 'Nuburg'
Pope John XXIII at the consecration of a new Mercedes in
    Rome, 1960
King George VI in an ancient Daimler
Henry Ford in his quadricycle
The first of the 'Docker Daimlers'

Between pages 188 and 189
The assassination of President Kennedy
The Marquess of Exeter's famous artificial hip-joint
Princess Anne in her Scimitar
H.M. The Queen and Prince Philip on one of their less formal
    motoring occasions
After fifty years of Daimlers, the present Royal Family went
    over to Rolls-Royces
The U.S.A. President's specially constructed Lincoln Continental
    Executive Limousine

Introduction

I had this idea to write a history of motoring as it has featured in the lives of a number of famous men and women. I wasn't sure how it would turn out. In the beginning, I thought, perhaps, there might be an atmosphere of comedy about it. As my research progressed, however, I found that I was discovering rather a lot of tragedy, and the story saddened me. I was, indeed, amazed at the amount of drama which has taken place in motor cars.

At first, it seemed to be necessary to define what qualifications were necessary for a man or a woman to be included in my collection. I jotted down such words as 'Royals' and 'Dictators' and 'Presidents' and 'Millionaires', and then I threw the list away.

It seemed best to go where the action was and the anecdotes bloomed, and to take people as they came.

Nevertheless, this book, in some ways, is a reaction against the swarm of motoring as it is today: against traffic jams and little processions which crawl along country roads at 30 m.p.h.; against overcrowded car parks and shoppers who overload urban streets on wet Saturday afternoons; against those sad lost Sundays spent slogging down to the coast and back in a metallic herd of vehicles, and the awful alikeness of the anonymous millions of cars which clutter the roads.

Once I thought it was going to be a history of motoring written especially for snobs, but now I don't think it is. It is the story of some remarkable people and some glamorous cars and some strange occasions. I have tried to make it as accurate as possible, though I am afraid that there must be some mistakes. The past seldom delivers its evidence neatly packaged and with all the facts intact.

Many people have assisted me. I would like to give especial acknowledgement to the work done by Commander Robin Bousfield, R.N., who helped me with the research, and whose death came with tragic suddenness before the book was completed.

I should also like to thank the following for their ready and patient assistance:

Mr. Hermann Ahrens, Mr. E. A. Bellamy (of the Montagu Motoring Museum's Library), Mr. P. L. Boxhall, Marquess Camden, Mr. S. C. H. Davis, Mr. G. W. Dench, Baron Philippe de Rothschild, Miss Rosemary Dennington (who typed the manuscript), Sir John Dring, Richard von Frankenberg, Mr. Nigel Guinness, Mr. M. A. Hashmi, Mrs. Thora Hornung, Mr. W. Housden, Mr. T. H. Kelly (of the *Daily Mail* Library), Mr. Erich Kemptka, Mr. Bernard Lee, Mr. Walter McNally, Sir Gerald Nabarro, Mr. Percy G. Parker, Mr. W. H. Pratchett, Sir Ralph Richardson, Mr. Osmond Rivers, Mr. Bruce Ropner, Mr. James J. Rowley and Mr. John W. Warner (both of the United States Secret Service), the O.C. 20 Squadron R.T.C., Dr. Alfred Schüler, Mr. Rolf Whetherich, Mr. A. J. A. Whyte (of Jaguar Cars Ltd.), Mr. D. E. A. Miller-Williams (of Rolls-Royce), Mr. B. G. Wilson (of the Ministry of Public Building and Works), Mr. T. Woodruff, my wife (who went over the manuscript for me when it was still in a very raw state), and to many other people who, in one way or another, helped to make it possible.

The extracts from Royal correspondence on pages 25 and 28 are reproduced by gracious permission of Her Majesty the Queen.

The extracts from Ian Fleming's *On Her Majesty's Secret Service*, which appear on pages 152 and 153, are published by permission of Gildrose Productions Ltd. and Jonathan Cape Ltd. The excerpt from *The Life of Ian Fleming* by John Pearson on page 153 also appears by permission of Jonathan Cape Ltd.

R.G.

Tunbridge Wells
1971

1   *Requiem for Obsolescent Horses*

It would be interesting to know why the early motorists in Britain were so persecuted by the law. Did people really love horses as much as that? Cars were certainly noisy and they stank, but was that a justification for putting such severe restrictions on their use? The original speed limit of four miles an hour in towns, and two in the country, was just sloppy thinking. The authorities had linked the car with traction engines, which, in any case, weren't capable of going very much faster.

The real irony, the ultimate mockery, was the ill-described Emancipation Act of 1896. It raised the limit to twelve miles an hour in towns (fourteen in the country), and did away with the unnecessary man who was supposed to precede the vehicle on foot. His purpose had been to soothe frightened horses, but the horses had already shown that they did not need to be soothed.

Nobody, not even the police, had paid very much attention to the earlier regulations—they were too stupid to be taken seriously. The new act was an entirely different matter. It meant that the law-makers had at last acknowledged that a motor car *was* different to a traction engine, and that, having done so, they proposed to make its use as difficult as possible.

Emancipation! The word was nonsense.

Not that such an attitude was altogether peculiar to Britain, though the authorities elsewhere seem to have been more tractable. For example, in 1893, seven years after Gottlieb Daimler and Karl Benz had produced their first cars, the government of the Grand Duchy of Baden in Germany suddenly had misgivings.

Benz was sitting at his desk one day, going through the mail, when he noticed a communication from the Minister of the Interior. It set down a number of conditions which had to be observed by motor vehicles travelling on public roads. It stipulated that, on the open highway, they should not exceed 7·5 miles an hour. When they were in towns, or going round sharp corners, 3·25 miles an hour was the limit. And if they met 'carts, dray animals or saddle horses' they had, if that were possible, to reduce their speed even more.

The document increased in menace as it went on. The minister took pains to point out that these regulations were only temporary. If, for any reason at all, it seemed desirable, still harsher rules would be enforced. It might even be that permission to drive automobiles would be taken away altogether.

Such words were scarcely music to the ears of Benz, who had spent many years of toil and frustration developing internal combustion engines and devising cars to put them in. He grabbed his pen and immediately wrote a polite but nevertheless sharp letter to the minister, pointing out why these steps were unnecessary. After the usual wrangle, he seems to have got his way. At any rate, the restrictions were eased and presently forgotten about.

In Britain a strong Labour lobby might have accounted for the harsh legislation. In the opinion of Alfred Harmsworth (later to become Lord Northcliffe), the poor were the real opponents of cars. They had nothing to gain from them, and they might appear to be symbols of all the things they lacked. Socialism has always been a puritan creed; these frivolous contraptions of the well-to-do may have seemed to be another smack in the eye for the underdog. In Harmsworth's opinion, working-class opposition would continue until motor buses were built. After that, the under-privileged would join hands with the over-privileged, and see the new invention for what it was supposed to be—a great liberator.

But there was not a strong Labour lobby. The Empire was in excellent shape, the nation was considerably more than solvent, and the poor—well, they could always eat cake. The day had not yet arrived when no corridor of power would be complete without a limousine parked outside, but it was coming. The day when no council house would be complete without one would come, too (though nobody seems to have envisaged it at the time).

In 1892 the Sultan of Morocco had become the first ruler to purchase a motor car. It was a so-called Daimler Steel-wheeler (to distinguish it from a wooden-wheeler), powered by a two-cylinder 0·97-litre, 1·65 h.p. engine, which gave it a top speed of just over 11 m.p.h. To provide a suitable touch of the exotic, it was fitted with a fringed canopy and side curtains. Steering was by a tiller.

How the Sultan came to buy it, and to what uses he put it, are mysteries which have been buried beneath the sands of the desert. He may have been at the Paris World Fair in 1889, and if he was, he would doubtless have seen Mr. Daimler and Mr. Benz demonstrating their wares. They were not billed as star attractions, and he might have had difficulty in finding them. However, it would have been worth the trouble, for he could have taken a ride in one or another of the cars. He might even have embarked in a motor launch at a special dock which Daimler had built to demonstrate this side of his business.

Probably, for this was a characteristic of many rulers, he was a fanatical collector, who had to possess an example of anything that was new and interesting and rare. In those days, a motor car would have fulfilled all these requirements.

At all events, he had one, and there may have been wise men at the court who shook their learned heads and said that the days of the camel were indeed numbered.

A year or two later, that scion of a noble banking line, Henri de Rothschild, purchased a Benz Victoria (if the going was good, it was possible to coax a top speed of 18·75 m.p.h. out of its 2·28-litre engine).Indeed, the Rothschild family were quick to appreciate the motor car and its potential. Lord Rothschild's son Charles was the first man to drive a car in Cambridge. He looked upon it as a convenient new tool in the hands of a naturalist and collector of insects. Baron Henri took part in the Paris–Madrid Race of 1904, and founded the car company known as Unic (or Unique). But unlike other members of his family he was not an astute business man. Renault outstripped Unic in manufacturing performance, and presently he sold the factory.

His son, Philippe de Rothschild, was also a motor racing man.

He twice took part in the Le Mans 24 Hours Race and also achieved successes in grand prix events. But more important to motoring, perhaps, was his invention of an early windscreen wiper, which worked off the exhaust system. Neither he nor Charles Rothschild's daughter Miriam, who was the first motorist to fix a seat belt to the driving seat of a car, patented their inventions.

At about the same time as Henri de Rothschild purchased his Benz, an example of Daimler's sturdy but inclined to be sluggish Phoenix of 1899 was bought by Emile Jellinek. Jellinek's name may not amount to very much these days. At the turn of the century, however, he had the keys to countless illustrious doors in the pockets of his frock-coat. Moreover, he and his wife had the wit to call their eldest daughter Mercedes.

Jellinek was a large man with a bushy black moustache and *pince-nez*. He was the son of a Leipzig rabbi. As a young man, he had sailed to North Africa and set up a business in Spanish Morocco. He married the daughter of a family that exported fruit to Europe; and presently he and his wife moved to Vienna, where he established a highly prosperous undertaking, importing North African delicacies for the dinner tables of the better-off members of Viennese society.

Towards the end of the nineteenth century, the Jellineks moved to the French Riviera.

Emile Jellinek was a man of charm: a by no means inconsiderable personality, who soon became appointed Austro-Hungarian consul general at Nice. He was well thought of in local society and he was a motoring enthusiast.

Whenever you scratched Jellinek, you found a business man screaming to get out. That, perhaps, in an exaggeration, for the commercial captive did not have to cry very hard to secure his release. Having met Daimler in 1897, he undertook to become a distributor of his cars. It was a shrewd move which, nowadays, is better known as 'getting on to the bandwagon'.

As it happened, Jellinek was not particularly pleased with his Phoenix. It was, he said, underpowered and he insisted that it should be redesigned. Gottlieb Daimler did not take very kindly to the idea. There are some doubts about whether he approved of high-speed motoring. In any case, he was a sensitive, restless man who, like most creative artists, preferred to have his own way.

But Daimler's health was beginning to fail, and Jellinek's letter about the Phoenix soon found its way on to the desk of his colleague, Wilhelm Maybach. Maybach had for some years been the designer who had translated Daimler's ideas into workable reality, and he was glad of the challenge. He produced an absolute beauty of a car, powered by a whacking great 5·93-litre engine and with a top speed of 45 m.p.h.

Jellinek was delighted. He agreed to take thirty-six of them in return for exclusive agencies in Austro-Hungary, France, Belgium and America. In these countries, he insisted, the car should be called Mercedes after his eleven-year-old daughter. Elsewhere in the world, it was to be known as the 'New Daimler'.

The Jellineks had another daughter whose name was Maja and she, too, had a Daimler car named after her. But her star never shone so brightly as the well-favoured Mercedes. Her namesake went out of production in 1908, and she slipped back into obscurity.

But the Mercedes—there was no holding its stampede into fame. It rapidly distinguished itself in the emerging sport of motor racing; and, equally quickly, it established itself as the motor car for top people. The mark two version was snapped up by such illustrious gentlemen as J. Gordon Bennett (proprietor of the *New York Herald* and creator of the Gordon Bennett car races), W. K. Vanderbilt (American millionaire and instigator of the Vanderbilt Cup races, which were to North America what the Gordon Bennett races were to Europe), plus a pair of princes and a Viennese nobleman. And when, in 1904, the Mercedes Simplex was introduced, the list of important owners was headed by H.I.M. Kaiser Wilhelm II of Germany.

Benz was also busy adding famous names to his clientele. His tonneau of 1902 (it had a 1·73-litre two-cylinder engine and a top speed of just over 30 m.p.h.) was bought by an archduke, three minor nobles and the current ruler of the house of Krupp—who was not able to enjoy it for very long, for he died that same year. Better still, when his Parsifal came out two years later, the Kaiser, who bestowed his imperial favours with a reasonable degree of impartiality, invested in one (it was similar to the Mercedes tonneau of the same period. Both cars had a top speed of just over 30 m.p.h. The Benz got there by way of a four-cylinder 2·80-litre engine, producing 18 h.p. at 1,280 r.p.m.,

B

whilst the Mercedes used a 4·08-litre unit that also produced 18 h.p. at 1,280 r.p.m.)

In Britain the Daimler was the senior car. People were waiting, though they did not know it, for the union between Mr. Rolls and Mr. Royce. At the end of the nineteenth century, Royce was busy at his small factory on the outskirts of Manchester, manufacturing electrical goods. Rolls was doing a great deal of motoring, and some of his experiences were preparing his mind for a meeting with a man like Royce.

On one drive from Paris to Calais, his car suffered from the following defects:

The joints in the water pipe came to pieces. The tyre on the offside front wheel had to be replaced. The chain worked loose. One of the rear tyres punctured. A cylinder developed a leak, and the upper ends of all of them became red hot. The water pump jammed. The radiator pipes leaked. The ignition tube burst twice. Oil got on to the brakes, and another tyre burst.

This sort of thing gave motoring a bad name, and the only consolation can have been that, among the élite of Britain, it was regarded as something very close to a sport. Most sports depend on some sort of challenge, and there was plenty of that in many of these early motors.

Perhaps this may have been why the authorities were so slow to see the benefits which the horseless carriage could bring to mankind. Or, possibly, they supposed that its power would develop more quickly than it did, and that the roads would become a mechanical hell, in which young tearaways frightened the living daylights out of horses and old ladies.

On the other side, there was no lack of articulate people who were ready to plead the automobile's cause. As the Hon. John Scott-Montagu (father of the present Lord Montagu) pointed out, it could even produce a saving in cash. Apparently, it cost no less than £50,000 a year to sweep up all the horse manure that sullied the streets of London. That was one bill which could be forgotten about, once the horseless carriage had completely taken over from its obsolescent four-legged competitor.

There was also the matter of safety. It was easier to apply the brakes (when they worked) on a car than it was to stop a horse. Furthermore, on a slippery day, you didn't find cars falling over in the way that horses did, causing traffic jams and generally creating havoc. A car was so much more reasonable, so much more, in a manner of speaking, *intelligent*.

To judge by a series of articles which appeared in a volume on motoring published by the Badminton Library in 1902, the ownership of a car was something which had to be attended by common sense and a certain awareness of style. You did not simply get out and buy *one*. You bought several. You had, the authors assumed, a place in London and a house in the country. For London use, electric cars (the Duke of Westminster was one of the first to cotton on to this idea) or steam cars were advocated. The only trouble with the former (which, in one writer's view, were 'almost as costly as horseflesh') was that there were no satisfactory accumulators on the market. This would seem to have been a rather considerable snag, but little was made of it. After all, when your man brought you home in the evenings, he could plug the vehicle into the electric light system and charge up the batteries for the following morning.

Indeed, there was more than mere motive power to be had from batteries, inadequate though they may have been. They provided light for the lamps, heat for the footwarmer—all this plus a means of lighting cigars.

In the morning, when the electric carriage took you from your house in Belgravia, or Kensington, or wherever, to your office in the city, you might with any luck make the journey in comfort. Scott-Montagu wrote: 'When your driver is careful and competent, has learnt the danger of skidding, and is content to take you round corners at a reasonable speed when the wood pavement or the asphalt is wet, you should be able to enjoy your newspaper or talk to your companion with as much serenity as if you were sitting in your favourite chair at home.'

If he insisted on cornering as if he were a competitor in the Paris–Madrid race, you could, presumably, fire the fellow— though this may not have been so easy as it sounds. The coming of the car brought about a need for new skills, and it was too soon for anyone to have learned very much about them. Many wealthy motorists attempted to train their coachmen for new responsibilities, and this worked well enough up to a point. The trouble was that the chauffeur was also required to have a certain amount of mechanical knowledge, and to be able to undertake simple repairs and servicing.

As Harmsworth not unreasonably pointed out: 'One would not dream of putting a coachman in charge of a printing machine, a steam launch or a cathedral organ. So—why a car? They can be taught to *drive* the cars, but not to maintain them.'

Electric carriages, it seems, were less demanding. 'A shrewd coachman or groom', Harmsworth conceded, 'can easily be trained to take complete charge (of them).'

So far as life in the country was concerned, the coming of the motor car certainly brought a most welcome feeling of freedom. Nowadays, it is hard to imagine how isolated a community living in a big house used to be. The nearest station was several miles away and train services, though admirable for getting backwards and forward to London, were totally useless for local journeys. Everything had to be accomplished at a horse's pace, which was not very fast. Even places twenty miles away were out of range unless you were prepared to make an expedition of it.

Life was correspondingly introspective, and the only way out of the problem was to import train-loads of guests at the weekends. The car, on the other hand, opened up a huge new social opportunity. You could visit friends (or make them) on the far side of the county, and hunting enthusiasts could indulge their sport at faraway meets—though one had to be careful about this. At one hunt, a distinguished lady rider had received the rough edge of the master of foxhounds' tongue for turning up in a car ('Damn stinkin' contraption'). Farmers, too, were apt to be rather sensitive to the new devices. For many years, they had made useful pin money out of the sale of forage to riders who had come from longish distances. If too many people arrived in motors, their takings would be sadly reduced (they had not, it appears, grasped the idea that they might sell petrol instead).

The notion that a car might be a general purpose vehicle does not seem to have occurred to the more illustrious pioneer motorists. Scott-Montagu, writing for the man who owned 'about half a dozen horses', suggested that, ideally, there should be a car for almost every task. There should be one for meeting guests at the station, and another for carrying their baggage. There should be a closed car for bad weather, and an open car for when the sun shone (though he was prepared to accept as an alternative one which had a detachable top, which could be fitted when it rained).

For shooting, there should be a 6 or 12 h.p. vehicle—a 'good, roomy wagonette' was how he described it—for the loaders, and a 12 or 20 h.p. 'flier' for the guests. The former should depart fifteen minutes earlier than the rest of the party.

Harmsworth pointed out that a long wagonette could be used for both beaters (to shoots) and baggage (from the station), and could also move heavy goods about the place. He, personally, used a Serpollet steamer for this purpose. It could travel at 25 m.p.h. even when it was fully loaded, and 200 miles could be covered in ten hours 'with ease and no discomfort'.

It must have been a very fine vehicle, for, on the whole, Harmsworth was against steam cars. He found them difficult to handle in high winds, and their thirsty habit of needing water at intervals of less than fifty miles made him impatient.

Whilst Montagu came out on the side of steam or electricity for town use, he favoured the internal combustion engine for the country.

According to the ideas of these affluent sages, the cost of motoring, at any rate in terms of capital outlay, seems to have been rather high. In 1903 a 10 h.p. Wolseley cost £430, and the price of a Daimler chassis in 1905 was £700. When, in December 1904, the first Rolls-Royce chassis were announced, they came in four versions (the Rolls-Royce 'one-model' policy was adopted with the advent of the Silver Ghost in 1907). The lowest price had a two-cylinder 10 h.p. engine and cost £395. For £500, you could buy the three-cylinder 15 h.p. version, and £650 secured one with a four-cylinder 20 h.p. engine. At the top of the range, there was the six-cylinder 30 h.p. edition selling at £890. On top of this, there was the price of a body, which was fashioned with loving care by a firm of coachbuilders, and might have cost almost as much again. It was understandable, for the standards were very high indeed. For timber, nothing but seasoned ash (and that had to be at least seven years old) was acceptable, and there was none of this nonsense of a quick flick round with the spray gun. Umpteen coats of paint were applied, and the whole thing was finished off with a carefully applied layer of varnish. Cellulose was a word that nobody had heard of.

One doubts whether 'lock-up garage' had been heard of, either. One of the early advocates of motoring was a baronet named Sir David Salomons, who lived near Tunbridge Wells. He was an extremely articulate gentleman, and he was (or seemed to be) continually writing letters about motoring to the *Daily Telegraph*. Sometimes he wrote longer pieces, such as the one he composed about 'The Motor Stable and Its Management'.

Sir David's own 'motor stable' appears to have been rather like an expensive health farm. The vehicles were accommodated in rooms which were clean, warm and, above all, dry (though the poor dears did have to share them sometimes). There was also a treatment room which could, and certainly not at a pinch, be converted into an operating theatre.

Explaining what has since become reasonably obvious, Sir David told his readers that a car could be examined by one of three methods. The first, and clearly the least acceptable, was by the mechanic lying on his back underneath it. The second was 'by raising the car up on a platform', and the third was by a man going down into a pit underneath it.

All told there were five rooms for the cars, which could accommodate a total of nine assorted sizes. They were long and narrow, with big skylights on the northern side. The siting of the skylights was important, for it ensured that the direct rays of the sun never touched the precious paintwork of the inhabitants. Another important factor was the quality of the glass. Sir David's was ¼-inch thick and was proof against hailstones. Apparently, some while earlier, the inhabitants of Tunbridge Wells had undergone a rather traumatic experience, when there was an exceptionally heavy storm, and stones one inch in diameter had fallen. The total cost was estimated at thousands of pounds in terms of broken glass, but anything ¼-inch thick or more had escaped.

The walls of the building were constructed of double nine-inch brickwork with two inches of airspace in between. Sir David explained that cemented walls would have done for the interior, 'but pointed brickwork looks nicer'.

To service and repair the vehicles, there was a pit, eight feet deep and 'slightly narrower than the distance between a motor car's wheels'. You reached it by means of a circular staircase, which also admitted the mechanics to a small basement, lit by means of a glass floor in the room above, and in which an assortment of spare parts and special tools (e.g. a grindstone) were stored. Upstairs, there were work benches, shelves for tools and spare parts and chests of drawers for smaller components. There was electric light in every room, and heating was by hot-water pipes.

Sir David had a number of rules and woe betide anyone who ignored them. All tools had to be duplicated, with one set contained in the cars on the strict understanding that it should only be used while on the road. Every puncture had to be mended at once 'and not left for chance moments', and the cars had to be cleaned daily according to a formula. Thus:

One: the mud had to be thoroughly moistened before any attempt was made to remove it. Two: a large Turkey sponge had to be used for cleaning the body and the wheels. Three: the aforementioned body and wheels then had to be dried, using a sponge cloth or a leather. Four: the engine should be cleaned with a damp sponge cloth and then gently wiped over with oily waste.

A hose might be used for washing the mud off, but the work should be done gently. There should be no question, Sir David said, 'of dashing it over a car—as is done with ordinary carriages'.

In case the cars happened to be out of doors during a rainstorm, each should be provided with a mackintosh cover (similarly, each had to have a dust cover for warmer weather). The former had to be neatly made 'so as not to be disfiguring'.

Perhaps Sir David Solomons was a little too fastidious; but, on his own experience, he had reason to be. He had noticed that far too many people seemed to have grown up in the belief that anything mechanical was tough, and could be knocked about and, more often than not, woefully neglected. This was utterly wrong. A car, whatever anyone cared to think, was a much more delicate object than a horse-drawn carriage. Any owner who ignored this fact did so at his peril.

Perhaps it was a reaction against the law, which—in Britain, at any rate—seemed to exercise an unfair bias in favour of horses. At all events, many a four-legged friend would have been grateful for the pampering which some of these early motor cars received. And, as I may have remarked somewhere else, if a car broke its wheel, there was no need to shoot it.

2 The Carriage Trade

On a summer's day in 1895, the Hon. Evelyn Ellis (another early motoring enthusiast) made a lonely journey from London to Windsor Castle with the object of introducing Queen Victoria to the motor car. Ellis's Daimler must have been one of the very few motor vehicles in the country at the time. And then, less than ten years later, the homes of the royal, the rich and the powerful seemed to be crammed with the things.

Alfred Harmsworth had been a keen cyclist in his youth, and it was with a magazine on bicycling that he laid the first brick in what became the colossal edifice of his publishing empire. He was almost completely unmechanically-minded, and yet he loved toys that worked. Sometimes he went to the extent of bringing them over especially from America. Gadgets delighted him, too. When the telephone was introduced, he seized upon it with delight, and installed one in every room of his house. It remained important to him, and he once observed that 'A car and a telephone and a good bed—what more do I want?' His editors no doubt sometimes thought that the car and the bed would have been sufficient.

Harmsworth's introduction to the horseless carriage came about during a trip to Paris in 1894. He examined the cars of Panhard and Levassor, De Dion, and Daimler, and immediately predicted that, within the next twenty-five years, the horse would become extinct.

In the following year, he went again to France and, this time, had the opportunity to ride a motor cycle. The experience was not a particularly happy one; for the bike ran away with him, somehow managed to jump over a hedge, and pitched poor Harmsworth off into a field.

However, his enthusiasm was undaunted. In 1896, he bought a Panhard and this particular car served him very well indeed. He was still using it in 1902—by which time it had survived his one and only car crash.

He had been driven down to Rottingdean on a visit to his friend Rudyard Kipling. The Canterbury cricket week was in progress, and, on the return trip, his car came up behind a dogcart crammed with slightly drunk enthusiasts. The noise of the vehicle seems to have startled the dogcart's horse, which reared up and then bolted across the road.

Harmsworth's small French chauffeur, Émile, took avoiding action by steering up a bank. Unfortunately it was too steep. The driver was flung clear, but the car overturned on top of Harmsworth. For some reason, the future press baron was clutching a copy of a Baedeker guide at the time.

He was taken into a nearby house, and the doctor was sent for. He diagnosed severe bruises and ordered a week's rest. The unfortunate Émile was discovered wandering around in a daze, uttering '*La route est barrée*' in a funereal monotone.

There were times when Harmsworth seemed to buy a new car every month. There were usually six in his garage at any one time, and a typical collection would include a Serpollet steamer (for the heavy stuff), a small Renault, a Daimler, a Napier, a Mercedes (he bought half a dozen of them in all) and a Rolls-Royce (he owned at least five of them).

Although he possessed some of the most powerful vehicles in the world, he was not—at any rate in the earlier days of his motoring— in favour of them for ordinary use. 'I consider that these heavy and powerful road engines', he once wrote, 'are a mere passing freak of the hour. Their weight makes them uncomfortable on rough roads, and the amount of petrol required to drive them is a serious item.'[1]

[1] At 7d. a gallon, which was the retail price at that time, one finds this hard to believe.

They were all very well for the long straight roads in France, he said, but on the winding roads of Britain they were a wanton waste of power.

Harmsworth had a sharp eye for the cost of motoring. On one occasion, he worked out an elaborate table on the relative performances of cars up a certain hill in relation to their prices and speed. He discovered what might have been safely assumed that, the cheaper the car, the less power it had. For instance, according to his reckoning, a vehicle priced at £240 would carry two people up this particular hill at a speed of 8·8 miles an hour, whilst a £380 car would take four people up at 10·8 m.p.h. and a £1,150 vehicle would ascend with four people on board at 18·5 m.p.h. Quite what this particular exercise contributed to the sum of motoring knowledge is not very clear, but Harmsworth considered the results worth publishing.

Tyres were a matter on which he had strong views. It is, perhaps, hardly surprising when one considers that his own tyre bill for a single year added up (in 1902) to £500. On the whole, he was 'inclined to think that the pneumatic tyre craze has been altogether overdone by motor-car owners'. Although a vehicle shod with them went faster than one with solid tyres, they were (in his opinion) less comfortable than the latter, and more expensive. They were liable to puncture in hot weather and were apt to cause skids.

He himself mixed his tyres with joyful abandon. On one of his cars, he had solid tyres entirely. On another he had solids on some wheels and pneumatics on the others. And, on a third, pneumatic tyres with metal spikes in them were fitted for town use.[1]

Just as he promoted aviation through his newspapers, so did he help to further the cause of motoring. The R.A.C. 1,000-mile trial from London to Edinburgh and back in 1900 was largely the result of his initiative. He had put money at the club's disposal to finance a suitable scheme, and one of his papers suggested that a trial of this nature might be the right thing to do.

After the first world war, he no longer drove himself, but his interest in motoring continued. Indeed, the last article in which he had a special interest was one for *The Times*, estimating the genius of Henry Royce. He had ordered a copy to be put on his

[1]Metal spikes, which find a present-day echo in snow tyres, were common in those days. Wooden road blocks in wet weather were uncommonly slippery. By biting into them, the spikes overcame this hazard.

desk in Printing House Square, so that he could re-write it if he thought necessary. No alterations were ever made to the piece. By the time the manuscript had been prepared, he was beyond making any lucid contribution to journalism. A few weeks later, he was dead.

In 1903 the 5th Marquess of Anglesey had caused the design of exotic motor cars to be taken very close to the limits with a huge and entirely special Mors, which was proudly displayed at the French motor show. The instructions had been that cost was of no account, and that every effort should be made to produce a car which had all the luxury of a railway Pullman carriage.

For the sake of the record, it was powered by a four-cylinder, 35/40 h.p., engine. The wheel base was ten feet six inches, but that is of little account. What matters is the limousine which was built on top of it.

The design was by Graham White, who had a very happy way with him on matters of body design, and the work was carried out by a Parisian firm of coachbuilders. There were especially large windows, with curved panes at the rear corners. Every one of them was fitted with a spring-operated sunblind. There were no such things as seats in the conventional meaning of the word. Instead, there were four revolving armchairs in the rear compartment, each upholstered in dark red Morocco leather. Between the chairs, on either side, there were small tables which, when they were pulled out to the full extent, turned into a single long table with green baize covering. Also at the sides were small cupboards and tiny chests of drawers. All the woodwork of the interior was in polished mahogany.

A dark crimson Wilton carpet graced the floor, and there were royal blue plush curtains at the windows. But the real triumph was the ceiling, which was done up in the style of Louis XV.

On the partition between the driver and his passengers there was a Morocco leather holdall, a clock, a barometer, a thermometer, a manicure set, one or two notebooks, and a looking glass. There was an electric telephone for communications to the chauffeur and, if that should fail, there was a device rather like the engine-room telegraph on a ship. By means of it, His Lordship could signal such pertinent messages as 'right', 'left', 'turn', 'steady', 'home' and 'quicker'.

The lighting arrangements were perfectly in harmony with

everything else. At the back, they amounted to two sprays of electric bulbs with glass shades. It required two sets of accumulators, producing sixteen volts apiece, to take care of their needs. And, on a somewhat more practical note, a heating system connected to the exhaust was installed for winter.

Up front, the chauffeur was not exactly slumming it, and nor was the footman. They sat in bucket seats covered in bright red Morocco with brass beading all around them.

The exterior was painted in dark blue with fine red lines, and the wheels were in pale yellow and lined in black. There were four big brass acetylene Bleriot lamps. With a full load on board, this amazing vehicle was said to be capable of averaging 25 m.p.h. on a long journey.

The Marquess was no doubt able to afford such a masterpiece, and he was a sufficient personality to live up to it. His main interest in life was the theatre and, for he never did anything by halves, he indulged it to the full. At his Plas Newydd estate on Anglesey he had a full-scale playhouse built, and he used to invite the great actors and actresses of the day to visit him. On these occasions he did the kind of thing that many people dream about, but only a man of his wealth and eccentricity could carry off. He produced plays with himself in the leading role, and with the stars in supporting parts.

'He no doubt paid them well', the present Marquess of Anglesey commented.

Unfortunately the 5th Marquess died fairly young and without issue. It seems a pity: characters on this scale are very rare. His car, of course, attracted a great deal of attention; and, inevitably, somebody wanted one like it. The person in question was the Countess de Carrié, about whom very little is known, though she sounds the right type to have one.

Possibly there were echoes of the Marquess's Pullman-inspired giant in the 1906 20/30 Renault, which took as its model the interior of a first-class French railway compartment. Although it was somewhat smaller than one of these carriages, the effect was very pleasing and the inhabitants were able to enjoy an extremely comfortable ride.

In those Edwardian days, peasants were still supposed to touch their forelocks to the gentry. They may even have uttered such idiotic phrases as 'Beggin' your leave, ma'am'. Horses were not so servile; and, now and then, they had their revenge on the four-wheeled usurper.

Lord Edward Churchill (a distant relative of Sir Winston Churchill) was not particularly interested in cars, but he bought one to please his daughter. They went for a drive in it, and the wretched thing broke down. Since it happened in the depths of the country, they had to wait for some time until a man turned up with a carthorse. He agreed to tow them home.

In outline, the tactical plot sounds simple and workable. The idea was that Lord Edward was to remain in the car and steer, and that the horse should take up a position in front, tethered to the chassis. Lord Edward sat down behind the steering wheel. The horse was made fast. Nothing happened. Its owner shouted something like 'Gideeup tha' ' (or whatever it was they used to say). Still the obstinate brute refused to budge. The man gave it a smart smack with his stick, and the horse jumped forward.

Unfortunately the road was on a slight downhill slope. After its great leap forward, the horse slackened its pace, but the car did not. The result was that the car rammed the horse in the rear, and the horse, disgusted, sat down on the bonnet of the car.

This horrible chapter of accidents was still not done. The horse got up, leaving a badly bent front end beneath it, and promptly got one of the ropes entangled round its nearside rear leg. This caused the car to spring at the stationary animal and to clout it on the fetlock.

By now an audience of delighted peasants had assembled. No doubt they should have been touching their forelocks. Instead they cheered on the drama with such comments as 'Whoa, Motor! That's the way to lead it home', which may not be high on satire, but was considered at the time (though not by Lord Edward) to be an amusing example of rustic wit.

A nobleman who was rather more successful with his early motoring was the Earl of Lonsdale. He was a personal friend of the Kaiser; and, on a visit to His Imperial Majesty at Berlin in 1901, he had been greatly taken with the Emperor's new Mercedes. The thing that impressed him most was that, during his stay, it never broke down.

The car was driven by a young German mechanic named Keiser;

and, before he returned home, Lonsdale had not only ordered a Mercedes, but had also persuaded Keiser to enter his employment (with, one must assume, the agreement of the German Emperor).

Some while later, the car arrived at Lonsdale's estate in Cumberland. It proved to be mechanically sound, and His Lordship was very happy with it until Keiser brought him a most disturbing piece of information. It seemed that all the fittings were not in silver (as he had expected), but were merely chromium plated. The vehicle was sent back to Germany on the next boat with the strict instructions that all the offending parts were to be replaced by solid silver at once.

Lonsdale was nothing if not fastidious. All his cars were painted in his racing colours of yellow and bronze blue. And they were *really* painted: he insisted that no fewer than eighteen coats should be applied.

Although he enjoyed motoring, this famous sportsman never trusted a car to the same extent that he would put his faith in a horse. But this did not prevent him, when the race track at Brooklands was opened in 1907, from leading a parade of vehicles around the track in his latest Mercedes. Nor did it stop him from accepting the presidency of the Automobile Association in 1910, when that organisation amalgamated with the Motor Union. Indeed, he gave the association permission to use his personal yellow, which has adorned its vehicles ever since.

One of the most important encounters in the history of motoring took place at an hotel in Manchester in 1907. Those present were a motoring enthusiast named Henry Edmunds, a young aristocrat named the Hon. C. S. Rolls who owned a business which represented a number of Continental makes of car, and a quiet, rather withdrawn, engineer named Henry Royce.

Just after the turn of the century, Royce had bought a 10 h.p. Decauville two-cylinder voiturette. It was considered to be one of the better cars of its day, but he disliked it intensely. The design, the unreliability, the smell and the noise—all of them disgusted him. At first he applied himself to the task of curing them, but this proved to be out of the question even after he had almost rebuilt the vehicle.

There was, he decided, only one thing to do: make a car of his own. Eventually he made three. He kept one for his own use, gave another to a friend, and the third to Henry Edmunds, who was associated with him in his electrical components business.

This car was the object of Rolls's trip to Manchester. Edmunds wanted him to try it out.

After a run round the city, Rolls returned to the hotel. He was, he said, enchanted by it. If Royce was in agreement, he would give up his other agencies and concentrate his selling ability on the output of the Manchester factory. Royce agreed and, on that day, Rolls-Royce was born.

The first Rolls-Royce to be manufactured commercially was delivered on December 12th, 1906, to an American millionaire named Paris E. Singer. It was a four-seater car with the entrance at the back, and the registration number was AX148. The body, which had been built by Mulliner, was in dark green.

Mr. Singer, who was the grandson of the inventor of the Singer Sewing Machine, was living in London at the time. Later he moved to Paignton in Devonshire, where he bought a large house which, nowadays, serves as an hotel. He was a man with a considerable taste for the exotic. He loved cars and he adored beautiful women. Among the latter was the famous dancer Isadora Duncan, by whom he had an illegitimate child.

The second Rolls-Royce was sold to Sir Oswald Moseley, Bt., who had not yet achieved political notoriety, and the third was ordered by a member of the Guinness family.

Lord Northcliffe bought his first Rolls in 1907 (one of the early Silver Ghosts). In the following year, the Marquis of Bute, Lord Montagu of Beaulieu (formerly the Hon. John Scott-Montagu), and the Duke of Northumberland all took possession of these magnificent cars. Already the list of Rolls-Royce customers was beginning to read like a page from a society magazine.

It wasn't long before the Rolls-Royce reputation had reached America. Pierpont Morgan had one delivered to a house that he owned outside Watford in England, and Andrew Carnegie's was delivered to his Scottish seat at Skibo Castle, Dornoch, Sutherland. Mr. Morgan's car was finished in 'claret'. There is no record of the colour of Mr. Carnegie's.

Even Henry Ford bought a Rolls-Royce. It was a seven-seater with a torpedo body, and was delivered to his British base at Trafford Park, Manchester. According to one account, 'When Ford came to England and travelled in a Rolls-Royce, interviewers asked him why. "All our T-models are sold," he replied, "so I used the next best car available." '

Now and again, a mystery crops up. For example, one would love to know what happened to the limousine belonging to a wealthy business man from Cheshire. In the Rolls-Royce guarantee book, a note appears to the effect that it was 'lost in Belgium'. To lose a lesser car might be regarded as a misfortune, but to lose a Rolls-Royce in Belgium in the year 1909 looks like carelessness of a rare and almost magnificent kind.

However, the gentleman in question must have been able to afford his loss, or else he was well insured, for he promptly ordered another.

The first car to be owned by the writer Rudyard Kipling (he didn't exactly invent the British Empire, but readers of his poems might have been excused if they thought he did) was a Lanchester. As time went on, he became a staunch Lanchester man, and even conjured up a thinly disguised version of the car (he called it the 'Octopod') in some short stories that he wrote about motoring. But even Kipling was not proof against the charm of Rolls-Royce and presently he ordered one. There seems to have been some difficulty about the chassis at first; but, eventually, a green and black landaulet was delivered to his home at Burwash in Sussex on December 20th, 1911. The instructions to Rolls-Royce noted that 'all accounts under £1 to be sent to the driver, Geo. Moore, but over that amount to Mr. Kipling himself'.

Whilst most distinguished clients of Rolls-Royce in those early days preferred to buy their cars brand new, there were some who had no objection to purchasing them at second hand. For instance, on the 1st of May 1911, a Mrs. de Quincey of Chislehurst took proud (one hopes) possession of a Thrupp and Maberley-bodied landaulet. In 1915 this same car was resold to the Governor of Bombay who, in his turn, sold it on April 1st, 1920, to the Maharajah of Nabha for the sum of £4,000.

Nobel and Pulitzer, those great givers of prizes both owned Rolls-Royces and so did A. G. Vanderbilt, who was drowned in the *Lusitania*. One can find little but praise to say for a number of owners who, at the outbreak of World War I, gave their cars to the armed forces. But how can one forgive that gentleman in Dundee, who possessed one with a Vanden Plas Colonial type body, and who, in 1926, sold it to a local farmer for use as a tractor?

3 Early Royal

Whatever may have been the reaction of the law-makers to the coming of the motor car, royalty took to it with relish. By 1910, King Edward VII, the Kaiser, the Czar of Russia, King Leopold II of Belgium, King Frederick of Saxony, King Manuel II of Portugal, King Wilhelm II of Württemberg, King Ludwig II of Bavaria, Queen Maria Pia of Portugal, and King Alfonso XIII of Spain (to mention but a few) had all bought cars. In addition to this, there were already too many motoring princes, archdukes, grand dukes, ordinary dukes, and minor members of the nobility, to count.

King Alfonso of Spain kept a Daimler permanently in London for his use when he came over to this country on shopping sprees. Prince Henry of Prussia organised a motor tour which took competitors on a devious route around Germany, and the Kaiser presented a prize for voiturette racing. King Edward VII had various distinctions in the motoring field. By no means the least of them was in 1901, when he gave his wife an electric vehicle valued at £1,000, and thus established (in its present sense) the first two-car household.

There are various suggestions about how King Edward first became acquainted with a car. One of them has it that it was during a holiday in the South of France. Another gives credit to an

c

exhibition held at the Imperial Institute in London during 1896.

Queen Victoria, so far as anyone can tell, never rode in a car: indeed she may never have seen one. Admittedly there was that drive of the Hon. Evelyn Ellis to Windsor Castle in 1895, but there is no record to show that the Queen actually met Mr. Ellis, nor that she came out of her castle to view the machine.

She must, however, have been aware of the automobile—if only because she put her name to Acts of Parliament regulating its use.

The occasion at the Imperial Institute was really an ambitious public relations campaign aimed at changing these laws. A number of cars were on show: they drove round and round the exhibition hall, went up and down the wooden ramps, and gave off a most fearful stench of burnt paraffin. Members of both Houses of Parliament were invited to view man's latest achievement, in the hope that they would find the demonstration reassuring. Edward VII (he was then Prince of Wales) was also asked if he would care to attend.

The future monarch accepted. He was driven through the gallery and out into the grounds by Ellis on a belt-driven Canstatt-Daimler belonging to F. R. Simms (it was he who had introduced the Daimler engine to Britain). His Royal Highness seemed to be interested, and Simms explained how the car worked.

Two years later, Edward was staying at Warwick Castle, and had his first experience of driving on public roads. The trip was a very short one. More important, perhaps, was an excursion in the following year, when he was staying with friends at Highcliffe Castle near Christchurch in Hampshire.

The Hon. John Scott-Montagu was invited over to lunch one day, and he drove the seventeen miles from Beaulieu in his 12 h.p. Daimler. After the meal, he suggested that they might like to go for a trip in the car. The Prince of Wales sat in the front with Scott-Montagu. Two ladies travelled in the back. They drove through the New Forest towards Southampton and, on the way back, touched 40 m.p.h. The ladies had to hold on to their hats and doubtless made delighted noises—a more refined version of the sounds that are uttered on a helter-skelter. The Prince joked with them and suggested that, for future motoring, they should wear more suitable hats. Afterwards, the local schoolmaster came round to the castle and took their photographs.

During the trip, he asked Scott-Montagu several questions, and wanted to know what type of car would be most appropriate for himself.

Edward VII had a gift for attracting novelty. Through a mistake on the part of his valet, he became the first man to have the creases in his trousers fore and aft instead of at the sides. He also pioneered the art of being operated on for an appendicitis, and it was this illness which, in 1902, caused his coronation to be postponed.

After that drive in Hampshire, it was clear that he was greatly attracted by the automobile, and it came as no great surprise when, a few weeks later, John Scott-Montagu was summoned to the prince's London home at Marlborough House. He was instructed to bring his car with him.

Court officials examined it, and the Prince asked some more questions. On December 1st, 1900, he finally made up his mind and ordered a Daimler. It was the first of an extremely long line of these vehicles to be owned by members of the Royal Family.

The car was delivered to Sandringham. It was a standard model, known as the 'A'—with electrical ignition, but with burners in reserve in case something went wrong. Steering was by means of an inclined wheel. There were four forward gears and a reverse, and the acceleration was controlled by a foot pedal. This feature was something of a novelty since, hitherto, it had been done by means of a hand lever. It had pneumatic tyres, wider-than-usual leather mudguards, and its phaeton body was painted in chocolate and black picked out in red.[1] The Prince's crest on a panel behind the nearside headlamp was the only indication of its royal ownership.

Somebody now had to be found to give the Prince driving lessons. Some years earlier, he had been taught to ride a bicycle by a gentleman of American descent named Oliver Stanton. Stanton was a thickset individual with greying hair and a rather theatrical manner. He used to smoke cigarettes in a long holder. Most days, he could be seen in Battersea Park, where he taught well-to-do people how to bicycle. When cars came on to the scene, he turned his trade to driving lessons and he also took commission

[1] Subsequently all the royal cars were in claret and black.

from selling insurance. Presumably, he found the work profitable, for he always gave the impression of being wealthy.

The Prince chose him for his motoring tutor and Stanton duly arrived at Sandringham. He said polite things about the car and then, with his royal master on board, set off round the estate. They did innumerable circuits, up and down the drive, negotiating the bends in the shrubbery, along the terrace, round and round, with the Prince's brow crumpled in a frown of concentration and, now and then, a royal grunt of satisfaction as a manœuvre came off well. He was not without aptitude, and Stanton was pleased with their progress. It took him very little time to master the art of driving in second gear. The other gears came later, but they came.

His Royal Highness was pleased with the motor car, and delighted with Stanton. Thereafter, he seldom so much as thought about buying a new vehicle without asking his advice. Clearly, though, there had to be a mechanic to look after the vehicles, and for this purpose a young man named Sydney Letzer was chosen. He had been employed at the Daimler company for two and a half years, and came to the royal household with the highest recommendations.

If there was going to be any problem about royal motoring, it was likely to show itself that summer, when the Prince, his Daimler and Letzer moved to Ascot, and the car took up residence in the royal stables. The question was: would the horses approve? Or would they, as horses were supposed to, go out of their minds with fear?

Nobody need have worried. The creatures regarded the car with a singular lack of interest.

The relationship between Edward and his father, the Prince Consort, cannot have been a very cosy one. The latter was always laying down rules, subjecting his son to a rigid and somewhat humourless routine, and giving him advice. Nevertheless, a certain amount of Albert's teaching stuck. One item was a cause which had been very close to his heart, the promotion of British industry.

Perhaps, by espousing the cause of motoring so eagerly, Edward was attempting to give the emerging British motor industry the encouragement it had so woefully lacked from previous governments. At all events, he bought another Daimler in 1901 and allowed it to be exhibited at a motor show held in the Agricultural Hall, Islington, in the following year. By 1905, he had acquired his seventh.

Queen Alexandra's vehicle of 1901 is now on display at the Montagu Motor Museum in Hampshire. It looks a horribly difficult thing to drive, but Her Majesty seems to have managed it. This may have been because she had a taste for speed. Certainly her trips around the Sandringham estate in a pony-cart are said to have been little short of terrifying; and, in a letter to her son, she remarked on how much she enjoyed being 'driven about in the cool of the evening at *fifty miles*!!'—though she did admit that she was apt to poke the chauffeur 'violently in the back at every *corner* to go gently and whenever a *dog, child* or anything comes in our way!'

The model was a Columbia as supplied by the Electric Vehicle Co. of Hertford, Connecticut. The 2 h.p. motor, powered by forty-eight (later this was modified to thirty) two-volt cells, was on the rear axle. There was a footbrake, tiller steering, wooden wheels, and solid tyres. The two-seater phaeton body was painted in dark red and black.

Once King Edward's enthusiasm for motoring had become apparent, there were several attempts by manufacturers to bring their wares to his attention. On one occasion, when he was staying at Homburg, an aide arranged a meeting with that giant of steam cars, Serpollet. The Frenchman had already sold one of his vehicles to the Shah of Persia and now he hoped to pull off a further coup with Edward. The idea was that he should drive the monarch over a distance of about six miles to Langenschwalbach, where the King had an appointment to take luncheon with the Grand Duke Michael of Russia.

It was a beautiful day, the roads were in excellent condition, and Edward sat in front and asked a great many questions. He must have enjoyed the trip, for, a few days later, Serpollet was asked to bring his vehicle over to Homburg again. This time, they made a journey of thirty-one miles to Frankfurt-am-Main. At Frankfurt, the King went into an optician's shop and bought a pair of goggles. Again, he asked innumerable questions, and he seemed to be particularly interested in the details of the Shah's cars. As a sales exercise, it was not very successful, for Edward never bought a Serpollet. However, the motor manufacturer was presented with a scarf pin of brilliants for all the trouble he had taken.

Later, in 1906, Edward was staying at Marienbad with his war minister, Viscount Haldane. The occasion was a kind of think-in for the purpose of discussing Army reforms.[1] One day, the King suggested that they should put on plain clothes and motor out into the country—just as if they were Austrians. They drove to a monastery some miles away, where they were entertained by the abbot. One of the purposes of the trip seems to have been to enjoy a good cup of coffee. Edward liked coffee, but preferred the Austrian way of making it. German coffee, he said, was horrible.

An occasional visitor to the royal household was Edward's nephew, the Kaiser. The story goes that, early in his motoring career, the German Emperor tried to sell his uncle the idea of running his cars on methane. But this sounds unlikely. Alcohol, which was a product made by German farmers, was much closer to the Emperor's heart. If Edward remained unconvinced, he was wise. Cars using this fuel were severely underpowered. Although the Kaiser bravely used it in his first three vehicles, he eventually had to abandon the struggle and use petrol.

On his visit to Sandringham in 1902, the Kaiser was given the use of Edward's 22 h.p. Daimler. He liked to drive at high speeds and so, for that matter, did his uncle. Although a contemporary observer loyally protested that Edward 'was no friend of furious driving', he had to admit that he was 'scarcely content to drive behind hay motors'.

Perhaps a more direct assessment of his attitude to motoring is provided by one of his biographers, Sir Philip Magnus, 'He loved to be driven fast [Magnus wrote] and was proud of having exceeded 60 m.p.h. on the Brighton road as early as 1906. He hated to see any car in front of his and would often urge his chauffeurs to pursue and overtake, and his gestures were normally as vehement as his actions were brisk.'[2]

His motoring certainly had style to it, and so did that of his friends. For instance, Lily Langtry, who was by no means un-known to the monarch, attracted a good deal of favourable

---

[1]It resulted in a considerable reorganisation in the light of lessons learnt in the Boer War.
[2]*King Edward the Seventh* by Philip Magnus (John Murray).

attention when she gave the press details of her motoring wardrobe. It consisted of a long sable coat, shaped to the waist and adorned with a deep, cape-like, collar of ermine. A Henry II muff and a sable toque completed the ensemble.

In 1907 the King gave his patronage to the Automobile Club, thereby making it the *Royal* Automobile Club. In the following year Prince Francis of Teck (a great-grandson of George III and brother of King Edward's daughter-in-law, who later became Queen Mary) became the club's chairman. Prince Francis had been a soldier of some distinction. He was educated at Sandhurst, served in the 1st Dragoons, was awarded the D.S.O. and two bars, and was twice mentioned in dispatches. He remained the club's chairman until his death in 1910. During his period of office, he showed considerable interest in the R.A.C.'s clubhouse which was being built in Pall Mall and, particularly, in the decorations.

Towards the end of his life, Edward VII made more and more trips to Brighton. Another car always accompanied him in case anything went wrong with his own. Sometimes it did. There is a retired chauffeur living in Kent, who was employed as an apprentice at a garage in Crawley at the time. On at least one occasion, he can remember his boss being called urgently away to carry out first aid on the royal vehicle which stood, stranded, a few miles down the road. By the time he reached the scene, there was no sign of the monarch, who had transferred himself into the other vehicle and carried on with the journey.

All the King really wanted at this time was peace and quiet, but getting it was difficult. Once, in the late winter's sunshine of 1910, he drove down to Worthing. He climbed unsteadily out of his car, and wandered over to the pier, where he settled down to read a newspaper. Presently he fell asleep. But the distinctive, claret-coloured car which was parked nearby attracted the crowd. Before very long, the sleeping king was awakened by a throng of people. With some difficulty, the police helped him back into his vehicle and he was driven away.

His son, who became George V, never shared his enthusiasm for motoring. George's first car was a four-seater phaeton, powered by an electric motor which could travel for ninety miles on one charge, and had a top speed of 25 m.p.h. He kept it at Sandringham. Later, he bought a Daimler, which went rather faster, though it seems doubtful whether the extra speed appealed to him very much.

His wife began by disliking cars. During a holiday at Mentone in 1898, she wrote to her Aunt Augusta, the Grand Duchess of Mecklenburg-Strelitz, that a drive she had made (presumably in a horse-drawn carriage) had been 'somewhat disturbed by an odious motor car which kept on passing us and then slowing down, it smelt so nasty and made such a noise'.

However, her views were to change. From Interlaken in 1903, she wrote to her husband: 'Do you know the roads are so good here that it would have been rather fun to have a motor car to go about—two people in the hotel have their own.'

And, on another occasion, to Aunt Augusta: 'Only think what George and I did this afternoon, we went in Lord Shrewsbury's *motor car* (driven by him) down to Hampton Court which George had never seen. I really enjoyed the drive very much and we flew . . . (we) have just returned at *7.15*, it took us *38* minutes to get back—I feel you will nearly have a fit at me going in a car.'

Aunt Augusta nearly did. She replied with alacrity: 'And now to your drive in a motor-car! yes, I very nearly had a fit and quite screamed out to myself . . . oh! dearest child, how could you?'

Undaunted by her aunt's observations, the future Queen Mary persevered. A few months later, she and her husband were down in Cornwall and making long drives in their own vehicle. As for Aunt Augusta, she never came to terms with the motor car. She considered it to be 'horrible', 'dangerous', and 'so un-royal'. Perhaps, if she had deigned to think about it, that would have been Queen Victoria's opinion as well.

The Kaiser was fond of fast motoring, and King Alfonso XIII of Spain was even fonder. In 1924, he was to drive round the racing circuit at San Sebastian at a speed only slightly slower than that of Henry Segrave when the latter won the Spanish Grand Prix that same year. His first car was a Panhard, and he quickly threw his court into a state of extreme agitation by his habit of leaving the palace at a rip-roaring rate, departing from the route that he had told people he would follow, and returning late at night and long overdue. On the one hand, his statesmen considered such conduct unkingly: on the other, they feared for his life and for the future of the Spanish monarchy.

*The first crowned head to own a car was the Sultan of Morocco,
who took possession of this canopy-topped Daimler in 1892. Contrary
to popular belief, it did not sound the death knell of the camel.*

*In 1900, King Edward VII discovered the pleasures of motoring
after being driven by the Hon. John Scott Montagu in the latter's
Daimler. The effect of a safety belt around His Majesty is, in fact,
produced by the top of a rug.*

Prince Henry of Prussia (seen at the wheel of his Benz) gave his patronage to motor sport when he sponsored the Prince Henry trials. The object was not so much speed as reliability and sportsmanship.

The Czar of Russia was a Delaunay-Belleville enthusiast to begin with—later he invested in Rolls-Royces. His transport for the 1911 manœuvres of the Russian army was a Mercedes-Knight.

The German Kaiser loved his cars and employed a well-known racing driver as his head chauffeur. When on army manœuvres (as below), *a special vehicle was equipped with a bed—to enable H.I.M. to sleep in the field.*

By 1910, no self-respecting monarch was without a car. The size of the vehicle seems to have been in proportion to that of the state he ruled. The occupant of this Mercedes 16/45 is King Ferdinand of Bulgaria.

The French President, as might be expected, has always favoured a French car. This Panhard and Levassor was used by President Fallières in 1913.

When he was married in 1910, Alfonso's queen delighted him by presenting him with an Hispano-Suiza. He already had two examples of this distinguished breed, and this latest—powered by a very potent 3·6-litre engine—pleased him enormously. When, shortly afterwards, the firm sought his permission to call the model 'Alfonso', he had no objection at all. Some years later, his wife had the honour (if that is the right word) of having a car named after her. Known as the 'Victoria' (after Victoria Eugenia), it was a comparatively small but by no means unsportsmanlike vehicle, powered by a 950 c.c. o.h.v. engine and fitted with four-wheel brakes. A thousand of them were manufactured until, in 1933, the company sold its controlling interest to an English firm, and the name was discontinued.

While he was Prince of Wales, the Duke of Windsor may have been pleased to know that an American product called the 'Prince' was named after him (it was about as far as anyone could go with the British Royal Family: actual christian names would have been taboo), but the one who came off best in this respect was Prince Henry of Prussia. There were two cars which bore his name: the Prince Henry Vauxhall in England and the Prince Henry Tourer, a Daimler product which was designed by Ferdinand Porsche in 1910.

In fact, if one has to be honest, these cars were not dedicated to His Imperial Highness so much as to a sporting event to which he had given his name.

Prince Henry was the younger brother of the Kaiser. For some years, he was supreme commander of the German Navy (Queen Victoria, who never ceased meddling in the affairs of her relatives, had suggested that he should go to sea in the vain hope that it would prevent a marriage of which she disapproved). Not very much is known about his naval career, and it was over and done with by the time the first world war broke out. However, he did acquire at least one priceless possession from this period of his life, and that was a stoker from his flagship, *Deutschland*, who turned out to be a most excellent chauffeur.

The Prince acquired his first car in 1903, when he bought a 14/18 Benz limousine. In the following year, this was joined by a 24 h.p. Benz tourer, which was much more lively.

At about the same time as Prince Henry took delivery of his

second car, a motoring enthusiast named Professor Hubert von Herkomer was busy drawing out a plan for an event that he hoped to organise with assistance from the appropriate automobile clubs. Herkomer was a portrait artist who had received a knighthood in England. Possibly this was secured by a painting he did of the Duke of Wellington, which was badly damaged when suffragettes set fire to the Royal Academy in 1914. Anyway, he was an artist and a motoring enthusiast, and he planned to organise an event which would take the competitors on a tour of Germany, with a speed test and a hill climb thrown in. Entries would be confined strictly to amateurs, and the first prize (consisting of a trophy and a portrait of the winner by the Professor) would be awarded on the basis of reliability.

In those days, motor sport was as much of a jungle as it has ever been. The works teams, always eager for publicity, just couldn't keep out of it—and when, one day in 1905, the cars arrived for scrutineering, there they all were.

The regulations insisted that every competing car should be a tourer: that it should be fitted with its proper body, able to seat four people comfortably, and in a fit condition to be delivered to a customer—which meant, among other things, that it had to have sufficient coats of paint and the final finish of varnish.

Presumably in an attempt to save weight, a number of cars were unvarnished and some had merely been given a swift smear of lead primer. The Opels and the Adlers were fitted with specially built light bodies, which at first caused them to be disqualified. After a lot of argument, it was presently agreed that they might take part if they carried forty kilogrammes of sand as ballast. All told, out of the 161 cars which were ready to start, no fewer than forty had to be brought into line with their standard specifications before they were allowed to compete.

In the following year, the Herkomer Trial was repeated. With an almost cynical disregard for the rules, the manufacturers again tried to cheat. At scrutineering, it was found that some cars had the steps leading up to the back seats removed, and others had been fitted with canvas doors. Twenty per cent of the entries had only been given a light coat of grey paint, and some of the vehicles were so modified that anyone sitting in their rear seats would have been thrown overboard on the timed sections. The theory of the entrants, it seems, was that any penalty marks incurred by irregular bodywork would be offset by bonus points they'd win in the speed trials.

Among those taking part was Prince Henry of Prussia in his new Benz. Prince Henry had motored from Berlin to Frankfurt to be present at the start, and popular opinion had it that he considered the antics of the manufacturers a serious threat to amateurism. One British magazine reported him as saying that he considered the entrants from the U.K. to be the 'only section who, as a body, were doing the thing as amateurs and gentlemen'. Since a dozen Daimlers had been entered from England, the word 'amateur' must be regarded with a certain amount of suspicion. However, everybody was delighted with the Prince. He was seen to pump up his own tyres and, during the overnight halts, he would talk to other competitors and exchange notes on where to change gear on the hillclimb. He also went to a good deal of trouble to ensure that the Daimler (British version) party's accommodation was satisfactory.

Perhaps because he was worried about the ungentlemanly conduct of some competitors, and felt that royal patronage might make them mend their manners, the Prince took over the event in 1908. Thereafter, it became known as the Prince Henry Trial. The organisation was handled by the Imperial Automobile Club in Berlin, and the regulations stipulated that 'the competing cars are to be driven by gentlemen who are members of recognised automobile clubs, and who must not receive any fees for driving'. Among the prizes were trophies given by Prince Henry himself, the Grand Duke of Hesse (for the hillclimb), H.R.H. the Hereditary Princess of Sachsen-Mainigen and the City of Lübeck. The entrance fee was £20 and competitors were assured that, sport apart, it was a very good way of touring Germany at a reasonable cost.

The service of issuing results at the end of each day was indifferent. A French journalist scoffingly described the event as 'a promenade of speeds of 20–30 m.p.h.'. And one competitor fell over a ninety-foot cliff. By some miracle, he wasn't hurt.

Otherwise, it was a great success.

In 1909 there was another Prince Henry Trial, and it was noticed that the Prince's own car had a squeegee mounted on the bottom offside corner of its windscreen for the purpose of cleaning the glass. Since windscreen wipers had not yet been invented, the idea seemed excellent, and many people copied it afterwards.

Nineteen-hundred-and-eleven was the year of King George V's coronation. Relations between Germany and Britain had become somewhat strained. Both countries were building battle-ships for all they were worth, and were regarding each other uneasily from behind barrels of gunpowder. Prince Henry had been a favourite of the late king, who, at the time of Queen Victoria's funeral, had made him an honorary vice-admiral in the Royal Navy. In that same year he made a trip to Canada and the United States in a bid to improve relations with Germany. Now, with a new monarch on the British throne, there seemed to be another opportunity for his role as a self-appointed diplomat.

His theory was that, if you could not get the statesmen to agree, you could at least build up goodwill between various sections of the two communities. In this case, his target was the motorists, with the armed forces as a side benefit. What he proposed to do was to make the Prince Henry Trial of that year an Anglo-German affair. Half the event would take place in Germany. The cars would then be taken from Bremerhaven to Southampton by steamer, and a roughly circular tour of the U.K. would follow. An officer from either the Royal Navy or the British Army would travel as an observer on each of the German cars. An officer from either the Imperial Navy or the German Army would travel on each of the British cars. All told, there were forty-two German cars entered and thirty-two British. Among those taking part were the Duke of Connaught, Sir Arthur Conan Doyle[1] (the creator of Sherlock Holmes) and Prince Henry himself. His Royal Highness was an honorary member of the R.A.C., and, accompanied by Prince Francis of Teck, had made a visit to the Daimler works at Coventry in the previous year. Thus he had a reasonable knowledge of his way around the British motoring scene.

Apart from Prince Henry's own prize, cups were presented by King George V (who seems to have viewed the event with some suspicion at first, until it was explained to him that it wasn't a race), Queen Mary, the German Emperor and the German Empress. A British car was the outright winner and the Prince

[1]Earlier on, Conan Doyle, who drove a de Dietrich, had been fined for speeding on the Portsmouth road.

Henry Cup passed into the hands of the R.A.C. In spite of plans for a Prince Henry Tour to Austria in the following year, and one to Russia in the year after that, the trophy never left the club. For some reason which has never been explained, and is now no doubt forgotten, the Prince Henry Trial was discontinued after its giant coronation edition.

4 The Emperor's Automobiles

Early in the twentieth century an ingenious accessory manufacturer produced a rather horrible motor horn. It had four notes, and they were arranged in such a way that they made up a little tune. This might have been bad enough, for any four-note melody becomes tedious after a while. Unfortunately, it was made even worse by the suggestion that, if you thought about it, you could fit some words to the tune. All that was needed was '*Der Kai-ser Kommt*' which, being translated, means 'The Kaiser is coming'.

The manufacturer chuckled happily, said wasn't that a good idea, and immediately had the notion of doing himself and his firm a bit of good. Having written a sufficiently sycophantic letter, he packed the horn up and dispatched it to His Imperial Majesty Kaiser Wilhelm II of Germany.

His Imperial Majesty was delighted. Indeed, he was so pleased that he immediately issued instructions that no one else in Germany should be permitted to use a horn of a similar type. This, of course, was a most bitter blow to the manufacturer, and not at all what he had in mind. He spent the next two years trying to get the restriction removed. In the end, he was partially successful. The Kaiser agreed that such a horn might be used when motoring in the country, but he still forbade its use in the cities.

The ban only applied to four-note horns. It did not prevent the King of Saxony from stealing a march on the Emperor, and having a *six*-note horn made for his car. Nor did it inhibit the Kaiser's son, Prince Augustus Wilhelm, from composing a small theme tune and commissioning the construction of a horn capable of playing it.

A thing one has to remember about the Kaiser is that he was an *enthusiast*. He never did anything by halves. If he liked a car horn, he liked it so much that he was quite prepared to turn a section of the accessory industry upside down to secure its exclusive use. Much the same thing applied to his ownership of cars. He didn't simply enjoy the things: he *revelled* in them.

Initially, they were a convenience. The Emperor had two palaces in Prussia: one in Berlin and the other at Potsdam. Travelling between the two used to be a rather tedious business. There had to be a carriage to convey the Imperial Family to the station at Berlin and another had to be waiting for them at Potsdam. Admittedly the court train was an extremely comfortable conveyance, but the Kaiser had to pay for it—just as any other German citizen had to buy a ticket to travel on the railways. It was expensive, and one of the advantages of the car was that it cut out this expenditure.

Instead, the family climbed into a cavalcade of vehicles, processed through the zoological gardens and out into the Grünewald. For much of the time, the horn on the Kaiser's own car played its little ditty, announcing to one and all that Himself was on the way.

When there was an emergency, of course, the cars were even more useful. One night, when the Empress was staying at Potsdam, one of the princesses gave birth to a child in Berlin. Without the well-beloved Mercedes, the situation would have been intolerably difficult. The carriages would have had to be got out, a train assembled in the station, and goodness knows what all. As it was, the car was brought round to the door, and the Empress was driven to Berlin just in time for the infant prince's arrival.

The imperial stables in Berlin were known locally as 'the first stables in the world'. It was a description with which the Kaiser's uncle, King Edward VII, might not have agreed and there would have been no lack of dissenting voices from other royal households. However, that was what they were known as, and the garage, which was added to cope with the Kaiser's growing herd of motor cars, was a very splendid affair.

Kaiser Wilhelm's first drive in a car had been during the army manœuvres of 1899, when he made a short trip in a Daimler. A number of observers thought the undertaking was extremely dangerous and that the ruler of the Fatherland had no business to be risking his neck. It was the sort of criticism that Alfonso XIII had to put up with in Madrid, though with rather less justification. Wilhelm seems to have enjoyed his trip, but it was not until 1904 that the designs of cars were considered to be sufficiently advanced for him to own one. It was a 28 h.p. Mercedes, built to be run on alcohol.

Down in the first stables in the world, the newcomer was regarded with disfavour. The car cleaners made bad jokes about its six-seater body, and there was a general atmosphere of hope that the wretched thing would break down and cure the Emperor of his latest craze.

Much to their dismay, it did not. Five months later, to the fury of those horse-loving stable hands, the Kaiser bought a second car, and in February of the following year, a third appeared. Like the first, these two ran on alcohol.

By stipulating this type of fuel, the Kaiser displayed an unusual sensitivity to public opinion. Like the rustics in England, German farmers disliked cars intensely. It was the usual story about love of horses, and how the cars stank, and so on. By providing them with an outlet for the products of their potato distilleries, the Emperor hoped to wean them away from their prejudice. With a bit of luck, he might even cause them to regard motor cars with affection.

Unfortunately for these praiseworthy objectives, it turned out to be impossible to overcome the internal combustion engine's antipathy to potato alcohol. It performed very badly on it and, in the end, the Kaiser, who was not a man to give in without trying, had to admit that petrol might be better.

The Kaiser's first petrol car was a 60 h.p. Fiat. Poor Wilhelm! The fact that he had bought an Italian car provoked a storm from the factories. Some of it was righteous indignation: quite a lot was self-pity. Were not German vehicles good enough for His Imperial Majesty? Were they not the finest in the world? How could the German motor industry hope to develop if it didn't receive royal support? And so on. The Emperor gave in and promised that, from then onwards, he would only use German cars.

Originally, the imperial stables had been under the management of a minor member of the nobility, who cared a good deal for horses and not very much for automobiles. By the time the car fleet had acquired four vehicles, it was decided that some changes were necessary. In terms of administration, the cars were separated from the animals, and the former were put under the charge of a captain in the German Army. Before very long, he found that he had seven petrol-driven vehicles to look after, two electric town carriages, and two large lorries. By 1912, the number had grown to twenty-five vehicles, of which twenty were based on the palace in Berlin and five at a residence the Kaiser owned on the Greek island of Corfu. Among them were the products of Mercedes, Benz, Adler, Opel, and N.A.G. Strangely enough, they did not include a Horch, which seems to have been an oversight on somebody's part.

The earlier cars had been tourers, but these were soon dismissed as unsatisfactory. After a long drive over dusty roads, the Emperor and his retinue were apt to arrive at an official engagement in a state which, according to one German eyewitness, could 'absolutely not be described as fit for court'. The open cars were replaced by landaulets. The roof at the back could be lowered in good weather, and yet it gave complete protection when it rained, or on a journey over dusty roads. It seemed to be an admirable compromise.

The Emperor's cars were upholstered with red leather: those of the Empress with beige cloth. The exteriors were painted in the livery of the royal train.

One of the objects of providing Wilhelm and his empress with distinctive colour schemes for their vehicles was that the police could identify them from some distance away, and this was supposed to make the work of controlling the traffic easier. Unfortunately, and this may explain the Kaiser's attitude to the melody of his car horn, other people thought that it might be fun to copy the royal household. The first person to do so was one of the palace staff. He had his car repainted in the imperial colours. His wife was delighted when, passing through the Brandenburg Gate in Berlin one day, the guards on duty smartly presented arms to her.

D

Eventually the whole thing got out of hand, and some other means of identifying the Kaiser's cars had to be devised. First of all, they almost smothered the vehicles in crowns: there were small ones on the headlamps, a big Prussian royal crown on the back, and, in case anyone had missed these, a further band of crowns was painted on the doors.

Later, a rather better idea—using flags—was employed. When inside Prussia, the Emperor flew the royal standard. Elsewhere in Germany, he displayed the imperial standard, and when he was in company with a foreign guest, the visitor's flag was flown from a small staff on the right-hand side of the car. A considerable stock was stored away in the stables. It included one for every ruler in the world.

At night, the Emperor's standard was replaced by a lamp on the roof of the car with the glass carefully tinted in the imperial colours.

To keep the car fleet on the move, a staff of thirty-one was employed. There were five head chauffeurs, seven junior chauffeurs, twelve escorts (probably a species of footman), three lorry drivers, one mechanic, one fitter, one labourer and one telephonist. The two top drivers were a man named Schroeder and the racing driver Christian Werner. Schroeder seems to have been one of the older palace hands. Apart from the trust which the Kaiser had in him, the most noteworthy thing about him was the variety of foreign decorations festooned on his uniform tunic. Whenever a foreign potentate visited the Kaiser, he gave Schroeder a medal as a reward for driving him. As one of his colleagues remarked, the row of ribbons looked rather like a royal portrait gallery. There was one from King Edward of Britain, and another from the Czar of Russia. A Spanish decoration, recalling a visit from Alfonso, was next door to a Swedish ribbon, and so on.

Werner had taken part with moderate success in a number of early motor races, including the ill-fated Paris–Madrid event and at least two in the Gordon Bennett series. His motor sport career continued long after the Kaiser had gone into exile. He won the 1924 Targa Florio, and he shared a Mercedes with Rudolf Caracciola in the 1930 Le Mans 24-Hour Race.

After the war, he joined Daimler-Benz as a test driver. One of his jobs was to report on Caracciola, when the latter applied to the factory for a job as a racing driver. Caracciola afterwards wrote that 'he had a long, sad face with a large nose and deep-set eyes. It was a face that looked as if it would never laugh again.' This may have been explained by the fact that Werner's wife had just died. What Werner thought of the would-be ace has not been recorded—except that he recommended him for work as a car salesman at 100 marks a month.

When the Kaiser was in Berlin, Schroeder and Werner shared the duties of driving him on the basis of eight days on and eight days off. They took it in turns to handle the longer journeys; and, when H.I.M. was on manœuvres, they worked on alternate days.

The Kaiser used to spend much of the winter on Corfu. In summer, there were the army manœuvres, when by no means the least of the problems was that of transporting him to a series of appointments with horses. On the mock battlefield, he liked to ride around on a charger, and this would have been simple enough if he had been content to confine himself to one area each day. Unfortunately for his hard-worked staff, he preferred to get around as much as possible. He would appear unexpectedly at one place, and then, within an hour or so, put in an appearance at a sector several miles away. Somehow the drivers, the aides, and all the rest of the retinue had to scamper around the countryside, collecting horses at map references, a smart thunder of hooves, some brisk military chat, and then back to the cars and away to somewhere else. It was all very exhausting. When visiting royalty was present, it was even worse, and anything from twelve to twenty cars were involved. They were usually loaned for the purpose by the Daimler factory at Stuttgart.

One of the better aspects of manœuvres were the meals, which were served by the imperial field kitchen. It consisted of two vehicles. One contained the kitchen itself, the other was a mobile furniture store. Apart from the tools of cooking, the kitchen car was fitted with capacious ice boxes in which meat, butter, plenty of beer and wine, were stored. Air-tight containers were packed with vegetables, spices, and other foodstuffs. The theory behind the kitchen car's contents was that, in the good open-air life of military exercises, the imperial appetite was liable to become twice as sharp.

The other vehicle contained a portable dining-room table (when assembled, it was about fourteen feet long and three feet wide) and a dozen folding wooden chairs. If it rained, a large awning was ready for instant erection over the table. Inside the van, there was a collection of seats, which could be folded back and turned into a bed if Wilhelm decided to remain in the field overnight.

To judge by contemporary reports, he used it a good deal, for he had a habit of dropping in unexpectedly, like an over-zealous scoutmaster, on parties of troops as they sat round their camp-fires in the evenings.

After the war, when he lived in exile in Holland, the Kaiser's fondness for cars continued—though it had to be on a somewhat reduced scale. With money that he had been able to take with him from Germany, he purchased several acres of woodland in the area of Doorn. He then ordered a huge supercharged 7·1-litre Mercedes, which was delivered to him personally by one of the Daimler-Benz directors. Like the 1904 Mors owned by the 5th Marquess of Anglesey, it had a signalling system between the rear and front seats. In the Kaiser's version, a switch at the back transmitted messages to an instrument, about the size of a clock, which was mounted on the dashboard. It was divided into segments: one had the word 'Left' printed on it—another 'Right'. There was 'House', 'Stop', 'Quicker' and 'Slow'. Whichever the Kaiser indicated with his switch was instantly illuminated.

The interior of the car also contained accommodation for two axes. Like Mr. Gladstone in an earlier though less unhappy political exile, the Kaiser liked to chop wood.

And that famous car horn melody, *'Der Kaiser Kommt'*, was taken over by the German fire brigade who used it on all their engines.

5 The Mysteries of Sarajevo

At 10.40 a.m. on Sunday, July 28th, 1914, a nineteen-year-old Bosnian High School student was standing on a street corner in Sarajevo. In one pocket of his jacket, he had a Browning pistol —in the other, a crudely made bomb. His name was Gavrilo Princip. His hair was dark and brushed straight back from his forehead. He had a sallow complexion and a small, carefully trimmed, moustache. But what attracted you about this rather intense young man were his eyes, which were large and blue and strangely innocent.

The street was crowded with people, for the heir to the Austrian throne, the Archduke Franz Ferdinand himself, had come to visit the town. It was a sunny morning, and the houses on either side had their windows open. In several of them, the inhabitants had come out on to their balconies to get a better view of what was happening.

When the Austrian emperor had come to Sarajevo six years earlier, the sides of the royal route had been lined with double rows of soldiers. There were no such lavish precautions for the protection of Franz Ferdinand. Members of the city's 120-strong police force were stationed at strategic points, facing the bystanders. But since the Archduke's route lay over a distance of four miles, 120 men were not very much use.

There was a ripple of cheering from up the road and a number of people began waving their hands. The first two cars in the procession slowed down and turned right at the cross roads where Princip was standing. The third car, in which the Archduke and his wife, the Duchess Sophie, were travelling, also began to turn right. But then there seemed to be a good deal of confusion. The man who was sitting in the passenger seat at the front began shouting at the chauffeur. The driver brought the car to a halt.

Princip had been waiting for this moment. It was better than he had dared to hope for. The range was short, the car had stopped, and the Archduke was a sitting duck. First of all, he flung his home-made bomb at the vehicle, but it never went off. Then he took out the Browning. A woman who was standing beside him noticed this action, and called to the nearest policeman. But it was too late: aiming the gun, the schoolboy Princip fired what have ever since been called the first shots of World War I.

In 1914 Sarajevo had a population of about 41,000. Eighteen thousand of them were Mohammedans, 4,000 were Jews, and, of the remainder, many were Austrians. The Austrians lived in the more expensive houses.

It was an attractive place, 1,770 feet above sea level, with hills rising to over 5,000 feet on either side. Just above the town, the river Miljacka burst out of a gorge. In Sarajevo, there were nine bridges over the Miljacka. Nowadays, one of them is named after Princip: another after Zerajic who, in 1916, shot an Austro-Hungarian official and then killed himself.

Because of the variety of religions, Sarajevo only really came to life on four days of the week. The Mohammedans celebrated Friday as the Sabbath; the Jews rested on Saturdays; and the Christians took Sundays off. The busiest day was Wednesday, which was market day, and the bazaar in the centre of the town was crowded with people. There were always plenty of 'oriental goods' to be bought at the stalls—though most of them were manufactured in Austria.

On Thursday evenings, a troupe called the Dancing Dervishes put on a show in one of the cafés. Tickets, improbably enough, were obtainable at the police station. There were three main hotels, of which the largest was the Europa. By 1914, the Europa had installed electricity and central heating, which gave it the edge on its competitors. The hotel porters were happy to take guests on short sight-seeing expeditions—a reasonable fee was considered to be a small sum of money and 'a few cigarettes'.

The main railway station was about two miles from the centre of the town. On the way in, you passed the barracks where 2,900 Austrian troops were quartered, and the Konak, which was the residence of the military governor. The Konak's gardens were open to the public on certain days of the week: the residence was not.

When the Archduke came to Sarajevo in 1914, his entourage was accommodated at the Europa. He and his wife stayed at a small spa some miles away called Ilidze. It was famous for its thermal baths and 'radio-active' waters.

Sarajevo was one item on a fairly busy programme. Before visiting the Bosnian capital, Franz Ferdinand had to attend the summer manœuvres of the Austro-Hungarian Army. Since he and Sophie had made the journey from Vienna by train, and had not brought any vehicles with them, there was a transport problem. It was solved by two noblemen: Count Franz von Harrach, who was a member of the imperial court, and Count Boos-Waldeck, who owned an estate about thirty miles north of Trieste.

The royal couple used von Harrach's 28/32 Gräf and Stift touring car, which had been delivered to the Count by its Viennese manufacturers back in 1910. It had a four-cylinder engine with four forward gears and one reverse. The gear shift was on the outside and with it there was another lever which worked the brakes at the rear. There were also two foot pedals, both connected to the prop shaft. One was for stopping in an emergency, the other produced a rather more gentle deceleration. This particular model was in production from 1908 until 1918. About 500 were produced in all.

Boos-Waldeck equipped the members of the entourage with vehicles which had belonged to one of his tenants. The man was a brewer from Trieste who had been killed, a month before the royal visit to Sarajevo, on a car journey to Munich. Among his possessions were six very expensive motor cars, and these seem to have fallen into the Count's possession. He also offered his chauffeur, Carlo Diviak, as driver to the royal car.

Diviak had grown up in Trieste. At school, he learned to speak German, though his native language was Italian. For the first few years of his career, he drove lorries for a brewery in Trieste. In 1912 he gave up this work, moved north and became Boos-Waldeck's chauffeur. He was twenty-four years old at the time of the Archduke's visit to Sarajevo, and extremely proud of the fact that he had been singled out to drive the heir-apparent's car.

Every morning, he reported punctually at the Hotel Bosna at Ilidze, collected his royal passenger, and drove off to the manœuvres. Count von Harrach also travelled in the car, whilst the Archduchess remained behind, possibly to take the waters. The car had the yellow and black standard, with the double-headed eagle of the imperial household, mounted on a small flagstaff next to the left-hand side of the windscreen.

Franz Ferdinand has been described as 'a heavy, gloomy and unbending man'—and 'Europe's proto-Nazi'. He certainly had no time for idle chatter with servants and, on these trips, he never spoke a word to Diviak. He was reputed to be interested in mechanical things, but he asked no questions about the car and there is some doubt about whether he was able to drive. Diviak found the imperial silence perfectly understandable. His passenger was, after all, heir to the Austrian throne. One couldn't expect much conversation from the likes of him.

On the morning of the 28th, the routine was much as usual. Diviak checked in at the Hotel Bosna. Since it was such a beautiful day, somebody asked the Archduke whether he would like the hood down. He replied that he would—not so much because of the weather, but because he wished the people of Sarajevo to have a good view of himself and his wife. He climbed into the back of the car, and the Duchess Sophie got in after him. Franz Ferdinand sat on the left-hand side: the duchess sat behind Diviak[1]. Count von Harrach travelled in front until they reached the Bosnian capital, when he was replaced by the military governor.

At no time was Diviak given any instructions about what route he was to take. He was simply told to follow the two cars in front.

In Sarajevo the main business thoroughfare was the Franz-Josef Street. The most beautiful, on the other hand, was the Appel Quay, which ran beside the river. It was here that the greater part of the crowd was congregated. Before the trip, Franz Ferdinand had been warned to expect trouble. There were a number of Serbian nationalists in the city and there was no knowing what

[1]The car had right-hand drive.

they might get up to. But he brushed the idea away. 'Do not worry,' he told the army officer who was in charge of the reception committee. 'These lesser breeds would not dare to do anything.'

Confidence is all very well, but the Archduke had rather too much of it. The first incident occurred when they were approaching one of the bridges over the river. A man was seen to throw what appeared to be a bouquet of flowers at the royal car.

In fact, he was a printer named Cabrinovic (described afterwards by *The Times* as a 'ne'er-do-well'), and, seconds before throwing the flowers, he was seen to prime a small bomb by knocking the cap against a lamp-post. Earlier, he had asked one of the spectators which car would be carrying the royal couple, and what the Archduke looked like.

Having set the grenade, he wrapped the flowers around it and had aimed it at the car. It landed on the folded hood, just behind the Archduke's head. With a sweep of his hand, Franz Ferdinand sent it flying down on to the road. It exploded by the left-hand rear wheel of the following car.

It was a somewhat crude kind of bomb, loaded with an assortment of ironmongery which included nails and small pieces of scrap iron, but there was plenty of explosive in it. A woman watching the parade from a first-floor balcony was hit in the face. Twenty other spectators were injured—some of them seriously. The car itself was holed in seventy places, and two of the occupants—an army lieutenant and Diviak's employer, Boos-Waldeck —were hurt. The lieutenant's injuries were severe.

Cabrinovic jumped off the parapet and into the river. A policeman went in after him, and so did a number of civilians. Between them, they hauled him back on to land. For the moment, there was chaos. The injured officers from the car had to be taken to the hospital, and the crowd was doing its best to lynch Cabrinovic.

Only the Archduke and his wife seemed to preserve anything resembling calm. But, then, nothing could shake the stolid heir-apparent to the throne. The military governor was all for calling off the rest of the day's schedule, and returning to his residence for a cup of coffee, but Franz Ferdinand dismissed the attack as the work of a lunatic, and gave orders for the programme to continue.

Somehow, the situation was got under control, and what remained of the parade continued on its way to the town hall.

The mayor was on the steps to welcome his distinguished visitors. But, instead of the polite greetings he had expected, he found himself face to face with a very irate archduke. 'What is the use of your speeches?' Franz Ferdinand demanded. 'I come to Sarajevo on a friendly visit, and someone throws a bomb at me. This is outrageous.'

But the mayor had not the least idea of what he was talking about. News of the bomb attack had not reached the town hall. He had heard a distant explosion, and had assumed that it was a cannon being fired in salute.

Under such circumstances, a man must keep his head, and the mayor decided that the best way of doing so was to act as if everything were entirely normal. He adjusted his spectacles and proceeded to read the speech of welcome he had prepared.

By the time he had finished, Franz Ferdinand had recovered as much good humour as he ever possessed. He acknowledged the speech suitably and then said, 'Let's get on with the programme.'

There were further suggestions that the rest of the tour should be abandoned. After all, where there has been one spot of trouble, there can easily be two. But no—His Imperial Highness was adamant. What had been begun must be completed. Nevertheless, he must have had some misgivings; for, as he climbed into the car, Diviak overheard him remark to von Harrach that they would probably 'also get a couple of bullets this day'. Of course, it may have been a rather bad joke.

The situation now becomes very confusing indeed. Before the cavalcade left the town hall, the Archduke demanded a change in the programme. They were to have visited the museum. Instead, he wished to look in on the two wounded officers who had been taken to the military hospital. In the enquiry which followed the assassination, von Harrach said that he alone was sitting in the front of the Archduke's car beside Diviak. Other, and more substantial, evidence suggests that the military governor was next to the chauffeur and von Harrach was standing on the running board—though why the Count should have bothered to make such a fabrication is a complete mystery.

Certainly nobody bothered to tell Diviak of any change of plan, nor of what emergency action to take if they ran into more trouble. He simply had to keep following the two vehicles in front.

The leading car carried the chief of detectives and he, too, does not seem to have received any other fresh instructions.

At about 10.30, the procession left the town hall. It turned into the Appel Quay and quickened its pace. At the junction with Franz-Josef Street, the two leading cars turned right, as if they were carrying out the original plan. Diviak made as if to follow them, but then the military governor (who *must* have been in the car whatever von Harrach may have said) suddenly yelled 'Stop!' He told Diviak that they were going the wrong way, and should continue along the Appel Quay. Diviak jammed on his brakes.

This gave Gavrilo Princip his opportunity. How many rounds he fired is another mystery. Diviak swears there was only one. It was, he said, a dum-dum type bullet which, having hit the Duchess, went on to tear open the Archduke's jugular vein. One suspects that he is wrong; for Franz Ferdinand was hit in the neck and in one of his legs, and the Duchess was wounded in the abdomen— all of which seems a lot of work for one bullet. Von Harrach went on record as saying: 'I can quite definitely recollect that, on the second murder attempt, only two shots were fired.' The military governor heard 'two, perhaps three or four shots' and a passenger in the car behind said: 'After the first shot, I heard two or three noticeably weaker shots quickly—one after the other.'

But the important question is: Why was there so much confusion? Did Diviak really make a mistake and, by following the two leading cars, provide the opportunity for one of the most disastrous murders in history? Obviously not. He had been told to follow them and that was what he did. Furthermore, he told a reporter many years later that the Archduke himself had *ordered* him to turn right, and that the idea of carrying on down the Appel Quay was entirely the governor's.

Whatever the truth is, after the shooting Diviak was ordered to drive as fast as he could to the governor's residence. Such break-neck methods cannot have done the condition of his gravely injured passengers very much good, but they may have been beyond medical aid in any case. The Duchess had scarcely been given the last sacrament before she died. Her husband followed a few minutes later.

Once the fatally injured couple had been taken out of the car Diviak was kept busy driving backwards and forwards to government buildings, collecting doctors and first-aid equipment. Afterwards, the vehicle was empounded by the authorities until the enquiry into the assassination had been completed. On July 27th, 1914, it was taken to Vienna and handed over to the Museum of Military History. It is still there today.

Carlo Diviak returned to his job with Count Boos-Walbeck until war broke out. He then joined the Austrian Army and, afterwards, went back to Trieste, where he raised a large family. He held down a number of chauffeuring jobs until his sixtieth birthday, when he retired on a pension. The mayor of Trieste presented him with a commendation recording the fact that, during the whole of his career, he had never been involved in a road accident.

In 1964 the Rome correspondent of the Swiss weekly *Die Weltwoche* visited him at his small flat on the third floor of a block in the old quarter of Trieste. His left arm and leg were paralysed, and he seemed to be lonely. But that is one of the less charitable facts of life: far more attention is given to historic cars than to historic chauffeurs.

Gavrilo Princip died from tuberculosis on April 28th, 1918, while serving a sentence of twenty years' hard labour (it involved living in an unlit cell and being deprived of food for twenty-four hours each month). Cabrinovic and three others involved in the plot were executed. Perhaps they were more fortunate than their young accomplice.

The story of Sarajevo is really one of monumental inefficiency. The assassins deserved no success at all. Princip's bomb was a failure and Cabrinovic's aim was poor (Cabrinovic seems to have been one of history's total incompetents: having delivered his grenade, he made two attempts to commit suicide. One was by taking poison, which didn't work, and the other was by jumping into the river—from which he was rescued or captured, according to how you like to put it).

In spite of this ineptitude, the luckless Franz Ferdinand was more or less handed over to the killers on a plate, partly by his own pigheadedness and partly by atrocious organisation which neglected all but the most elementary security precautions (what was the point of those 2,900 soldiers confined in the barracks up the road—or were they not yet back from manœuvres?) And yet, in spite of this, Princip's attempt might still have failed, if only the royal entourage had been able to make up its mind in advance which route to take—and then had stuck to it.

The chauffeur Diviak was rightly awarded a citation for umpteen years of accident-free driving. And yet, one cannot help feeling, he was an unwitting assistant at one of the biggest chapters of accidents the world has ever known.

6 The War Game

The British Army loved its horses. Even when the first world war was well advanced, there were military commanders who would sooner have entrusted their troops to unprotected chargers than to the steel-plated security of tanks. Ironically, the first people to appreciate the possibility of armoured cars were at the Admiralty, a fact which caused a number of the earlier vehicles to be prefixed with the initials H.M.S.

Obviously there was a role for the internal combustion engine to play in time of war, and the Automobile Association was the first motoring organisation to take heed of it. With assistance from a Member of Parliament, and in a desperate attempt to convince the authorities that the car had a military future, the association organised a run from London to Hastings on March 17th, 1909. Its members provided the vehicles and the War Office (grudgingly, one suspects) supplied a fully equipped battalion of Guards. Each car was crammed with soldiers, and the entire unit was transported over a distance of sixty-three miles.

It not only gave the Army Council something to think about: it also helped to convince the public at large that the motor car was not entirely evil.

Three years later, an experiment was conducted in which a number of Delaunay–Belleville taxis were equipped with Maxim guns and wireless sets. It was never taken any further, which was probably just as well. Although a very elegant and sturdy vehicle the Delaunay–Belleville would have presented a huge target to enemy machine gunners, and, in terms of protection, it would have rated very poorly indeed.

In that same year, after putting up a particularly fine performance in trials organised by the St. Petersburg Automobile Club, the Vauxhall Motor Company received a contract to supply staff cars for the Russian Army. Each was fitted with a folding map table and a basket in which the officers could park their swords.

When war broke out on August 4th, 1914, there was a patriotic stampede to give things to the nation in its hour of need. Mothers gave their sons, employers gave their chauffeurs, young men gave their lives, and Rolls-Royce owners gave the most precious thing they possessed—which was, of course, their Rolls-Royces. The Maharajah of Patiald in India had a particularly beautiful specimen with a teak and aluminium torpedo body mounted on a colonial-type chassis. Like so many other people, His Highness made the supreme sacrifice, and had his car shipped to Europe for the use of the British Expeditionary Force. A French Rolls-Royce owner who seems, by some devious means, to have acquired it from Emile Jellinek, presented his car to the French Army, for the use of Marshal Foch. And a gentleman in Abergavenny offered his Barker-bodied saloon (the body was blue and the black seats were edged with white) to the Admiralty. Possibly the senior service had learnt to beware of charity: at all events, their Lordships bought the car and ear-marked it for the First Sea Lord.

During the retreat from the Marne in 1914, when the Germans nearly captured Paris, the day was partially saved by Renault taxis, which were commandeered to rush reinforcements to the front. But, on a somewhat smaller scale, Rolls-Royces assisted as well. Just as the retreat was beginning, three of these cars and their owners were landed at Le Havre to transport an English general and his staff to the French headquarters at Le Cateau.

Major Hugh Davnay was a cavalry officer who was killed leading a charge in the first battle of Ypres. But, before that, he had a brief moment of glory, when he was driven about his duties by the Duke of Westminster in His Grace's own Rolls-Royce.

Another member of this noble breed had been presented to the Army by a wealthy young gentleman living in Chile. Its body was finished in natural wood which, one supposes, made it easier to camouflage. It was allocated to a signals officer, who seems to have used it in much the manner of a scout car. On one occasion, it came under fire from a German infantry unit and only escaped destruction through its ability to accelerate rapidly over an extremely muddy road.

Baron Robert de Rothschild presented his Rolls-Royce to a French general named Hugnet. Louis Chiron, who became famous as a racing driver during the years between the wars, was called to the colours and employed as chauffeur by General Foch and, later on, by General Pétain. But the military leader with the fastest car was Field Marshal von Hindenburg. Indeed, the German commander's vehicle was more than an automobile: it was almost a secret weapon, for it was a modified version of that celebrated racing car, the Blitzen Benz. In a somewhat different form, a Blitzen Benz had set up an unofficial World Land Speed Record in 1911, when it travelled at 142 m.p.h. at Daytona.

Some years later, when he became Chancellor of Germany, von Hindenburg invested in a six-cylinder 3·92-litre 116 h.p. 'Super Mercedes'. Although by no means inclined to hang about, it was certainly more conventional.

Field Marshal Sir John French, who was in command of the British Expeditionary Force when it first landed in France, had a 30 h.p. Maudslay. Earlier, this vehicle had been used by King George V and Queen Mary when they attended army manœuvres. The Queen liked to sit bolt upright in a car, and so it was fitted with a special back to the rear seat.

Their Majesties left the Royal Daimlers at home when they went on manœuvres, and possibly the royal chauffeur also enjoyed some leisure on these occasions.

One year, the manœuvres were scheduled to take place in Northamptonshire. Normally the top brass employed N.C.O.s as drivers, but, since the King and Queen were to be the passengers, it was decided that an officer ought to perform this function. Eventually a young lieutenant, who seemed to have the right social graces, was selected. What the authorities overlooked was the fact that he had never driven a car with anything larger than a 12 h.p. engine.

The royal couple were staying at a large house belonging to Earl Spencer, and the first signs that all might not be entirely well appeared when the lieutenant brought the car round from the rear of the building to the front door. A rather tight corner had to be negotiated, and a flower bed received a severe battering in the process. However, anxious officers reassured themselves with such remarks as 'There's always a first time', and 'He'll improve when he gets used to the car'.

In theory, the roads had been cleared of traffic to let the royal car through. Through some oversight, however, a lorry had got through the cordon. About five minutes after the royal party had set off, a dangerous situation developed. The lorry was approaching from one direction, and the Maudslay from the other. This might have been all very well, if the road had been wider at this point. As it was, there was just about room for the car to get through—or there would have been, if the driver had been more experienced.

To make matters worse, he was extremely nervous, for it is not every day that a young officer suddenly finds himself driving the King and Queen. Possibly he panicked: certainly, he misjudged the gap, took the Maudslay up on to the pavement, where it came to a halt with its wheels jammed against a wall.

This sort of thing obviously could not be allowed to continue. The young officer was instantly relieved of his 30 h.p. command. However, the King, always generous, later presented him with a pair of gold cufflinks for his services. The sergeant who took over from him was given gold and enamel cufflinks and a signed photograph of Their Majesties.

In spite of war, business of a kind had to continue. One of the more impressive—though, in view of the slaughter which was taking place in Europe, almost totally unremarked—feats of 1915 was the sale of a Rolls-Royce to His Majesty the King of Afghanistan. It was a limousine painted in bronze brown picked out in black. That, at any rate, is what one hopes it was. The various components had to be shipped out to India, taken over the Khyber Pass on pack mules, and then assembled in Kabul.

In 1916, Lord Kitchener, who was Secretary of State for War, had a Rolls-Royce on order. Before it could be delivered, however, Kitchener was killed when his ship struck a mine on a voyage to Russia. David Lloyd George, who had just become Prime Minister, took the car over, and it was delivered to him at number 10 Downing Street.

E

Kitchener had specified that the Rolls should be in green with black edging, which was an usual departure for him, He always used to insist that his cars be painted bright yellow. Before discovering the charms of Rolls-Royces he had been a great admirer of Delaunay-Bellevilles. The rather garish colour scheme may have been due to a personal preference for bright things: it may, equally well, have been explained by the fact that it was easily recognised. Pretty well every policeman in London knew the Field Marshal's car, and held up the traffic to let it pass.

Once, in Whitehall, an inexperienced member of the law ignored (or did not recognise) the illustrious presence, and held up the car to allow somebody to cross the road. Impatiently, Kitchener told his chauffeur to 'knock the bloody fool down'. Most people would have intended this as just a rather testy remark. Kitchener probably meant it.

Most of the military top brass had their little fads. Field Marshal Sir Douglas Haig, for example, was apt to be cautious. He had two Rolls-Royces, one permanently at his command at the War Office, and another based on his home at Kingston-on-Thames. A chauffeur who was assigned to him temporarily was chided for driving too quickly. And the commissionaire at the Horse Guards in London was once roundly rebuked for slamming the car's door.

Sir William Robertson, who was the first British general to have come up from the ranks, liked to be driven very fast. As ill luck would have it, one of his early drivers when he became Chief of the Imperial General Staff was a man who, in civilian life, had served as coachman to a couple of old ladies. It was hatred at first sight. The general had to be taken to Brighton and, in spite of angry comments which were blasted into the chauffeur's right ear through the speaking tube, the journey was undertaken at a snail's pace. Robertson concluded his business, went up to the car, and said to the unhappy man: 'Think I'll go home by train—it'll be quicker. Take me to the station, if you can get this damn thing up there.'

Back at the War Office, the General demanded that the driver should be replaced. A sergeant was found who was just back from a long period of service at the front in France. He arrived at Robertson's office wearing a pair of frayed puttees and blue mittens. When his blood pressure had recovered from the shock, the General suggested that he might return to his unit and persuade the quartermaster sergeant to kit him out in something more suitable. An hour or so later, the N.C.O. returned, wearing breeches, brown leggings and brown boots. He looked a very picture of military smartness, and Robertson was satisfied.

Field Marshal Sir Henry Wilson had a kind of phobia about taxi drivers. He owned an open Rolls-Royce, which he used to enjoy driving. One of his amusements when motoring in London was to break just about every rule in the book in attempts to force these vehicles on to the pavement. If this makes him sound a mean, unpleasant, character, the impression is probably wrong. It was just his idea of boisterous fun, though the cabmen cannot have agreed with him.

During his career, Wilson held a number of positions, from Chief of the Imperial General Staff at the end of the war, to Member of Parliament for Donegal. He also acted as military adviser to Northern Ireland, and was responsible for establishing the special constabulary over there.

He was a large man with a thick moustache, who (as his chauffeur put it) liked to dress 'as if he was an out-of-work gardener' when off duty. He had a London house at 36 Eaton Square and a place in the Home Counties at Bagshot. His passion in life was gardening, which may have accounted for his taste in clothes. At Bagshot, he gardened the living daylights out of the soil, and used to return to London with the back of the Rolls-Royce loaded with vegetables.

Once when he was down there, a clerk from the local station telephoned. There was, it appeared, a gun addressed to the Field Marshal awaiting collection. Thinking it was probably a twelve-bore he had ordered, Wilson summoned his chauffeur and hurried down to take possession of it. They were met by the station master, who said: 'You'll never get it in there, sir. It's a tidy size.'

The gun turned out to be a German long-range sixty-pounder, which somebody had decided to give the Field Marshal as a tribute to his wartime service. It was eventually taken up to the house on a lorry and mounted on the lawn.

Wilson was a sometimes amusing, often relaxed individual, who treated his driver as a member of the family. As a passenger, he was easy-going, and one retired soldier told me: 'He was the only man who never worried about how he was driven.' Once, on the way to Bagshot, they ran into thick fog at Staines. Very obligingly, the Field Marshal told his man: 'I'll get out and walk in front of the car.' For the next few minutes his huge, six foot four inches tall, figure could be seen in the headlamps, waving a pocket handkerchief and running on ahead. Once, he was nearly run down, and things became even worse when it was presently discovered that they were on the wrong side of the road. They made the best of a bad job, and went back to London.

If you were a common soldier, it never did to take anything for granted. One afternoon, Wilson was on his way through Camberley in his Rolls-Royce. He was sitting in the front, chatting to the driver, when they came up behind a large army lorry. The lorry was hogging the centre of the road and no amount of hooting could persuade the driver to get out of the way. Presently a gap appeared Wilson's man accelerated, but, at that moment, the lorry pulled right across to the far side. The driver jammed on his brakes and fell back. Shortly afterwards, they did manage to get through and Wilson flagged the lorry to a halt. He was wearing plain clothes at the time, but this did not stop him from getting out of the car and demanding the lorry driver's name, unit and number.

The private soldier at the wheel glanced at him with disdain. 'Look, mate,' he said, 'I'll give you mine, if you'll give me yours.'

Wilson regarded him through hard, steely eyes and revealed his identity. The soldier was reported to his commanding officer, and afterwards spent a period confined to barracks—doubtless reflecting that it might pay him to be more considerate while driving. Wilson's driver considered the punishment as merciful. 'If it had been Kitchener,' he recalls, 'he'd have had the man shot.'

Shortly after he had relinquished his duties as C.I.G.S. (field marshals never retire), Wilson had to go to Liverpool Street Station to unveil a memorial to railwaymen who had been killed in the war. He used a taxi for the return trip to Eaton Square, and at 2.30 in the afternoon he alighted outside his house, paid off the fare, and walked up to the front door. The square was almost deserted.

He was searching for his key when, suddenly, a shot was fired. Wilson ducked, and it smashed through a panel in the door. A second shot followed and, in a vain glorious gesture, the Field Marshal turned round and tried to draw his sword. The gunman fired three more rounds. This time the bullets found their mark. Wilson was hit in a leg, an arm, and in his body.

The noise attracted a crowd. Lady Wilson, who was in the house at the time, hurried to the front door, and helped to get her husband inside. He died soon afterwards.

Meanwhile, the assassins had made off with the crowd in full pursuit. They boarded a taxi that was coming into the square, and then jumped off it again and ran round the corner. From time to time, they turned round and fired. For a brief period, they even walked backwards discharging their guns, and a policeman was wounded in the stomach.

A group of workmen was taken by surprise and did nothing. A milkman was more effective. He threw a milk bottle, which hit one of the killers. But, by then, their escape was out of the question. The sound of police whistles had brought reinforcements from a nearby station. A constable threw his truncheon at one of the men and it caught him on the side of the head. Within minutes, the two assassins were in captivity. One of them, it transpired, had a wooden leg. They gave their names as James Connolly and James O'Brien, but it turned out later that these were false and they were really Reginald Dunn and Joseph O'Sullivan. Both were twenty-four years old. They were members of the Irish Volunteers, which was a forerunner of the I.R.A. The motive for their crime seems to have been Wilson's responsibility for organising the specials in Northern Ireland. The newspapers referred to the killing as 'cowardly', though 'suicidal' might have been a more apt description. In this case, British justice worked very quickly indeed and, within three months of the assassination, both men were hanged.

The final comment comes from the man who had been Wilson's chauffeur. If the Field Marshal had made the journey to and from Liverpool Street in a staff car with an army driver, he assured me, the story would have been very different indeed. These men were trained in how to act in such a situation, and Dunn and O'Sullivan would never have been able to commit their crime.

Field Marshal Sir Henry Wilson was superseded as C.I.G.S. by the Earl of Cavan. Whilst Wilson had been tall, Cavan was very short—about five feet four inches was one estimate. He inherited the official Rolls-Royce, but presently decided that it was too large for him.

'Look,' he told his driver, 'I'm going to change this car. I can hardly see out of it.'

He replaced it with a Vauxhall Prince Henry, which suited him much better. The car was beautifully got up, with inlaid mahogany tables, solid silver flower vases, and carriage lights on the outside. It was one of several that had been given to the government at the outbreak of war.

To protect his person against attack, a plain-clothes member of Scotland Yard's special branch was assigned to Lord Cavan. He carried a gun in his pocket, looked (so his colleague, the driver, told me) 'like a farmer', and had a rather unenviable job. Lord Cavan liked to play bridge at his club until well into the night, and it was often two o'clock in the morning before he got home and could be left to the security of his own house, Furthermore, he did not enjoy being guarded, and often used to assert that his chauffeur provided more than sufficient protection. On one occasion he told the special branch man to go home, and the unhappy police officer had to protest that 'If I did that, sir, I'd lose my job'. Cavan relented and allowed him to stay on—provided he kept out of the way.

Cavan, who had been a Guards officer, was very regimental. He always addressed his driver as 'Sergeant' and everything had to be just so. Nevertheless, he did relax sometimes, and he and Lady Cavan used to play a kind of game. Both prided themselves on their knowledge of London's streets, and they used to devise devious itineraries, hoping to catch the chauffeur out. It was all done in a spirit of fun and became a kind of competition in the end.

Certainly, if one was going to be a chauffeur, service chiefs seem to have been more companionable than civilian employers; and in many instances a spirit of comradeship grew up between the driver and the driven. Indeed, about the only person who was not totally in awe of Lord Kitchener was his chauffeur, and that is saying a very great deal.

7 Russian Roulette

In 1918, after the Tsar of Russia and most of his family had been murdered by the Bolsheviks, units of the Royal Navy entered the Black Sea. One of them, a battleship named H.M.S. *Marlborough*, presently put in at Odessa. Her mission was to rescue the Tsar's mother, the seventy-two-year-old Dowager Empress Marie Fedorovna. The large warship was accompanied by two cruisers, H.M.S. *Grafton* and H.M.S. *Theseus*.

Among the officers who went ashore from *Grafton* was Lieu-tenant-Commander W. R. Leycester, R.N. In the course of his duties, he was patrolling the docks when he came across a Rolls-Royce abandoned on a quayside. History is vague about the details. Whether or not the car was brought back to Britain aboard *Grafton* is not known. But, whatever the circumstances, the chassis number was identified as 2503. A glance at the Rolls-Royce records later revealed that it had been delivered on July 23rd, 1913, to a gentleman living in Moscow.

Presumably he had fled by car to Odessa, had somehow got away in a ship, and had been compelled to leave his vehicle behind him.

In this respect, he may have been more fortunate than most of the Russian Rolls-Royce owners, whose cars (and, one assumes, themselves) had remained at Moscow or St. Petersburg and were eventually taken over by the Bolsheviks.

The first of this breed to be sold to a Russian was a Hooper limousine, built to the order of Count Soumarakoff, who had residences in St. Petersburg and at 44 Curzon Street in London. It was dispatched to his St. Petersburg home on December 3rd, 1910.

Other Rolls-Royces followed. In 1912, Baron Nicolas Korff of St Petersburg took delivery of a vehicle with a seven-seater torpedo body by Barker; and, in the following year, a number were sent to Moscow. The Tsar himself bought his first Rolls-Royce in the summer of 1914, when a chassis was dispatched to the garage of his Tsarskoe Selo Palace (translated as 'the Tsar's village' and situated about fifteen miles from the centre of St. Petersburg—as opposed to the Winter Palace, which was in the middle of the city).

The Russian Emperor discovered the beauty of Rolls-Royces rather late in his life. Previously, he had been an ardent admirer of Delaunay-Bellevilles which, until the British car usurped them, were generally regarded as the finest vehicles in the world.

A typical example was the car delivered to him in 1910. It was a large limousine painted in dark blue with cream lining, and picked out with gold. The engine was a six-cylinder unit and, unusually for that period, was fitted with a self-starter.

The body was by Kellner: it had two seats right at the back and, in front of them, two armchairs facing forward. The Tsar himself always sat in the nearside armchair.

A clerestory roof at the rear provided ventilation and, to some extent, improved the lighting. All the rear windows were fitted with blinds, manufactured, so a contemporary account said, 'after the manner of the tops of American writing desks'. There was also a sliding blind in the partition behind the driver, which was fitted with a metal gauze screen. The object of the screen was to keep out insects when the car was travelling at speed.

The floor at the rear was insulated against the heat from the exhaust system and, in winter, the cold. Warmth was provided by a hot-water system in which the radiator water circulated. Fittings included a cupboard at the back containing a silver luncheon service. Underneath the body, there was a sliding rack able to accommodate two large travelling trunks.

Specifications, as issued by the Director of the Imperial Garages at St. Petersburg, insisted that it had to be possible to

Archduke Franz Ferdinand of Austria and his wife made their last journey in a Graf and Stift. The scene here is outside the town hall at Sarajevo—after the first attempt on the Archduke's life and before the second (and successful) murder bid.

Franz Ferdinand and his wife at Sarajevo shortly before the assassination.

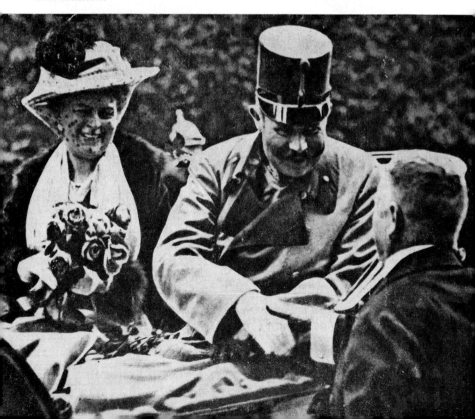

When Queen Mary went over to France to visit the troops, she was driven in a half-tracked Citroën.

King Alfonso XIII of Spain was a motoring enthusiast who preferred to occupy the driving seat. On this visit to Spanish Morocco in 1919, however, he allowed himself to be driven for ceremonial purposes.

In 1933, the Sultan of Morocco invested in a 14 h.p. Panhard, but his son, Prince Moulay Hassan, was not overlooked. He received this very fine model of a sports version.

When rajahs (or, indeed, representatives of the British raj) went tiger shooting in India, their cars were fitted with special seats for tiger-spotters—and, sometimes, trailers to carry spare parts.

Manufactured in Lowestoft to the order of a British subject in India, this remarkable car did more than, simply, look like a swan. When the occasion demanded, it could behave like one.

start the car from the driver's seat, and that it must move off 'without the least sign of an explosion'.

This sounds like a fairly difficult assignment. However, Delaunay-Belleville solved it by a device which worked off compressed air.

At the time of this particular vehicle's delivery, the Tsar owned about twenty cars. He maintained four palaces, and each of them was equipped with impressive workshops in which the machine tools were mounted on marble plinths. He was said to be a keen mechanic, though one views this statement rather cautiously. In spite of all his vehicles and his elaborate facilities for their maintenance, he had (in 1910) only 'honoured' the garages with one visit. Had he been a real enthusiast, one might have expected him to put in rather more appearances.

Taking the Tsar for a drive was a most complicated operation. His car was always preceded by several other vehicles of the same type, and the route was lined by Cossacks. Stationing the troops was, in itself, difficult; for, before the royal party set out, only the police were vouchsafed any knowledge of what the route would be. It all sounds a somewhat paranoic attitude, but, in view of what was to come, there may have been a good reason for it. Certainly it makes a mockery of those two armchairs, which must have been placed there to give the people a better view of their emperor.

During the final years of his life, the Tsar purchased, or attempted to purchase, three Rolls-Royces. The last of them was completed in March, 1918, by which time he was a prisoner. Four months later, he was dead. The car never left England, and was taken over by the War Office in London for the use of distinguished visitors. In November, 1919, it was sold to a Rolls-Royce enthusiast living in Mayfair.

Cars may have played an important part in some revolutions— once they had been sparked off. But prominent rebels seldom seem to have driven by motor vehicle to the scene of conflict. When Mussolini seized power in Italy in 1922, for example, he 'marched' on Rome. Wisely, perhaps, he left the footslogging to his 30,000 supporters and made the journey by train (though he always liked people to believe that he had walked at the head of the column). Lenin accomplished his return from exile by rail;

and it was left to Alexander Kerensky, head of the ill-fated pro-
visional government which ousted the Tsar, to find an important
role for the car in the Russian revolution. He used it on at least
two major occasions, though there is a certain amount of doubt
about the vehicles in which he travelled.

One of these times was during the night of October 24th, 1917,
when he was in the Winter Palace at St. Petersburg with his
cabinet. Sentries belonging to the hostile Bolsheviks' Red Guard
were patrolling the streets. All telephone communications had
broken down, and it seemed unpleasantly probable that Lenin's
supporters were about to seize power. Kerensky had ordered
troops back from the front, but there was no sign of them. By the
morning of the 25th, the palace was completely cut off.

There seemed only one thing to do: Kerensky decided to
drive across the city and out into the country. On the way, he
expected to meet the troops. Although it is unlikely that he
could have persuaded them to march any faster, it was the understandable act of a normally impatient man who was being subjected
to almost unreasonable tension.

One story afterwards had it that he left the Winter Palace
disguised as a nurse. This account always angered Kerensky, who
considered it belittled his heroic status. According to his own
version, he was dressed in 'semi-military' uniform; and, in any
case, he saw little danger in the trip. The people of St. Petersburg
were used to seeing him travelling about the city in a car. They
would, he believed, hardly notice him.

The American and British embassies were less sanguine. The
former ambassador offered him safe conduct across the city in an
American car flying the United States flag. Kerensky appreciated
the thought; but, according to his own account, turned it down.
In his memoirs, he wrote: 'I thanked the Allies for their offer,
but said that the head of the government could not drive through
the Russian capital[1] under the American flag.' He decided to use
his own vehicle, with his driver and adjutant up front: himself,
the commander of the troops in St. Petersburg, and two aides, in
the back.

However, there was still not room for all his retinue and the
car offered by the Americans was used by one of his officers,
who travelled at a short distance behind him. Conceivably this

[1] Moscow was not adopted as the Russian capital until March, 1918.

man was mistaken for Kerensky—in which case, it may account for subsequent reports that he did, indeed, use the American vehicle, and that he departed from the Winter Palace in a Pierce-Arrow. This was the leading American prestige car of the period, and was used by embassies overseas and by the heads of government departments within the United States.

There is, of course, another possible explanation: that *two* Pierce-Arrows were involved in the expedition—one belonging to the United States embassy and the other owned by Kerensky himself, though there is no evidence to suggest that he possessed a vehicle of this make.

His instructions to the driver were to take it easy through the city, for, above all things, he wanted to avoid any suggestion of panic. The chauffeur did as he was told, and the journey through the Russian capital went off without incident. Indeed, several of the Red Guards unthinkingly stood to attention as he drove past.

At the Bolshevik check point on the edge of St. Petersburg, things were different. In spite of the breakdown in communications, news of his departure must have reached the Red Guards, for they fired rifle shots at the car. Fortunately for the occupants, they missed. The driver accelerated, and they travelled at breakneck speed until they reached the town of Pskov, about 150 miles away, which was the headquarters of the commander-in-chief, Northern Front.

They arrived at nightfall, and Kerensky moved into an apartment belonging to his brother-in-law. The commander-in-chief came round, and immediately made it clear that the mission was in vain. This general, who doubtless had been watching events on the home front even more carefully that he had been regarding the Germans, had apparently decided that the Bolsheviks were bound to win. At all events, the troops Kerensky had gone to meet had never set off for St. Petersburg. They had been halted on the general's own orders.

Faced with such duplicity by a man who should have been his ally, Kerensky set about raising a force of his own. He drove off down the road for another thirty miles until he reached the headquarters of the Russian Third Corps at Ostrov. There he found about 500 Cossacks and a handful of field guns. He decided to use them in an attempt to break through the girdle which the

Red Guards had established around St. Petersburg, and to regain the centre of the city.

They reached one of the Tsar's palaces at a place named Gatchina without any difficulty, and Kerensky set up his base in the main building. Unfortunately for him, however, events had moved even faster than his car. The remaining members of his cabinet, who had stayed behind in the Winter Palace, had been captured in one of the biggest non-actions of history. Whatever pictures which have since been painted may suggest, and they always show it as an heroic feat of communist courage, the deed was accomplished with very little difficulty. As for the luckless politicians, they were removed to the Fortress of St. Peter and St. Paul. This, in spite of its saintly name, had been one of the most horrible of the Tsarist gaols.

Not unnaturally, once the contingent of Cossacks heard of this, they began to have doubts about their own security, and decided the time had probably come to switch roles. Instead of being the spearhead of Kerensky's strike-force, they suddenly became his gaolers. In return for the promise of safe conduct to their homes, and a guarantee that they could keep their horses and their firearms, they undertook to hand him over to a former sailor in the Russian Navy named Dybenko. Dybenko later became commander-in-chief of the Red Army, but eventually fell foul of Stalin, who caused him to be executed in 1937.

When the news of this treachery reached Kerensky, he gave up hope. In the gloom of a late autumn evening, shut away in a back room of this huge, ghost-ridden palace, he decided to kill himself, His aide, a stalwart named N. V. Vinner, affirmed that he, too, would shoot himself rather than surrender.

The drama in this small room reached theatrical proportions. Elsewhere in the palace, the Cossacks and a party of Red sailors were searching for them. In the room itself, Kerensky and Vinner had their guns out. One or two people had called to bid them a final and surreptitious farewell, when suddenly the door was flung open. Standing on the threshold were a civilian and a sailor.

According to the newcomers, it would take the searchers about another half-hour to discover their hiding place. If they acted quickly, they might be able to escape. How Kerencky must have wished that a Pierce-Arrow flying the American flag was ticking over alertly outside. The time for heroics was long past.

The leaders in this conflict seem to have been adept at assuming disguises. Lenin had shaved off his beard and, on his occasional train journeys in and out of Russia, he used to wear a wig to cover his all too unmistakably bald head. Kerensky had no time for such refinements. He borrowed the sailor's cap (it was too small for him) and jacket. He also found that he still had his goggles with him.

If ever there was a lost cause, this seemed to be it. Wearing his too-small sailor's cap, his goggles, and with his nautical disguise rendered more ridiculous by the fact that he was wearing brown boots and puttees, he said a suitably grateful farewell to Vinner. Then he applied himself to the task of getting out of the palace.

It was not going to be easy. The buildings had been designed to resemble a medieval castle by an eccentric Tsar named Paul I (the son of Catherine the Great, he had disliked his mother so much, that he changed the law of succession in such a way that only men could inherit the Russian throne). The effect was no doubt reasonably pleasing in more tranquil times. But, to a man in Kerensky's position, it had one enormous snag. True to its concept, it was surrounded by a large moat, and the only way out was over a drawbridge.

The obvious answer was to rush the bridge in a car, and that had been the idea of Kerensky's rescuers. But somebody bungled the directions, and the vehicle never turned up.

Thus, the former head of government—looking like an actor who is unsure whether he is playing in *H.M.S. Pinafore* or *Journey's End*, and who is prepared to go motor racing after the Saturday matinée—had to cross the bridge and melt into the background of a far from friendly mob.

He walked over the drawbridge with surprisingly little difficulty, but then onlookers outside were attracted by his somewhat singular appearance, and he might well have been detected. The situation was saved by an officer in the crowd who obligingly fainted just as his companions were becoming suspicious. This served as a distraction, and enabled Kerensky to run off down the street until, luckily and very improbably, he came across a prowling horse-drawn cab. The offer of a 100 rouble tip persuaded the driver to take him to one of the gates at the entrance to St. Petersburg, where, to his delight, he found the car which should have been in the palace yard. An officer was seated behind the steering wheel, and there were five soldiers armed with grenades to act as bodyguards. They set off at full speed with the officer whistling to himself as he drove, *en route* to a cottage situated in the midst of a forest several miles away.

Within thirty minutes of Kerensky's departure, the Red Guards at the palace discovered that he had slipped away. The effect of the news seems to have produced a situation not far from pandemonium. Cars were sent off in almost every direction to find the wanted politician. Fortunately for Kerensky, one man kept his head, and that was his own driver.

This loyal servant explained the most likely route his fleeing master would take, and suggested that he should pursue this line of investigation since he had the fastest car. The Red Guards agreed with him: he set off as if his life depended on it, and then, when he had covered a few miles, he pretended that the engine had broken down. Several minutes of groping under the bonnet gave Kerensky all the time he needed. He reached the lonely cottage safely and hid up there for the next forty days. Some while afterwards, he was smuggled out of Russia, and spent the rest of his life in the United States.

Lenin, the new master of Russia, certainly could not drive, and all the evidence suggests that he scarcely knew the difference between a spanner and a sparking plug. Nevertheless, he must have had a fairly shrewd eye when it came to judging the quality of a car.

When the Bolsheviks came to power, they requisitioned every vehicle they could find. This included the output of a small factory on the edge of Moscow, and a substantial hoard of imports from abroad. Some (such as an Austin armoured car that Lenin once used as a platform from which to deliver a speech) were taken over by the Red Army: a number were directed into a car pool attached to the Kremlin for the use of senior officials. Among the latter were two Rolls-Royces. One of them (painted dark green) was fitted with snow tracks at the rear and skis at the front for winter use. The other was entirely standard. Whatever his political creed may have suggested to the contrary, Lenin seized upon them with delight. They became his standard means of transport, and nobody seems to have thought any the less of the workers' champion for using strictly non-working-class vehicles. Both cars are preserved—one in the Central Lenin Museum in

Moscow, the other at Gorky in a collection of the Soviet leader's relics at the country house where he died.

Lenin enjoyed travelling by car, though he never made long journeys (about sixty-five miles was the furthest). According to the curator of the Central Lenin Museum, he 'often took a trip as relaxation'. The journeys, in contrast to those of the Tsar, were made with no fuss at all, and his only bodyguard was his chauffeur. He used to like hunting, talking to peasants (especially when they did not realise who he was), and spending the occasional night in a barn—huddled in the straw and getting, as it were, closer to a life of utter simplicity.

In the morning, he compromised this spartan regime by moving on in his Rolls-Royce.

Like a number of other world leaders, he was extremely considerate to his chauffeur, and displayed an almost fatherly concern for his well-being. Possibly because he himself was almost useless with his hands, he admired the skill with which the latter looked after the vehicles.

Lenin knew that idealism may be very well for an intellectual few, but the mass of the population requires a more concrete reason for rebellion. It may be revolt *against* something, or it can be in the hopes of obtaining something. Usually, it is a mixture of the two.

When the Bolsheviks turned Russia upside down, there was a mass of people who were eagerly awaiting any coins which might fall out of the nation's pockets. At first, everybody dreamed of an eight-hour day and a forty-four-hour week. Then they heard that, over in America, Ford employees only worked a forty-hour week. They decided that, whatever else was wrong with this capitalistic country, there was a great deal right about Henry Ford.

Thus began one of the strangest examples of one man's admiration for another, the most improbable search for a union of minds that has ever taken place in the whole of history. Lenin himself came to the conclusion that Henry Ford was one of the great men of destiny.[1] He caused *Pravda* to print articles under such headlines as 'The Fordisation of Russian Factories'. Ford's own *My Life and Work* was used as a textbook in Soviet universities

[1] An admiration which he shared with Lord Northcliffe—it must have been the only thing that the communist dictator and the press dictator had in common.

and technical schools, and the highlight of many a village wedding
was when a Fordson tractor towed the bridal cart.

By some ingenious distortion of logic, Henry Ford was regarded
not as a capitalist but as a revolutionary. This, perhaps, is all
the more strange when one recalls that American trade unions
were absolute anathema to him.

An American smallholder's dream may have been to own a
Model-T and a Fordson tractor. In this respect, a Russian peas-
ant's became very similar—though with considerably less chance
of being gratified. The Soviet Government's first order of Fordson
tractors came in 1920 after a wretchedly bad harvest. During the
next six years, they bought 25,000 and, by 1927, 85 per cent of
the trucks and tractors in Russia were American built.

A factory on the outskirts of Moscow was manufacturing a rather
poor copy of a Fordson, and claimed to be turning out two a day.
In fact, only about twenty a month were produced. No passenger
cars were manufactured in Russia at this time, and it was not
until 1933 that Stalin put his foot down and let it be known
that the Soviet Union ought to have a substantial automobile
industry. Significantly, perhaps, the two Russian prestige cars
which came many years later—the Zim and the Chaika which
replaced it—seemed to have depended for style entirely on the
inspiration of earlier American models.

Stalin himself, no matter what ideological differences there
may have been, appears to have been content to put at least some
of his motoring requirements into the hands of Daimler-Benz.
In 1928, he received a very powerful Mercedes SS (six-cylinder,
7·02-litre engine, top speed getting on for 120 m.p.h.); and,
in 1934, a Big Grosser Mercedes was delivered to him. This was a
kind of dictators' special, for the ownership of this particular
model included Mussolini, Hermann Goering and Adolf Hitler.
But who could (even if he had dared) criticise him? Had not
Lenin, the God-substitute and very father of the revolution,
driven around in that absolute symbol of capitalist success—a
Rolls-Royce?

8 A Cockade of Chauffeurs

On the morning of August 5th, 1914, twenty-four hours after
Great Britain had declared war on Germany, a certain wealthy
gentleman called his male employees together in the library of his
house in Sutherland. There were several of them, including the
butler, three footmen, a seventeen-year-old hall boy, two chauffeurs,
a number of gardeners, and a gillie. With the exceptions of the
head gardener and the senior chauffeur, who were both elderly,
he dismissed the lot of them. 'You've got to leave here,' he told
them, 'and go and fight for your country.'

He was an old man, and it seemed unlikely that the war would
require his services. But his son was on the reserve of officers and,
before very long, was killed in action. And so, for that matter,
were the hall boy, two of the footmen, and one of the gardeners.
The second chauffeur survived, though he was gravely wounded
during the week before Armistice Day.

It is, perhaps, characteristic of the times that these men went
obediently to the slaughterhouse in Flanders, never questioning
their master's orders—almost eager, indeed, to carry them out.
Nor should it go unnoticed that the gentleman, according to
his own lights, was making a considerable sacrifice by releasing
his employees. All his life he had been accustomed to an entourage of servants. Now he proposed to make do with just one

F

gardener and one chauffeur, and these men were only spared because of their age.

On the female side, of course, the situation was less drastic. No doubt, later on, the women would leave him to work in munitions factories. For the moment, the complement of cooks and ladies' maids and parlour maids and house maids was intact.

For a great many people, the first world war demanded, and received, sacrifices. For some, however, the situation was not nearly so bad. Whatever the jingoism and the flag waving and the guns may have done, they could not destroy the fundamental urge, which flourishes in a number of less scrupulous minds, to make a quick fortune while the making was good. Quite a few astute business men did very well out of the conflict—to such an extent that, in the immediate post-war years, Rolls-Royce had to increase its production of cars.

Before the hostilities, they had been turning out about five or, perhaps, ten a week. Now they were building twenty or thirty. Their owners wished to enjoy all the trappings of wealth; and, if a man was able to afford a Rolls-Royce, it followed that he should have a chauffeur. The trouble was that there were not enough to go round. For this reason, in 1921, Rolls-Royce started its school for drivers. As the present head of the school points out, in those days, even a Rolls-Royce 'was very difficult to drive. Changing gear was a major operation, and going from one to another was a very skilful job'. You could not pick up an untrained man and just set him down behind a steering wheel.

The early students were mostly recruited from the ranks of grooms, who knew a great deal about horses, but next to nothing about the internal combustion engine. The course lasted for two weeks, of which about seventy per cent of the time was spent out on the road. Much of it was devoted to going up and down hills and changing gear. Off the road, they were instructed in mechanics and how best to wash a vehicle—with particular attention to the care of its paintwork.

The new breed of employer does not seem to have been nearly so popular as the old guard. They were, one chauffeur said, lacking in consideration and courtesy. And, from another: 'The old gentry used to treat you well. There wasn't all the side you get today. After the war, people got on through the money they'd made—what I call "jumped up". But the old gentry always called you by your christian name—they used to treat you as one of the family.'

Another, who was employed by a duke and, later, by a marquess, went along with this view. He said: 'There wasn't equality —there can't be—but they talked to us servants just as you and I are talking to each other, and they passed the time of day with us. So long as you carried out your orders, it didn't matter what happened.'

Possibly the newcomers to the ranks of those who employed chauffeurs felt less assured. At all events, with the old gentry there wasn't (in one chauffeur's words) 'all this master and servant business'.

Before the first world war, men came into chauffeuring by various ways. One man, who spent sixty-two years in private employment, was engaged as second chauffeur to a medical officer of health in 1908. He got the job largely because he had been helping the head chauffeur to look after his master's cars. On a stretch of road behind the council offices, the head man had taught him to drive an 8 h.p. De Dion and, once he had mastered that, a somewhat more powerful Darracq.

Another attended a school instituted by one of the early car manufacturers (not Rolls-Royce) in the West End of London. Before undergoing instruction, he had already obtained a position as chauffeur to the wife of a wealthy business man. After three months, he was assigned to drive his lady across London to one of the big stores. He got her there all right; but he was so nervous, that she suggested he should go back to the school again. He was tutored for another month, having been told by the school's principal that 'I'll break your neck, if you don't finish this time. I'll *make* you drive this car'.

A number served apprenticeships at garages, and several had previously been employed as grooms or coachmen. But possibly the most singular graduate into the chauffeur ranks was a Suffolk man named Billy Burrell. He was a seaman by profession, and had served with the Orient Line before joining the crew of Louis Renault's yacht. One day, there was a mutiny, and Burrell was the only man on board who remained loyal to his master. What is more, he quelled the uprising by hitting the dissident sailors over their heads with a belaying pin. Renault was so pleased with his performance that he instantly made him his chauffeur and gave him a cottage on his estate outside Paris.

In 1901, an eminent shipowner in the north of England was approached by a young man for a job as coachman. The applicant had, it appeared, been employed by Buckingham Palace, but was discharged on the grounds that he was too short in stature. The shipowner studied his credentials, and decided to take him on.

After eighteen months, the man handed in his notice. 'What's the matter?' his employer asked. 'Aren't you happy here?'

'Oh yes,' he said. 'But people are now using cars and they have a future. I want to learn about them.'

'And if I buy one,' the shipowner said, 'will you stay?'

'Yes, sir—I'd be very happy to.'

The shipowner bought a Gladiator: the former royal coachman became a chauffeur and remained with the family for fifty-two years. 'He became,' the magnate's grandson told me, 'a friend of us all.'

There was one noble duke who never bought a Rolls-Royce because, his man told me, 'He always said that he could afford to look poor.' Instead, he owned such vehicles as a 60 h.p. four-cylinder Mercedes, a Bollée, and a 45 Fiat. Earlier, he had used a steam car and electric brougham, but, by 1911, he had got rid of them.

According to one retired chauffeur, 'All the early cars were heavy to drive, but you had to make do with what you had. When I joined my gentleman, he had a big Delaunay-Belleville limousine. It was a beautiful car to drive. It had a round radiator—like a barrel. The suspension was good, and it was a most comfortable car.'

But, better still, he liked his employer's Mors. 'There was nothing to touch a Rolls,' he admitted, 'but the Mors was the easiest to drive. You could put the gear lever anywhere you wanted and you'd never make a noise. I've never had such a car in all my life. It did twenty-three miles to the gallon, and it didn't half go.'

Less successful, in his opinion, was the Albion, on which he had trouble with the igniters. After every 350 miles, the engine would begin to misfire, and they had to be taken out, cleaned with emery paper, greased, and then put back again. 'After that,' he said, 'they were as right as rain until you'd covered another 350 miles.'

In the same car, the acetylene headlamps had a tiresome habit of going out whenever it went over a bump. By the time the chauffeur had stopped the vehicle, and gone round to the front to re-light them, a good deal of gas had built up. Unless a great deal of care was taken, there was apt to be an explosion.

The world in which these men lived had its own customs and a protocol which was extremely rigid. The head of the indoor servants in some very large households was the steward, but few establishments ran to one. Usually, the top man was the butler, whom the others deferentially addressed as 'Sir'. The scale of things is well illustrated by the 7th Duke of Newcastle, who died in 1928. His Grace maintained three establishments: a large estate in Nottinghamshire, a flat in Mayfair and a house at Windsor. At Clumber, his Nottingham home, he employed a personal chaplain, had his own chapel, a school for the children of his employees, a telephone system with a switchboard and twenty-two extensions, three dining halls, two kitchens, and a great deal else. The large kitchen catered for what was known as 'the Front' (in other words, the Duke and Duchess and their friends): the small kitchen provided the meals for the steward's room and the servants' hall. To take your meals in the steward's room, you had to be what might be described as the head of a department. The butler ate there, and so did the cook and the housekeeper and the groom-of-chambers and the valet and the ladies' maids. The junior footman used to wait on them and also carried out the duties of valet to the butler.

Lesser mortals, such as the footmen, the other maids, and the second chauffeur, took their meals in the servants' hall. The head chauffeur, in common with the head gardener, the head gamekeeper, and other senior members of the outside staff, had his own cottage, and ate at home.

Keeping their employers contented and well nourished was a masterpiece of detail. In many households, the valet did not stop at cleaning and polishing the tops of his master's boots and shoes: he polished the undersides as well, and even ironed the laces. Every morning, before laying out the day's delivery of newspapers in the dining room and the billiard room, the groom of chambers would fold them carefully, making sure that no page overlapped at the corners, and then ironed them. The idea seems to have been that it helped them to hold together better.

Among the groom of chambers's other responsibilities was that of ensuring that there was always clean blotting paper on the writing desks, a supply of note-paper and envelopes, and that the inkwells were full. He was not concerned with putting coal on the fire: that was the job of a footman.

At table, the footmen waited. If there was an under-butler, he would do the carving, while the butler attended to the wine (the corks were drawn in the steward's room). If there was not an under-butler, the butler carved the joint.

Second chauffeurs lived outside—usually in a room over the stables. However, the conditions were by no means bad, and at least one big house provided a billiard room and a smoking room in these quarters. The second chauffeur's duties, apart from driving, depended upon the nature of the head chauffeur.

One retired driver, who had served under a particularly villain-ous member of the species, recalled that he had to clean his chief's boots, and wipe the dust off them once he had climbed into the car. He was made to wash *all* the cars (there were six) and to do all the maintenance work. 'The head chauffeur never got his hands dirty,' he said.

Other head chauffeurs were more amenable. They would share in the work of servicing the vehicles and would even wash cars that they had been driving. Washing, indeed, was a very important part of the curriculum. In most households the routine was that, no matter what time a car was brought back at night, it had to be cleaned and leathered before the chauffeur went to bed. But one man had a routine, which he described as 'set fair'. He arrived at the garage never later than eight o'clock each morning—and some-times a good deal earlier. He would then top up the oil and check tyre pressures, fill up the petrol tank and, if the car had been out exceptionally late the night before, wash it.

At another household, the chauffeur had to be present at family prayers before he could begin work. These took place at 8·45 a.m. in the room of the housekeeper (who usually conducted them). An ordinary suit had to be worn. Afterwards, he had to make a quick change into uniform (navy blue: a fawn overcoat with a blue collar was worn in winter).

Everything—and this included days off and holidays—depended on the movements of the master and mistress. The methods used to transmit instructions to the chauffeurs varied. In some cases, both employers had their own order books. They used to fill in the details for the day at breakfast, and these were handed on to those concerned by the butler or else by the groom of chambers. At other times, the telephone system would be used. And, if something cropped up during the evening, which required a car early in the morning, details would be left in the pantry.

In some establishments, the head chauffeur had to present himself at the pantry each morning at ten o'clock for a briefing by the butler on the day's activities.

A chauffeur was on stand-by duty for twenty-four hours a day, seven days a week. In theory, he received ten days' holiday a year, though it did not necessarily follow that he was able to take it. It depended upon whether the master and mistress were away without their cars for a sufficient period. Perhaps it sounds a hard life. In the early days, the wages were in the order of 30s. od. a week with everything found including two suits of uniform a year. If a man married, the pay would probably go up to £3 a week, and he was given a rent-free house with free coal and light.

It was, of course, a nomadic existence in many ways. Wherever a man's employers went, he nearly always went too. In London, a fortunate few had apartments over the mews garages where their cars were kept. For others there was bed and breakfast accommodation to be had at a boarding house which was run especially for chauffeurs in the centre of the city.

But even if the hours sometimes seemed long and the pay was not altogether princely, most chauffeurs agree that theirs was not a bad life. They also point out that their incomes were sometimes substantially increased by tips from their masters' guests.

One retired veteran of many years' driving told me: 'A big house was a colony on its own. I think we were a jolly sight happier than most people are today, but it was a job you had to like.'

And, from another, who worked at an establishment where there were twenty indoor servants plus gardeners, stable lads and a gamekeeper: 'It was a free and easy life, and we used to live well, too. They were long hours, but you had to make up your time off when you could.'

Certainly they took an immense pride in their work. Here is what one man said: 'We used to leave the bonnets up when the cars were in the garage—just to show the engines off. The pipes were polished and even the crankcase. All the aluminium was polished. You wouldn't find a speck of oil anywhere. Mind you, a lot of it was brass. On a wet day, it might take one and a half or two hours to do the brass on the big cars. Going into Birmingham when it rained, and a lot of chemicals came out of the air, was the devil with the brass. The best idea was to take a cloth and soak it in paraffin before you set off, and to smear all the brasswork over with it. It took a bit of the shine off, but that didn't matter. When you got home, you washed it off, and leathered it off, and it came up beautifully.'

The chauffeurs themselves were as smart as their cars. They dressed according to the taste of their employers. One man always wore dark blue. When he was employed by a duke, he wore ordinary trousers and black boots. On the death of his master, he moved into the service of a marquess, and the latter insisted that he should wear breeches and leggings.

During the mornings in a shopping street, you would sometimes see a number of chauffeurs waiting on the pavement for their ladies. One might be wearing a green uniform, anothere fawn. There would be a man in blue and a man in grey—and you could always tell old So-and-so's man, for he always wore black. There was one lady in the Midlands whose driver was dressed in a dark blue jacket with a scarlet collar. The scarlet was included in the colour scheme as symbolic of her hunting interests (she owned a pack of hounds).

Footmen used to have their hair powdered, and wore breeches, stockings and pumps. In the early days of the twentieth century, however, this get-up tended to be modified to tailcoats with buttons bearing the master's crest upon them, and striped waistcoats. When one of them went out in the car, he wore a livery similar to that of the chauffeur—though the latter always wore a peaked cap and nearly always wore breeches. The footman was dressed in a frock-coat, trousers, and might wear a top hat (though many of them wore peaked caps).

When she was in the country, the lady of the house was usually taken out by the chauffeur alone, and he was responsible for wrapping her up carefully and gently in a rug. During the London season, a footman usually went along too in the afternoons.

Part of the social round was a ritual known as 'calling'. The idea, though it would never had been expressed in such informal terms, was to pop in on your friends and acquaintances unexpectedly. The lady of the house drew up a suitable itinerary. Sometimes several calls were made in one afternoon: at others the expedition was fruitless. These visits were never prearranged, and it might easily be that the first one or two attempts drew blanks—either because the ladies in question were also doing the rounds, or else because they were not in a mood to receive visitors.

When the car drew up outside a house, the footman—who had been sitting beside the chauffeur, bolt upright and with his arms folded—descended to the pavement, advanced up the steps to the front door, and rang the bell. The door was opened by another footman (employed by the lady who might reasonably be described as 'the target'), who was almost immediately joined by the butler (who might be called 'the ambassador'). The latter inquired who was there, and then padded off discreetly into the interior to find out whether his lady was at home (sometimes the ladies really were out: at others, they said they were—simply because they did not feel inclined to entertain the uninvited guest). If the prospective hostess was unavailable, the butler conveyed the fact to the visiting footman, who brought the bad news back to the car. Another name and address was produced from the list, and the quest continued.

On fine days, those who were fortunate enough to own landaulets would have the roofs at the backs lowered, and would put up their parasols. They might then order the footman to tell the chauffeur to drive round one of the London parks. They travelled at a speed of about 10 m.p.h., looking for other ladies of their acquaintance to whom they would wave very prettily. Having done a few circuits in one direction, they would turn round and travel the opposite way. At about 3.45, they would order a return home, where tea would be served by the footman.

A footman only used to accompany the lady on her afternoon expeditions. When she went shopping in the mornings, the chauffeur would be on his own up front. If they stopped at a large store, a commissionaire opened the door, and helped her out. At smaller establishments, the chauffeur did this. Unless her purchases were urgently needed, they were always delivered by the store. But if she had to take them back with her, there was no question of her carrying the parcels. They were always brought to the car by the assistant who had served her. The chauffeur then packed them inside once his mistress was sitting comfortably.

In the evenings there were balls, dinner parties, and visits to the theatre. An evening at the theatre suggests that the chauffeur had to spend a long time hanging about; but he usually managed to find out what time the show ended. Then he would either go back to the mews for the next two hours or so, or else 'have a noggin with some of the other chauffeurs' (though not, presumably, very many).

Long journeys usually meant that a night or two had to be spent on the way. One retired chauffeur recalls that a trip to Scotland had to be broken up into several stages. On the first night, they stopped at an hotel at Grantham. The second night was spent in York, the third at Northallerton, the fourth in Edinburgh, and the fifth either in Perth or Inverness.

At these halts, the chauffeurs used to take their meals in the stewards' rooms of the hotels, and they were usually accommodated in bedrooms set aside for this purpose in the attics. On the whole, the food seems to have been reasonably good, though there was one hotel in Yorkshire which they all dreaded. Said one victim of its kitchen: 'At this place, it was really bad. You couldn't eat the stuff after a long day's driving, it was so badly cooked. No—I don't think it was the same as they served in the hotel restaurant. They'd never have stood for it.'

Usually a man had a room to himself at these overnight stops, but sometimes they had to share. And, at Braemar at the time of the Highland Games, the steward's room was always so crowded that the hotel had to put on two sittings for meals. On these occasions, there were nearly always a number of foreign chauffeurs present. Once, through a language difficulty, an Italian driver was served roast beef, potatoes, plums and custard—all on the same plate. His colleagues were amused, though he cannot have shared their enjoyment of the situation.

Stewards' rooms survive in a number of hotels, though they are not used so much as they once were. Quite often employers invite their men to join them for meals. The chauffeurs usually sleep in the cheaper guest rooms. At a large hotel in the south of England, they receive a 50 per cent reduction on their room charges. At the Adelphi Hotel in Liverpool, the top two floors used to be reserved for hotel staff and for visiting chauffeurs—though valets and ladies' maids slept next to their employers to be within easy call. Nowadays, they occupy the less sumptuous guest rooms, and they eat in the so-called 'Couriers' Room', which is reserved for chauffeurs and coach drivers.

In the largest hotel at Chester, there used to be a separate dining room for valets, maids, and chauffeurs, and the back part contained special accommodation for them. It was almost as if there were two establishments in one. Nowadays, they eat in the main restaurant, just like anyone else.

At Claridges in London, there are special single bedrooms known as 'chauffeurs' rooms', and there is a large 'Couriers' Room' for meals. But they may, if they wish, have their food served in their bedrooms.

For many households, an invariable part of the year's routine was a summer migration to Scotland. One lady (a wealthy widow) had a large estate on the Island of Mull. Getting the car across from Oban in the days before the drive-on ferry service was a difficult business. The vehicle had to be driven on to the steamer down two planks. When the tide was low, this was a somewhat dangerous undertaking, and a rope had to be attached to the back of the car. It was then gently winched down the steep slope.

Scotland was synonymous with the slaughter of deer and grouse, and chauffeurs could usually please themselves whether they assisted in these executions. Since they had to go up to the moors in the course of their driving duties, they generally (though, so far as I can discover, there was no extra pay for it) made themselves useful as beaters or loaders. It was, after all, a way of filling in the time.

One retired chauffeur told me sadly that, nowadays, 'we are antiques'. Most admitted that theirs was a vanishing occupation. There are all manner of theories about why this has happened, but the one I like the best comes from an elderly man now living in retirement on the edge of London.

'The rot,' he told me, 'set in when self-starters were invented.[1] The old cars had to be turned by a handle, and the ladies, certainly, weren't strong enough to do this. Those early engines had terriffic

[1] No date is available as to when the first self-starter was introduced. According to Lucas: 'In the years immediately following the 1914–18 war, when intense competition was arising between vehicle manufacturers to supply the demands of a public eager to participate in the new pleasure of motoring, the incorporation of a "self-starter" was featured as an important selling factor.' The first car to be fitted with a windscreen wiper as standard equipment was probably a Pierce Arrow.

compression and, if they backfired, you went up to the roof. There were scores of broken wrists and arms from backfiring.'

Perhaps it is a pity that the privately employed chauffeur is a species doomed to extinction by the levelling of society. One has only to talk to men who have done this work, to realise what pleasure they got out of it. They speak of 'His Grace', or 'Her Ladyship', or 'My gentleman', or 'My lady', with respect, loyalty, and certainly not without affection. They served them well, with the meticulous care of a good craftsman. And the loyalty was a two-way affair. For example, one of the men I interviewed when doing the research for this chapter, now lives in a comfortable pleasantly situated cottage in Kent. His car is a fairly old Humber Sceptre in excellent condition, which he still drives (although he is over eighty). Both the cottage and the car were bequeathed to him by his lady when she died.

These employers—the good ones, at any rate—looked after their staff, and many a chauffeur remembers being called up in the middle of the night when some child on the estate had been suddenly taken ill and had to be rushed to a doctor. If they themselves were sick, they seldom wanted for anything, and there are countless stories of hampers of goodies being brought round from the big house.

Forty years' service with one employer was by no means uncommon, and a man would only move on to better himself. This was usually done through recommendation, but, as one man told me, 'You had to know your job from A to Z, and you had to have good credentials.'

It was, perhaps, a small, enclosed world; but, as communities go, it worked very well. But so many things have changed. According to a recent press cutting, a certain viscount was having to drive himself. The reason given was that his chauffeur had gone on unofficial strike. That sort of thing would have been unheard of in what many of my informants shamelessly described as 'the good old days'.

9 The Indian Car Trick

In the late summer of 1970, it looked as if the radically inclined government of India had hammered the final nail into the coffin of an already obsolescent institution known as the rajahs. There were 278 of these rulers, each of whom (until India was given self-government at the end of the last war) lorded it over an independent state. From time to time, under the British regime, they received a fond pat on the head, or else an admonitory frown as if from a vexed parent. Otherwise, their status stopped only a few yards this side of divinity.

The wealth of the rajahs once appeared to be unlimited. Now, it seemed, they were to be shorn of their titles, their power, and their privy purses which had been costing the Indian government something in the region of £250 million a year. Admittedly, for anyone who was able to see it, they had put on a show which was marginally more extravagant than that of a Hollywood epic (in motion pictures, the door knobs appear to be made of gold: a self-respecting rajah would insist that they were made of the real thing, and high quality gold at that).

If their government's attempt to cut them back to more reasonable proportions had succeeded, the rajahs would have lost more than just their titles and the annual hand-outs to their privy purses. When there were elections, it was quite out of the question for them to mingle with ordinary mortals in order to vote. Special booths were constructed for them and their families. They had the right to order public holidays to coincide with their birthdays; to fly their own colours; to mount guards outside their palaces; to help themselves to free water and electricity; and to import anything they liked without any nonsensical talk about paying duty on it. Nor could they be sued in court.

The last man to inherit the title of rajah can reasonably be put down as the Maharajah of Jaipur, whose father died during a polo match in England on June 24th, 1970. Within three months of receiving the title, it seemed possible that he might be reduced to plain Mr. Sing. His highness took the news philosophically, and told the press that he was not quite sure what it entailed. His younger brother, on the other hand, knew very well. He told a reporter that (if the de-rajahisation had gone forward): 'It means that we can't race round Jaipur the wrong way in one-way streets. Now we can be taken to court for traffic offences. We couldn't before—that was one of our privileges.'

It also meant that they would have been appreciably worse off. Some of the rulers had already seen it coming. To prepare themselves for a social and economic deluge, a number had turned their sumptuous palaces into hotels. The Maharajah of Bikaner conceived the idea of transforming his by no means inconsiderable fleet of cars into a taxi service; and several of them looked sadly at their collections of Rolls-Royces, Bentleys and Hispano Suizas, saying, 'These will have to go.'

Cars were part of the rajah legend. They bought their Rolls-Royces by the dozen—not because they were cheaper that way, but because it created a bigger impression. They had them painted in their royal colours and fitted them, for this was another of their privileges, with their private number plates.[1] And they had everything that money could buy (and, in some instances, what it could not buy) done to improve their luxury. They would fit out a shooting brake for tiger hunts until it looked more like a gunboat. Or they would encrust a limousine with such exotic trappings that it seemed too valuable to drive. Of course, it was not: and, if anything became damaged, they could always throw it away and buy another.

The rajahs loved their motor cars. One couldn't describe them

[1]Another was that they did not have to pay tax on their vehicles.

as status symbols, for they already had all that and more. On the other hand there was, perhaps, a sense of keeping up with somebody—or, possibly, a strong desire to be fashionable.

It was, for example, noticeable that, at one point, one or two of these princes foresook their royal colour schemes in favour of mauve. It may have been a coincidence, but it ought to be recorded that, at the time, the current Viceroy's wife had a passion for this colour. She even, according to a well-informed source, used it for the decoration of her lavatories.

Before the last war a New Delhi firm had a Rolls-Royce and a Barker (the coachwork people) representative attached to their staff. These two men were really only fully employed for about two weeks in the year. Delhi Week and Princes' Week were two occasions when the rajahs swarmed. Each no doubt wished to impress his peers that his fortune waxed as fat as ever, and that he had still not heard about such low-caste furnishings as chromium plate. At all events, these two representatives would invariably sell anything up to about fifty Rolls-Royces on these occasions, and would live very comfortably off the proceeds for the remainder of the year.

The motor car came gradually to India. Initially there were only a few vehicles, and their ownership was described by a motoring writer in 1903 as being 'among the wealthy natives' (how the rajahs must have hated those words if ever they read them). One of the earlier troubles concerned carburation during the heavy monsoons. The air was almost at saturation point, and it became virtually impossible to vapourise the petrol.

In an attempt to solve it, a European living at Ahmedabad conceived the idea of building a carburettor which would enable him to use paraffin instead of petrol. By some piece of apparatus, the fuel was fed directly to the cylinders and 'no carburisation in the accepted sense of the word was required'. It would be nice to put it down as a very early instance of the fuel-injection principle at work, but there are not enough details available to be positive about this.

To celebrate the accession of Edward VII to the throne, a Durbar was held in January, 1903, at Delhi. This was a kind of massive, super-sumptuous, jamboree to which all the rulers came flocking with their maid servants and their men servants, their wives and their concubines, and just about (bar their palaces) everything that was theirs. On this particular occasion, they did not bring their limousines and their touring cars, their shooting brakes and their wagonettes, for the simple reason that very few of them possessed such vehicles. Nevertheless, by rail and by elephant and by whatever other means they could think of, they came in their masses to pay homage to the new king, and to ensure him of their continuing loyalty.

The relative scarcity of cars must have caused some people to wonder whether enough was being done to introduce the automobile to India. The result was that the Motor Union of Western India decided to organise a trial to be held during Christmas week 1904. The cars were to set out from Delhi on Boxing Day and to arrive at Bombay on January 2nd. The distance was 880 miles, and the objectives were as follows:

1. To show the Indian public that cars were now suitable for their country.

2. To attract tourists and to persuade them to bring their cars with them. Two powerful selling points in this respect were the 'perfect' roads and the fine weather between October and March.

3. To provide car manufacturers in Europe and elsewhere with an introduction to India's motoring needs.

There was also an undeclared arrow of persuasion aimed at the government. Cars were clearly ideal for district officers and executive engineers, who had to travel over large areas where there were no railways. The trial might very well give proof of this and, with proof, might come the orders.

Lord Curzon, who was then Viceroy of India, gave the event his official patronage and was later joined by Lord Kitchener and the Governor of Bombay. The Gaekwar of Baroda promised a 'handsome and valuable' cup for the outright winner. Other rulers offered examples of similarly exotic hardware as class awards.

The rules, as originally written down, explained that the competition for the Gaekwar's cup would be judged entirely on the grounds of reliability. In addition to this, there would be prizes for the competitor whose car was in the best condition at the end of the trial, the car which was best suited to district work (an ill-disguised dig at the government), and the car with the quietest performance.

Only amateur drivers could take part, and each had to take an observer with him to record how many stops he made. The car which made the least number of unauthorised halts would be the winner. In the case of a dead heat, a hillclimb would be held to determine the outcome.

Any make or model of privately owned car could take part, but motor cycles were excluded.

Later, the regulations were re-examined and the expressions 'privately owned' and 'amateur driver' were considered to be ambiguous. Somebody had to find definitions for them, and presently it was decided that, to be 'privately owned', a car must be entered by an individual and not by a firm of dealers or manufacturers. An 'amateur driver' was deemed to be anyone who was not a mechanic or a chauffeur, but he could be a member of a motor firm who was not paid for driving, or who was recognised as an amateur in British motoring circles.

So far as the Viceroy's patronage was concerned, there were further conditions. According to a report in *Autocar*, he could not have given his approval if it had applied 'to the insensate and even criminal criterion of mere speed! To fly across the country at a velocity greater than the average train upon rails, destroying the roads, causing danger to men and animals, obliterating the scenery amid a cloud of dust, and drowning every sensation amid a roar of sound appears to be a prostitution of what is, in itself, a most benevolent institution.'

Then came a sharp attack on 'those horrible competitions which are gradually, but happily, alienating the public sentiment of European countries'. That, it was made clear, would certainly not to be countenanced in India.

The Viceroy need not have worried. The rules stated quite clearly that the minimum average speed between controls was 12 m.p.h. and the maximum, 30 m.p.h. Under such conditions, the sensations were unlikely to be drowned and little was likely to be prostituted.

During the days before the event, everything seemed to be going fairly well. The only antagonists to the idea were the holy men, who warned people against the car as something inherently evil, and officials of the Indian railways, who were understandably lukewarm about an event which was calculated to rob them of passengers. Something like £500 was received in the way of entry fees, which helped to pay the cost of erecting three temporary bridges over rivers, and the wages of two men for every four

G

miles of the route, who were employed to remove stones from the road.

When the final list of prizes was assembled, there was the Gaekwar's cup (valued at £66) for the outright winner, a lesser trophy for the best performance by a car costing not more than £500, another for the most economical car, a consolation prize, and the other awards already mentioned.

The Rajah of Pudukotal entered a Gardner-Serpollet steam car, and the Maharaja of Scindia took part in a De Dion. The railway company swallowed its dislike of the affair, and ran special car trains to Delhi. Since Bombay stands on an island, a lot depended on the efficiency of the ferry boats, and a good deal of work had to be put in at the last moment, clearing a road to the embarkation points.

Presently, on December 26th, thirty-three cars started from Delhi; and, on January 2nd, twenty-one of them reached Bombay The most common causes of breakdowns were punctures from nails that had fallen out of the shoes of bullocks. The crankshaft on one of the Panhards broke. In spite of the stone pickers' efforts, a De Dion's petrol tank received such a peppering, that it could no longer hold any fuel; and a solid-tyred vehicle was so shaken up that it virtually fell to pieces. Most of the smaller cars were described as 'semi-wrecks' afterwards. But these were mere nothings to the rows which, in the best tradition of early motor sport, followed the event.

Much of the trouble seems to have centred on the car which won the Gaekwar's cup and, also, the award for the vehicle most suited to Indian motoring conditions. It was a Darracq; and one has the impression that the English entrants felt that an event organised in a land under British sovereignty ought to have been won by a British car.

Most of the accusations were hurled at the judges, who, it was said, knew nothing about motor cars and, in any case, had not been informed about certain changes to the regulations. The panel was made up of three army officers and two civil engineers, which makes the accusation of mechanical ignorance rather hard to believe—especially since one of them was head of the motor transport depot at Quetta.

There was also an argument about the reports from the official observers. Some people said that they should be kept in locked boxes and seen only by the adjudicators. Others protested that the secretary of the organising club and at least one committee member should have a sight of them.

The winning car, it was said, had at least two serious breakdowns. One of the vehicles running on paraffin was said to have cheated by switching to petrol at some point. The driver of another vehicle reported one completely trouble-free day's motoring, but later qualified this statement by saying that 'we had to get off and push her up all the hills'.

When the driver of a Wolseley was awarded a consolation prize, he refused to accept it. Then he was accused of being a professional, which poured further fuel on to the blaze. It transpired that he was twenty years old, had only driven a tricar before, and that the Wolseley had only arrived in India fourteen days before the event.

Several committee meetings were held to consider a peace formula, but (reported *Autocar*) 'owing to clashes of trading interests the proceedings were too acrimonious for anything to be achieved'. The secretary of the club resigned; and the dinner at the Taj Hotel in Bombay, which should have brought everything to a joyful conclusion, was described as being 'more like Banquo's feast'.

Wrote *Autocar*'s man: 'At the dinner, the cheers were too forced to be pleasant, and the toast-makers were confined to . . . a small clique of the "you pat my back and I'll pat yours".'

Some of the pats, whatever impression contemporary reports may have given, must have been sincere. The roads of India turned out to be much better than any of the visitors had expected. The catering arrangements were generally conceded to have been excellent. A motor gymkhana was held in the grounds of a rajah's palace *en route*, and was said to have been great fun; and the Wolseley, which caused some of the trouble, took a party up a 1:4 gradient to a fort 500 feet above the road. This was a record for Indian hillclimbs.

In all fairness, if one forgets about the trial's claims to have been a sporting event, it was a success, and it certainly achieved its foremost object of introducing the automobile to India. Not only did it convince the rulers and the administrators and other influential members of the raj that the car could *do* something for the country: it also demonstrated to the visitors that, whatever they may have thought back home, this was not a wild man's paradise, with a cannibal lurking behind every tree, but a tolerably civilised nation and a splendid place for touring.

When, in 1911, a Durbar took place to celebrate the coronation of King George V, the rajahs went on a huge shopping spree beforehand, laying in Rolls-Royces at the rate that lesser mortals laid down bottles of port. During this highly colourful occasion, something like 2,000 cars and 200 motor cycles were assembled within an area of ten square miles. The former were wonderful to behold, for each was painted in the colours of its owner's state, and a more picturesque assembly of automotive might can seldom have been seen. One rajah, possibly anxious to outdo all the others, had no fewer than thirty-six vehicles in his retinue. A six-cylinder 50 h.p. Wolseley and a 38 h.p. Daimler were put at the disposal of the King, who took the opportunity to do a little sightseeing, and visited the famous Elephanta Caves near Bombay.

From then onwards, no rajah's establishment was complete without its stud of motor cars. They took many different forms, and one of them was the 'purdah wagon', which was specially designed for their ladies. To render them invisible, it either had curtains draped all around the compartment at the back, or else the windows were in black glass. Whichever it was, journeys in the purdah wagon were usually abominably uncomfortable for the sweating mass of womanhood crammed into the back. Custom apart, the object, according to one expert on Indian affairs, was 'to keep them quiet'.

Some rulers, of course, had more wives than others. The record in this respect seems to have been 365. When this particular rajah died, his women were, in a manner of speaking, bequeathed to his son, who turned them out of the palace. If this seems harsh, it was almost benevolent beside the action of one ruler, who became displeased with two of his wives. He locked them in a room over his stable of polo ponies, and then burned the whole place down. It seems an awful waste of horseflesh; but, in India, women had to be kept in their places.

They were no doubt kinder to their cars, though it was possible for a vehicle to lose face. Immediately after the last war, a certain rajah made a visit to Britain, where he had a house at Farnham. Driving down from London one evening in his 1938 Bentley, he was overtaken by two young sailors on a motor cycle. The rajah depressed the accelerator a little bit more, and overtook them. Then the boys put on a spurt and flashed past the Bentley. This sort of thing went on for several miles, with the speeds getting faster all the time.

Eventually, when they were doing well over eighty and the boys were in the lead, the rajah's prime minister, who was travelling in the car, decided the time for diplomatic action had arrived.

'Why race them, your highness?' he asked. 'These are just young boys who are back from the war. What's the point?'

The rajah eased off and let the youngsters roar on ahead. But, once they had reached his house, he would never use that car again. According to his standards it had been beaten by the motor-cyclists. Somehow, it had let him down, and eventually he gave it away.

This particular rajah had 150 cars of one kind and another. Among them were no fewer than eighteen Rolls-Royces. He seldom bought just one at a time, but purchased them in handfuls of three or four. And you never knew what he was going to buy next.

One year, he came to London and visited the motor show. He was particularly impressed by the current Docker Daimler, which was on display. 'I want one like that,' he told his prime minister. That ill-used individual pointed out that it was strictly one-off, and 'Why doesn't your highness come and see what they've got on some of the other stands?'

At this point, a Daimler representative offered them cups of coffee. Now the rajahs had a strict code of hospitality. Daimler's had given the ruler a hot drink: the ruler must now do something for Daimler's. He promptly ordered a car with a Hooper body and a plexiglass roof.

This particular ruler was a Moslem, and it is (or used to be) dangerous to lavish polite admiration on a Moslem's possessions. You are likely to find that they have suddenly become your own. The most simple illustration of this concerns an army officer, who was stationed in the Middle East. One evening, he was bidden to dine with a sheik. At some point in the meal, when conversation was beginning to flag, he filled in a gap by admiring his host's daughter. The sheik promptly said: 'Take her—she's yours. I will arrange a wedding.' To have refused would have been the height of bad manners and, at the end of the party, the officer was compelled to sneak back to his unit without saying 'goodbye'.

Once, when the prime minister of Pakistan visited the rajah with the Hooper-bodied Daimler with the plexiglass top, he remarked what a nice car it was. 'You really like it?' the latter asked. 'Most certainly. It is very fine.' 'Then—please. You take it.'

The cars accumulated in the royal garages, and were sometimes neglected by their owners. One year, a rajah bought a Bentley. He had it shipped to India, and it was duly stored away in his palace. A year or two went by before he actually got around to sitting in it. Then he decided that it was too small for his liking. 'Get me something bigger,' he said. 'That car must go.'

Even if there were over one hundred cars on the establishment, every one had to be meticulously maintained, for there was no knowing which the ruler would demand next. He might suddenly say: 'Bring me such-and-such to the paddock.' It had to be there within a minute or two, in perfect working order and well polished.

For tiger shooting, they bought touring cars with highly individual bodywork. The chassis was invariably a Rolls-Royce. In a fairly typical car, there was a mounting for a gun on top of a windscreen, and another gun on a swivel at the right-hand side. The battery of lamps up front would make the average rally driver's car look as if it were lit by candlelight. The Lanchester version had a pair of seats mounted outside the body for 'tiger spotters'.

The Nizam of Hyderabad, who had a passion for gold and filled his palace with the stuff, had a throne mounted on a Rolls-Royce for state occasions; but, for everyday use, he was more inclined to use an ordinary Ford. But, in many ways, the Nizam was a man of simple tastes. He used to wear inexpensive clothes and nearly always smoked cheap cheroots, which could be purchased for 1s. od. a hundred.

Just once in a while, a European would strive to outdo the rajahs in the extravagance, or else the eccentricity, of his cars. Such a man was Mr. R. N. Matthewson, a one-time resident of Calcutta. By a curious whim, Mr. Matthewson decided that his vehicle should be built in the shape of a swan. He commissioned a firm of engineers in Suffolk to make it from his own designs. It was, one had to admit, highly ingenious. By operating a lever, you could cause the car's 'beak' to open. By means of compressed air and water from the radiator, it could then be made to emit an extremely lifelike hissing sound.

But hissing was by no means its entire repertoire of sound. Using a two-way valve exhaust system, Mr. Matthewson enabled a Gabriel horn, with eight organ pipes and a keyboard, to be installed. Presumably it was impossible to drive and play an organ voluntary at the same time—but, given a musical co-pilot, the possibilities were immense. The 'swan' (or 'car') was shipped out to India fifty-nine years ago. When last heard of, it was stored in a Calcutta garage.

Some time after the last war, a traveller visited a disused airfield in India. Parked in the centre of one of the runways was an old Daimler which was clearly beyond restoration. The traveller looked inside it, and discovered, in the rear compartment, the rotting remains of an armchair set in front of the back seat.

There was only one person who could have ordered such a car as this, and that was King George V, who always insisted that his detectives should travel on the back seat, and that he and Queen Mary should occupy armchairs mounted amidships. Another point upon which the monarch insisted was that he should be able to get into his cars without having to bend down.

What was good for Buckingham Palace was also good for the Viceroy of India—though, perhaps, for different reasons. When the Viceroy was clad in his full regalia, and wearing his high hat, there was apt, in any more average vehicle, to be a marked shortage of headroom. Consequently the representative of the King had the habit of buying his cars at second-hand from the royal household, and the vehicle found on the runway must have been one of them.

No car was ever quite so good for this purpose as a Hooper-bodied Daimler, and the records in the Royal Mews record the sales of several to Viceroys. After the partition, the wisdom of this became even more apparent when one of the British High Commissioners to Pakistan was provided with an official Rolls-Royce. It was a huge, ambassadorial-type limousine, and seemed ideal for its purpose—until Mrs. High Commissioner got inside it. She was a tall lady and she found that, when she was dolled up in her finery, her hat was apt to hit the roof.

She complained about it to the local Rolls-Royce agent, who took the car away, and caused a large oval hole to be cut in the floor beneath Her Excellency's seat. The idea was to take it down a few inches. Predictably, the car became known in Karachi as the 'flying commode' or, sometimes, the 'flying thunder-box'. But—unfortunately, perhaps—the story does not end there. Once the modified car had been inspected, it was taken back to the agents for final preening and polishing before the official delivery on the following day. It was parked beneath a fig tree, and during the night there was a sudden thunderstorm. The tree was split by lightning and a large bough fell on the car, making a most fearful dent in its roof. It had to be shipped back to London for repairs, and when the officials at Rolls-Royce saw the hole which had been cut at the back of the body, they promptly nullified the warranty.

Rajahs had a passion for possessions. There was Hyderabad and his gold, and the Maharajah of Jind who had a passion for dogs. At one time, he had 500 pedigree pets, and even built a cemetery for the remains of those which were dear but departed. One Rajah had his own stamps, but the biggest status symbol of all belonged to the Rajah of Bahawalpur. On a trip to London, he had admired the soldiers from the Household Cavalry who were on sentry duty in Whitehall. Presently an idea began to germinate in his head and, before very long, he insisted that he, too, should have just such a bodyguard. The troops were decked out in near-imitations of the British uniforms. To command them, he recruited a retired Indian Army colonel, whom he promptly promoted to general.

The Rajah of Faridkot had a passion for motor cycles. During the last war, he loaned his palace in New Delhi as a mess for senior officers of South East Asia Command. Among those who used it was Lord Mountbatten.

When the war was over, Mountbatten decided that it would be a nice gesture to present the rajah with an item for his collection. He had nearly every kind of motor cycle under the sun with one exception. This was a tiny machine, called the 'Welbike', which had been developed round about 1942 at a research station in Hertfordshire for the use of airborne troops. It was powered by a little 98 c.c. Excelsior engine, which gave it a top speed of about 30 m.p.h., and its fuel tank could accommodate $6\frac{1}{2}$ pints of two-stroke mixture, providing a range of about ninety miles. The whole thing could be folded up and packed in a cylindrical container for dropping by parachute. On landing, it could withstand a considerable shock.

During the lean winter months of the 1931 depression King George V helped to keep the Daimler works busy by ordering these new vehicles for the Royal fleet.

Others might sit where they liked in the Royal Daimlers, but King George V always occupied an armchair situated amidships. In this picture, Queen Mary is in the nearside rear seat.

When Hirohito was crown prince of Japan in 1921, he made a journey in this Panhard and Levassor. Years later, when he was Emperor, a bullet-proof Mercedes (below) was produced to imperial specifications. Before delivery, it was tested by Japanese detectives, who fired revolver bullets at it.

Above: *King George VI was a Lanchester enthusiast and owned several before coming to the throne.* Below: *When he became King, he did away with the armchair amidships and occupied the rear seat. A sheet of glass was introduced into the Daimler's roof to improve lighting.*

It may have been contrary to the spirit of the revolution, but Lenin enjoyed travelling in this Rolls-Royce. Even the 'winged lady' mascot was retained. Another Rolls-Royce, fitted with caterpillar tracks, was kept at his country house outside Moscow.

When King Alexander of Yugoslavia landed at Marseilles in 1934, he was shot dead within a few minutes of coming ashore. The car was a Delage. The killer was a Macedonian terrorist.

It was the forerunner of the Gorgi and Lambretta and all the rest of the scooters.

Mountbatten got hold of a 'Welbike', invited the rajah to dinner, and duly made the presentation. His Highness was delighted, and insisted on trying it out at once. Like many of these palaces, the building had a large gallery running right round the centre well, with the bedrooms leading off it. He caused the small machine to be taken up to this gallery, and spent the rest of the evening happily riding round and round it.

The rajahs were masters of subtlety and were not above using their vehicles to convey, variously, approval or criticism. If, for example, you went on a visit to one of them, he would always send a car to meet you at the nearest railway station. If it was one of the best examples in his collection, you knew that you were welcome. But if, as happened on a number of occasions, it was a somewhat delapidated member of the tribe, you realised that you should not expect very much. And if the car's condition was such that it actually broke down on the way to the palace, you were probably in real trouble.

And, of course, they had their little fads. The Rajah of Bwalpur hardly ever went out of doors; but, when he did, everybody had to turn his back to the royal vehicle. It was as if, in some mysterious way, their eyes might have defiled him.

Sometimes the princes' tastes caused them to waste money at at most fearful rate. One ruler spent £¾ million on a palace in Pakistan—simply to slay bustards. He had a fleet of jeeps and Land-Rovers, which roamed the desert with guns and hawks, hunting the wretched birds down. But the bustards became extinct in that part of the world—leaving their murderer with an enormously expensive house on his hands, a fleet of vehicles, and arsenal of ironmongery, a cage of falcons, and no birds to kill.

When one considers the schools, the hospitals, and the other necessities of civilised life which were crying out to be built in India, it is, perhaps, easy to criticise the extravagances of the rajahs. They certainly put on a sumptuous show; but, in the end, it went sour. And, in any case, their thunder was stolen times without number by a small man who lived in the utmost simplicity, who seemed to spurn possessions, and who disliked (and could not drive) motor cars. His name was Gandhi.

10 *Life and Death on Two Wheels*

To most people, T. E. Lawrence is either the hero of Arabia or else that strange misfit of the between-war years who wrote a disturbing novel about life in the R.A.F. entitled *The Mint.* Since his death in 1935, he has been a favourite target for those who enjoy taking the stuffing out of legends. One somehow doubts whether these attacks would have disturbed him, especially as they have invariably been made by writers who were never within thousands of miles of the desert campaign.

But there is one aspect of Lawrence that has never received much publicity, which is, perhaps, strange, for it involved him in work which gave him enormous pleasure. He was an extremely good mechanic; and if he had chosen to make engineering his career, he would have no doubt been successful at it.

During his service in the Royal Air Force, for example, he was stationed for a while at a base on the western shore of Southampton Water which, many years later, became the centre of hovercraft development. How Lawrence would have loved that: it would have provided just the kind of mechanical challenge he enjoyed. As it was, he carried out valuable work on new powerboats for the R.A.F., producing, at one and the same time, more speed and greater manoeuvrability. We have his own word for it that this was one of the few periods after the first world war when he was completely happy.

In the desert campaign, his earliest form of transport was, appropriately, a camel. Later on, however, something more sophisticated was required, and he was equipped with a fleet of vehicles. It included seven Rolls-Royce armoured cars, two Rolls-Royce tenders, and a number of Ford trucks. Lawrence himself always travelled in one of the tenders. His driver was S. C. Rolls (no relation to the car maker), who became governing director of the Imperial Autocar Co. of Northampton, and proprietor of the Rolls Motor Company in that town.

To Rolls, Lawrence was the very stuff of heroes. In a contribution to *T. E. Lawrence by His Friends* (published by Jonathan Cape in 1937), he described him as possessing 'a power (which) seemed to command one's very soul, of charming persuasive manner, to seduce one's rebellion, and counteract all obstinate ideas. He talked as he rode by my side in the Rolls-Royce tender, he explained the Revolt, he discussed the great job which lay ahead, he spoke of his difficulties, or his hopes and fears, of his misgivings and good fortune.'

Lawrence was almost equally respectful of Rolls, whom he described as our 'strongest and most resourceful man'. As for the vehicles, his admiration knew no bounds. 'Great was Rolls, and great was Royce!' he once exclaimed. And: 'A Rolls in the desert was above rubies.'

When one considers the enormous mileages those vehicles put up, travelling over rough country, and loaded down with guns and ammunition and men and gold (as gifts to the Arab leaders), one can see his point of view. Nor was he inclined to pamper a car. As Rolls wrote: 'T.E. had a craze for speed and with delight he watched our speedometer 30–40–50–60–70–, there was nothing here to stop one travelling at any speed; other cars came along and T.E. shouted encouragement. We raced neck and neck, but the only danger was the strain on our tyres through the terrific heat.'

Whatever may have been his other hardships and anxieties during the campaign, these vehicles gave next to no trouble. The only occasion that so much as approached a disaster occurred during one of the later actions. It followed a raid near Deraa, in which they successfully blew up a railway bridge. Enemy patrols were in the vicinity, which meant that they had to make a quick getaway.

Unfortunately, it was too quick. As they jolted over a water-course, there came a sickening thud from beneath Lawrence's tender. The vehicle sadly slumped backwards with a broken spring. At first, according to Lawrence, his driver 'was nearly in tears over the mishap'; but, then, 'even the stubble on his jaw seemed to harden in stubborn determination'. There was, Rolls presently announced, just one chance. They would have to jack up the end of the damaged spring and wedge it back into position with slats of wood.

The car had a couple of lengths of wood on board for placing under the tyres when it became stuck in the sand or in mud. If three blocks could be chopped off one of them, they would produce just the kind of wedge that was needed. The trouble was that they had no saw with which to do the job.

This was one of those times when Lawrence's ingenuity revealed itself. Taking his revolver, he fired two rows of shots across the planks in such a way that the necessary lengths could be snapped off. The approaching Turkish patrols heard the explosions, and halted. Rolls fixed the pieces of wood into place with captured telegraph wire. The repair was so effective that the tender did normal work for the next three weeks, and was used to enter Damascus at the end of the campaign.

During one of his visits to Cairo, Lawrence had ridden a Triumph motor cycle. By all accounts, he found the experience very pleasing. In 1922, when he was serving as an aircraftsman in the R.A.F., he bought a Brough Superior. This was the first of seven machines of this make that he owned. He called the first 'George I', the second 'George II', and so on. One of them, improbably, was a present from Mr. and Mrs. Bernard Shaw.

Three years later, he met George Brough, the manufacturer of these bikes, and the two men became friendly. Mr. Brough later recalled that Lawrence was not only very able technically, but that he was also careful and well mannered when on the road.

He visited the Brough works on several occasions, and it became a kind of ritual that, whenever he arrived there, his machine was immediately taken away and cleaned. Once, when making a tour of the factory, he came across a boy laboriously polishing the spokes of the bike's wheels. He stopped and spoke to the lad, and told him how good it was to see somebody doing the difficult parts. 'It is quite easy for me to clean the easy parts like the handle-bars and tank, isn't it?' he said. The boy, of course, was delighted. As soon as Lawrence had departed, he asked permission to run home to tell his parents about the encounter.

Lawrence's detractors have been people who hardly knew him. Anyone who had anything approaching a close acquaintance with him immediately came under his spell. One impression which many of them had was of his amazingly blue eyes. Even when he was dressed in his motor-cycling get-up—normally a uniform cap, a storm suit made out of black rubber (it had been designed during the war for the crews of minesweepers), and highly polished black boots—it was those eyes which made the first impact.

Although he was, as George Brough said, careful on the roads, there was no denying his passion for speed. After an unpleasant day, when he had been at the mercy of some witless sergeant who was entirely without sensitivity, his escape would be to ride for 'a hundred fast miles'. Once, on a trip between Salisbury and Winchester, the speedometer stuck at 103 m.p.h., but the machine was 'rock-steady' and he loved it. On another occasion, in 1923, he averaged 44·5 m.p.h. for a round trip of 250 miles.

On the front cover of the original edition of *Seven Pillars of Wisdom* were engraved the words 'The sword also means cleanness and death'. A motor cycle, ultimately, meant death; but it is tempting to see it also as a cleanser. It may have been that, when Lawrence surrendered part of himself to the pleasure of speed, he experienced some feeling of purification—as if he were escaping from all the complications and frustrations which had surrounded him since the war, and which must often have seemed like a tangle of dirty cobwebs.

Certainly, in 1923, he was describing his motor cycle as 'a temporary escape', and the danger appealed to him as well. In a letter to his friend Lionel Curtis, he wrote: 'When my mood gets too hot and I find myself wandering beyond control I pull out my motor bike and hurl it top speed through these unfit roads for hour after hour. My nerves are jaded and gone near dead, so that nothing less than hours of voluntary danger will prick them into life: and the "life" they reach then is a melancholy joy at risking something worth exactly 2s. 9d. a day' (his pay as an air-craftsman in the R.A.F.).

'It's odd again, that craving for real risk: because in the gymnasium I funk jumping the horse, more than poison. That is physical, which is why it is: I'm ashamed of doing it and of not doing it, unwilling to do it: and most ashamed (afraid) of doing it well.'[1]

Sometimes, there were accidents, and at least two members of the 'George' family were disposed of in this way. In the spring of 1923, when he was serving as a private in the Royal Tank Corps,[2] he ran over some glass from a broken bottle outside Bovington Camp in Dorset. The front tyre burst: the machine ran up the bank and turned over. Lawrence was unharmed, but the bike was damaged. Later that year, the Brough was stolen. It was afterwards found abandoned in a ditch and ruined beyond repair.

In December 1925, on another 'George', he set off on a trip from Cranwell where he was serving with the R.A.F. It was a cold day, and he hit a patch of ice at 55 m.p.h. The machine skidded out of control. The damage to Lawrence added up to one injured knee, one ankle, and an elbow. So far as the motor cycle was concerned, the front mudguard, the name-plate, the handlebars, and one of the footrests had to be renewed.

Almost exactly one year later, he was even less fortunate. He was riding through Islington in North London. It had been raining heavily and the streets were greasy. Somehow, he slid on the wooden paving, fell heavily, and injured a knee-cap. Harm to the bike involved the footrest, the kick-start, the brake levers, half a handlebar and the oil pump. To Lawrence's way of thinking it was a write-off, but he managed to sell what he described as 'the wreck' for £100.

The final crash occurred at about 11.30 on the morning of Monday, May 13th, 1935. He had recently been discharged from the R.A.F. and was living at a cottage called Clouds Hill which he had built near the village of Moreton in Dorset. At the time, his friend, the novelist Henry Williamson, was going through agonies about the threat to peace in Europe. Williamson believed that it was possible to achieve 'pacification . . . through friendship and fearless common sense'. He wanted to discuss this idea with Lawrence and, in particular, the possibility of holding

[1]*Letters of T. E. Lawrence* edited by David Garnett (Jonathan Cape).
[2]This may sound confusing: during the post-war years Lawrence served in both the Royal Tank Corps and the Royal Air Force.

a rally of ex-servicemen at the Albert Hall. On Lawrence's table at Clouds Hill there was a letter from Williamson asking whether they could meet.

Lawrence (or T. E. Shaw, as he was known at the time) got out George VII, and set off on the short journey down to the post office at Moreton. There, he addressed a telegram form to Williamson, and wrote: 'Lunch Tuesday wet fine cottage one mile north Bovington Camp SHAW'. He then went outside and climbed back on to his machine. He kicked the starter and the engine burst into life. With that peculiarly satisfactory roar which was a characteristic of a Brough, the bike sped back up the road towards Clouds Hill.

Suddenly he came to a dip. As the machine hurtled over the top, Lawrence saw that there were two errand boys ahead, riding side by side on pedal cycles. He swerved to avoid them: braked hard and was thrown off. The bike was hardly damaged, but Lawrence lay unconscious by the roadside. One of the lads, the local butcher's boy, was taken to hospital with minor injuries. He was soon reported to be making good progress.

An ambulance driven by a Royal Tank Corps soldier collected Lawrence and took him to the hospital in Bovington Camp, where a fractured skull was diagnosed. A cable was sent to his mother and brother who, at the time, were travelling down the Yangtze River in China bound for Shanghai.

On the day following the crash, he seemed to be making some slight progress. He had been in excellent physical condition and it appeared possible that this might help him to recover. Furthermore, a formidable gathering of medical experts had been assembled at Bovington. Among them were Sir Farquhar Buzzard—Physician-in-Ordinary to the King, H. W. B. Cairns—the London Hospital's brain specialist, and Dr. Hope Gosse—a London lung specialist.

By the Friday, there still seemed to be hope, although he had not recovered consciousness and his body had to be turned over and tilted at hourly intervals, to drain off saliva and phlegm which were congesting his respiratory system. The crisis came late on the Saturday, when he had to be given oxygen. By seven o'clock on the Sunday morning, his condition had worsened considerably. His pulse had almost gone, and his breathing was very weak indeed.

T. E. Lawrence died at 8 a.m. on Sunday, May 19th, 1935.
At 8.30, Captain C. P. Allen, R.A.M.C., the camp's medical
officer, formally confirmed it. He was buried in Moreton Church
two days later. Had he lived, he would have lost his memory,
been almost totally paralysed and unable to speak.

But the hero of the desert, who had often sought anonymity,
could not even be permitted to die without suggestions of drama
bubbling through the mud of hearsay. A corporal from the Royal
Army Ordnance Corps had been standing near Clouds Hill at a
point about one hundred yards away from the road, when he
saw Lawrence go by at a speed of between fifty and sixty miles
an hour. He noticed that he passed a black car travelling in the
opposite direction just before he heard the crash. On the other
hand, neither of the errand boys—whose evidence was, admittedly,
rather confused—had any memory of a car being in the area at
the time.

At first, information about the accident was withheld from the
press, which may have helped to foster a story that Lawrence
was not in hospital at all. It was, this rumour had it, a trick to
divert attention while he slipped out of the country on a mission
for the secret service.

Of course, the black car had to come into it at some stage,
and this seems to have been regarded as the murder weapon
of a foreign power. Fiction then went really wild, and suggested
that Lawrence's brain, and his alone, stored all Britain's war
plans. Somehow, it had to be destroyed. Just in case there were
any plans elsewhere, there were tales of foreign agents breaking
into Clouds Hill and taking away secret books and papers, which
they burned on Moreton Heath. It was, of course, all a lot of
nonsense.

At the Brough motor-cycle works, George Brough looked
unhappily at George VIII, which Lawrence had ordered some
while previously and which was nearing completion. In memory
of the man for whom it was built, Mr. Brough refused to sell it,
but always rode it himself.

11 *Sporting Gentlemen*

One of the nation's most distinguished hip-joints will go down to posterity as a mascot on the bonnet of a Rolls-Royce. Both are the property of the Marquess of Exeter, who, for a good many years, has suffered from arthritis. In 1960, an artificial joint was installed in His Lordship with entirely satisfactory results. It performed its function so well that when, in the summer of 1970, it had to be replaced, the Marquess was unwilling to have it thrown away. Shortly afterwards, he told a reporter from the *Daily Telegraph*: 'When the joint was taken out and I saw it, I thought it was so attractive I couldn't possibly let it go on the scrapheap. It seemed as if it had been designed for another purpose—my car, for instance.'

Before he inherited his present title in 1956, the Marquess was Lord Burghley and, as such, was famous as a hurdler. He won eight British Championships and the 400 metres event in the 1928 Olympic Games. No doubt the artificial joint had a hard time standing in for what must obviously have been, in its heyday, a most immaculate natural unit. The Marquess must have realised this, and he was generous in his treatment of the redundant spare part. For its role as a mascot, the words 'A devoted supporter, 1960–1970' have been engraved on it. What finer tribute could any hip-joint hope for?

H

The Marquess of Exeter was one of the very few members of the British aristocracy to win fame as an athlete. Nor is there much evidence of noble impact upon other sports, with the exception of motor racing. Today's top driver is a professional and depends upon the game for his income. But this, in Britain at any rate, is largely a post-war trend. Before 1939, there were some works drivers; but, if you spent a day at Brooklands, you were likely to see such blue-blooded aces as the Earl of March (now the Duke of Richmond and Gordon) and Earl Howe in action, and driving very well. After the war, Lord Howe became chairman of the Royal Automobile Club's competitions committee, and he was succeeded by Marquess Camden, who is still in the chair.

In the very early days of motor racing, the starting lists of events glittered with great names. One of the first car manufacturers was that scion of a high-ranking Belgian family, Count Albert de Dion. When sent by his parents to Germany to learn the language, he achieved a sufficient degree of fluency, but, which was more important, he also learned how to construct steam engines. One day, on a shopping expedition in Paris, he noticed a beautifully built model of an engine in one of the windows. He was told that it had been made by a firm named Bouton and Trepardoux on the outskirts of the city. With typical impetuosity, he drove over to the tiny factory and promptly bought the concern up. The first de Dion-Bouton rattled and wheezed on to the roads soon afterwards, and the Count rapidly distinguished himself as a racing driver. He won second prize in the Paris–Rouen race of 1894, and, with his friend Baron de Zuylen de Nyevell, was largely responsible for founding the Automobile Club de France.

The first man to establish a speed record on land was the Marquess de Chasseloup-Laubat. At 39·24 m.p.h., he does not seem to have driven very quickly and, within a month, the record was snatched from him. But, all told between 1898 and 1899, he held it three times. When he finally gave up, he left it at 57·60 m.p.h.

There were the Chevalier René de Knyff, Baron de Caters and the Marquess de Montaignée. They were chivalrous competitors, who were always ready to give a novice good advice, and to help or encourage a driver in distress. In one big event, René de Knyff saw one of the competitors standing dejectedly by the roadside. He stopped, asked the unfortunate driver what his trouble was, and then spent several minutes trying to cheer him up.

When, in the Gordon Bennett race of 1903, the steering on Charles Jarrott's car failed and caused it to overturn, Baron de Caters, who was behind him, pulled up at once and asked whether there was anything he could do to help. Jarrott said that his sister was in the grandstand. He wondered whether the Baron could possibly tell her that he was not badly injured. De Caters did so, and then went on with the race.

A year or so after this episode, the Guinness brothers came on to the motor racing scene. Their father was a member of the Irish family which is renowned for its stout. He decided to break with tradition and, instead of going into the brewery, joined the Household Cavalry. Presently, he became a captain in the Blues, and is said to have ridden beside Queen Victoria on some state occasion.

He had three sons. The youngest, Nigel Lee Guinness, is living in retirement down in Surrey. The elder two, Algernon and Kenelm (more commonly known as 'Bill'), have been dead for some years.

It would, presumably, be possible to find two more fundamentally different characters who were, nevertheless, related and shared a common interest, but it would be difficult. Algy was educated at Eton and Oxford. According to Nigel Guinness, he was 'gay, carefree, but he was no good with money. It just went through his fingers.' That veteran motoring writer S. C. H. (Sammy) Davis, who knew him well, speaks of his 'dancing, humorous, blue eyes', and recalls an occasion when he had done well in one of the Tourist Trophy Races on the Isle of Man.

In order to celebrate the success in suitable style, he decided it was necessary to take his car, with three pretty girls perched on the bonnet, into his hotel. That might have been all very well, if the building had not been fitted with revolving doors. The ensuing technical struggle was hilarious, but a Guinness never gave up. By some means (the nature of the miracle has not been recorded), the victorious vehicle, girls and all, duly arrived in the lobby.

Guinness himself used to tell a story about an early bid by a Frenchman to capture the Land Speed Record. In those days, these attempts were made over one kilometre on a stretch of open road. The French prided themselves that, whatever might befall the franc, the statutory kilometre was sacred. It was quite unnecessary to measure it out: if one simply departed from one kilometre stone and drove on to the next, one would have travelled the exact distance.

On the first day, the Frenchman was unable to travel fast enough to beat the record. At the end of his second attempt, Guinness came up to him and whispered: 'Tell them you're having trouble with your carburettor, and that you'll have another go tomorrow.'

'But,' the Frenchman protested, 'it isn't true. The car won't *go* any faster.'

'Nevertheless,' said Guinness, 'do as I say.'

The authorities put away their stopwatches and the car was returned to its garage, presumably to be tuned up. At dead of night (according to the Guinness version), a small party went out on to the road, dug up the second kilometre stone, and replanted it slightly nearer the starting point. Then they carefully put back the turf and returned to their hotel.

On the following morning, the Frenchman tried again. This time, he was delighted to hear that he had broken the record.

The truth of the tale has never been established, but Algy Guinness used to enjoy telling it. Certainly there was some anxiety during the speed bid, when one of the conspirators noticed that the turf which had been so carefully replaced, had turned brown. It is unlikely that the officials noticed this, though perhaps somebody did have an inkling of what had happened; for, thereafter, the kilometre stones were not trusted. In all future speed record bids, the distance was meticulously measured out.

Bill Guinness had been delicate as a child. With most people, a cold in the head is simply an inconvenient and uncomfortable minor illness. For him, however, these complaints frequently turned to pneumonia. The rumbustuous life of Eton and Oxford was ruled out. Instead, he was educated by private tutors.

Possibly because of his sheltered youth, he lacked the spontaneous fun of his elder brother. One acquaintance has described him as 'cold as cold' and another as 'very serious. You could enjoy being with him, though not in the same way as with Algy.' He was also, unlike his brother, 'clever with money'.

The latter part of his life was marked by tragedy. In a race on the Spanish circuit at San Sebastian, he was involved in a crash, and his mechanic was killed. Guinness himself fractured his skull, and he never seemed to be the same after this incident. He became more and more introverted, and eventually took his own life.

Bill Guinness began his motor racing career as his brother's mechanic, and there is no doubt that the two were devoted to each other. As drivers, perhaps Algy was the more successful. He drove a car on the simple theory that it should be made to go as fast as it possibly could. His performances on corners were utterly hair-raising. By using up the entire road, he always managed to get through and, protected by whatever gods look after the brave and the reckless, he never had an accident. In 1906, he drove a 200 h.p. Darracq at a record speed of 117 m.p.h., though, through some fault in the timing, it was never officially recognised. After the first world war, his brother was more successful. Using a large 350 h.p. Sunbeam, he set off on a blustery day at Brooklands in 1922, and returned a speed of 133·75 m.p.h. Presumably the arrangements were more efficient than those made for Algy's bid: at all events, the record was accepted and remained unchallenged for the next two years.

Algy Guinness was never concerned with the tiresome business of making a living. He was a sportsman, and he lived in considerable style. As became a man of his wealth and position, he owned a steam yacht, and he used to keep his racing cars and three mechanics at the large house he owned in the home counties. When a machine with a 200 h.p. engine and open exhausts is started up, it is apt to make a most fearful din. His neighbours, however, appear to have been sympathetic—or else very long suffering. All they asked was that, before the roar of his motor tried to shake them out of their wits, they should be given a little warning.

Bill Guinness was not content to enjoy a sportsman's life. Racing was all very well, but he was determined to earn a living. The opportunity occurred when he was driving for Sunbeam. The sparking plugs of those days were manufactured out of porcelain and they were useless in a racing engine. One day, Louis Coatalen, the brilliant and tempestuous head of Sunbeam's racing activities, suggested to him that he might care to investigate some better design.

The first experiments were made in a potting shed at the end of his garden. Later, he bought an old inn in south-west London, took out all the floors, and installed a gas engine in the cellar for testing purposes. Unlike his rival, he eschewed the use of porcelain and, instead, insulated the electrode with rings of mica. At first, there were problems, but it soon became clear that he was working on the right lines. The firm which was to become world famous as K.L.G. Sparking Plugs had been founded with a capital of £50,000. By the time Bill Guinness left it, it was employing 8,000 people. One early order came from the Mercedes team, who insisted that a consignment should be sent out to Stuttgart as quickly as possible for use in a forthcoming grand prix. One of the German cars won the race, and the victory of mica over porcelain was complete.

Nigel Guinness told me that 'our people had a *feeling*—they wanted to go faster and faster. Speed was the thing.' The feeling had been born with the coming of the automobile, and one of the earlier sportsmen to experience it was a remarkable gentleman of Polish-American descent named Count Eliot Zborowski. Count Zborowski's Polish ancestors had emigrated to the eastern seaboard of the United States, where they had acquired valuable masses of land in New York and New Jersey. The Count himself lived in England and became famous as a horseman. He was, by any standards, an extremely colourful character, and once rode his hunter through the front door of his house and upstairs to the door of his bedroom.

When Mercedes became established, he invested in one of these vehicles. It pleased him so much that he sold off his stable of horses and devoted himself to motor sport. He took part in the Paris–Vienna race of 1902 and always believed that, had there been any justice in the world, he would have won it.

In the following year, he took his Mercedes down to the South of France for a hillclimb at a place named La Turbie. He was in one of his fatalistic moods that day and, as he sat beneath a tree smoking a cigarette, he observed to a friend that he doubted whether he would ever come back. Possibly this unhappy frame of mind can be accounted for by a visit he had made, some days previously, to a fortune teller in Nice. According to her, the omens were decidedly unpropitious, and he would be well advised not to take part in the event. Ever a superstitious man, he drafted his will, and yet he cannot have felt sufficiently convinced to withdraw his entry. At all events, he sat there brooding, elegantly dressed in a dark suit, with a white shirt and gold cufflinks, and wearing a pair of spotless white gloves.

Presently, he and his mechanic (another nobleman: his name was Baron de Pollange), and their 60 h.p. Mercedes, set off up the hill. Zborowski was in a reckless frame of mind, and the soothsayer's warning went completely unheeded. He virtually *threw* his car at the hill. On the first sharp corner, when he should have been slackening his speed, his gold cufflinks jammed the throttle lever wide open. The car went out of control, threw its driver overboard, and crashed into a rock face. The Baron, who somehow managed to retain his seat, was not badly hurt. Count Eliot Zborowski, on the other hand, had been pitched head first on to some large stones. His skull was fractured and he lay by the side of the road, dead.

He left a widow and an eight-year-old son, Count Louis Zborowski who became known to his wide circle of friends as 'Lou'.

According to S. C. H. Davis, Louis Zborowski was 'a poet, an artist. He was like a prince out of a musical comedy.' Darkly handsome, his moods ranged between the gay and the profoundly gloomy. He lived on an allowance which seems to have come to him from New York via Spain at monthly intervals. For the first half of each month, he lived like a prince, throwing wildly extravagant parties and buying up whatever took his fancy. During the second half, he was apt to be broke until the next instalment arrived.

He was fascinated by anything mechanical. He owned an aircraft, though he never flew it; he was one of the first men to produce home movies; he introduced electric light to the estate he owned in Kent; and he installed a fabulous model railway system to take guests round the grounds. Later on, this formed the basis of the narrow gauge railway which runs between Romney, Hythe and Dymchurch and of which, at one time, Bill Guinness was a director.

When his local fire brigade became worried about its continued dependence on horses (a fact which was causing it to arrive late for some of the farther-flung blazes), an officer called at Zborowski's house to ask his advice. His solution to this, like most problems, was lavish and immediate. He had a Rolland Pilain racing chassis in his coachhouse, and he instantly dispatched it to a Canterbury firm of bodybuilders. It was equipped to carry ten men, a large amount of hose, and was fitted with a coupling so that it could haul the steam pump. It was probably the fastest fire engine in the country, and Zborowski was made an honorary captain of the brigade for his generosity.

Inevitably, his attention eventually turned to racing cars. 'He liked,' Davis told me, 'big, horrible, things like that terrible Chitty, which was a jungle of enormous ironmongery.' The idea has developed that there were four of these cars, of which the third was a big Mercedes and the fourth was otherwise known as the 'Higham Special'. But, as David A. Paine pointed out in what is clearly the definitive article on the Zborowskis (it appeared in the December, 1969, issue of the *Veteran and Vintage Magazine*), 'the White Mercedes is sometimes referred to, quite wrongly, as Chitty III, for the sources that I have found all indicate that Louis only ever referred to the first two cars as Chitty, the third was always the White Mercedes'.[1]

The name 'Chitty-Chitty-Bang-Bang' was the invention of a music-hall comedian during the first world war. It was the title of a song and the words (somewhat improper by all accounts) like the name of its composer have been forgotten. If you ignore the film of that name, it lives on in the legend of those thunderous cars which were part of the private paradise in which Louis Zborowski lived. Chitty I and Chitty II were both powered by aero engines, were chain driven and huge. The top speed of Chitty I was 120 m.p.h., and Chitty II got up to 115 m.p.h. According to Mr. Paine, who made a journey to London in Chitty II, 'the only noise one could hear, as we journeyed west in the small hours, was the soft swishing of the chains, punctuated occasionally by the deep bark of the exhaust when a down shift was required. The ride, even at the legal limit, was surprisingly smooth and unexciting, not dramatic as one might expect.'

Both the Chittys had pronounced Mercedes elements in them. Like his father, Louis Zborowski was devoted to this make and, eventually, he joined that firm's racing team. His first race at the wheel of one of these cars was the French Grand Prix of 1924, which was held at Lyons. Zborowski was then twenty-nine.

---

[1] The fourth was used by Parry Thomas for an attempt on the land speed record in 1926. On the last run, the chain snapped and killed Thomas. The car was interred in the Pendine Sands until 1969, when it was exhumed by Professor O. Wyn Owen.

S. C. H. Davis rode with him as mechanic, and the two of them stayed at a small country inn some miles out of the city. Zborowski was restless that evening, filled with the darkest forebodings about the race on the following day. Somehow he had the notion that he was going to be killed. Since Davis was to travel with him, he can hardly have found the presentiment comforting. But he is a calm and very patient man. He encouraged his gloomy companion to bring his fears out into the open. Throughout the long hours until early morning, the two men walked round and round the hotel discussing philosophy. Much of the conversation had to do with infinity, a fact which is probably explained by the night sky which was clear, packed with stars and inviting in its promise of unending distance.

Zborowski's fears were allayed, and he woke up on the morning of the race with no more misgivings. As it happened, however, his fears of the night before might easily have been justified. On the sixteenth lap, looking up from his instruments, Davis noticed that the front suspension was about to come adrift. He quickly pointed this out to Zborowski, who stopped the car. The damage was beyond immediate repair, and they withdrew from the event. If Davis had not looked up at that particular moment, they would certainly have been involved in a very serious crash.

In September of that year, Zborowski presented himself at Monza to drive a Mercedes in the Italian Grand Prix. The new works car was not ready for him and the team manager, Professor Ferdinand Porsche, suggested that he should use a vehicle which was normally only taken out for practice. He agreed.

Louis Zborowski lived in two dimensions: in the every day, opulent, world to which his allowance gave him title, and in the very bright and very dark, but never grey, realms of his imagination. Like his father, he was intensely superstitious, and he had always refused to wear the gold cufflinks that Count Eliot had worn at La Turbie. On the day of the Italian Grand Prix, however, he suddenly decided to put them on.

If it hadn't been all too horribly real, it would be tempting to believe that Zborowski's death was a thing of his own imagining. To begin with, there was the feeling of impending disaster that he had experienced at Lyons. Now here he was—wearing the gold cufflinks, almost as if he were preparing himself to play the part of a victim in some sacrificial rite. Indeed, he was even dressed in a black suit, just as his father had been at La Turbie.

All went well enough for the first forty-seven laps of the race. Then he came into the pits to refuel and change his tyres. He was offered a glass of water, but he refused it. He did accept a cigarette.

When the car was ready, he had a good deal of difficulty in getting the engine to start. Eventually, it fired satisfactorily, and he set off in chase of Antonio Ascari, who was leading the race. On the far side of the first curve after the pits, one of his tyres burst. The Mercedes went out of control, shot across the track, plunged through a wire fence, ricocheted off a number of wooden posts and presently came to a halt with its nose embedded in a tree. The mechanic survived. Count Louis Zborowski died in the ambulance on the way to hospital. The gold cufflinks, the black suit, the fractured skull which caused his death, it was all too frighteningly like that day at La Turbie twenty-one years earlier.

There was a kind of dedication to speed. Some were content to go motor racing, others had to carry the obsession to its limits. Two of the foremost protagonists in the struggle to be fastest man on earth were Malcolm Campbell and Henry O'Neal de Hane Segrave. Both men were knighted for their triumphs.

Campbell was the son of a diamond merchant. At the age of eighteen, he left home—spent two and a half years on the continent and then went to work in the City of London as an insurance broker. One of his ideas was to offer publications coverage against libel actions. The first firm to take out such a policy was Odhams Press.

His first racing car was named 'Flapper' after a horse he fancied at the time. It was not very lucky, for neither the car nor the horse won any events.

'Flapper' was followed by a line of 'Bluebirds' and it was in cars with this name that he broke the World Land Speed Record on several occasions. It was borrowed from Maeterlink's opera, *The Bluebird*—a piece that Campbell had enjoyed. He considered that it symbolised hope and success.

De Hane Segrave lived exclusively for speed. He had an aluminium foot which was the result of a flying accident in the first world war. Otherwise, he was a tremendously fit individual, more than comfortably off, and very serious about his profession.

In long-distance races, his attitude did not serve him very well. The secret of winning at Le Mans, for example, is to drive no faster than you need to. This did not suit Segrave's temperament and, on one occasion, he wore out a car during practice. Somehow, he had mixed up his objectives and had become so determined to break the lap record, that he forgot the event was a test of endurance as well as speed. The vehicles have to be considered, and even nursed a little bit. Possibly it was because he, himself, would have been well able to drive close to the limits for a full-twenty-four hours, or even for forty-eight. He may have made the mistake of judging the stamina of his machinery by his own.

But he excelled at Land Speed Record attempts and he was also successful as a racing driver. It was, after all, he who won the French Grand Prix in 1923 and the Spanish event of 1924. The former had never before been won by an Englishman, and it was not until Peter Collins came first with a Ferrari in 1956, that the National Anthem was again played at the end of a grand prix in France.

He had what Davis calls 'a sprinter's mind'. Out of the cockpit he had a somewhat oblique sense of humour and it often took a minute or so before people saw his jokes. During the practice period for the 1925 Le Mans race, he threw his colleagues in the Sunbeam team into a state of acute anxiety. They were sitting at a café table, drinking coffee, and watching the cars go by. Segrave had a large stopwatch, and he was amusing himself by timing what should have been one of the slower vehicles. Suddenly he pointed to the dial of his watch and explained that, according to his calculations, it was travelling a good deal faster than the two Sunbeams had done.

Coatalen was in a state of near despair and so were the other members of the team with the exception of Segrave, who seemed to find the information amusing. Then he explained that it was all a lot of nonsense, and that the car in question had not travelled anything like so fast as his watch had suggested. It was, indeed, a somewhat elaborate practical joke, for he had juggled with the mechanism in such a way that it gave a false reading. None of his colleagues found it very funny, but Segrave enjoyed himself.

For much of his career, he worked with the present Marquess Camden, who became the director in charge of Sunbeam's Service, Research and Racing Department. Although, as the

Marquess says, 'my father almost detested motor cars', he himself took pleasure in them from a very early age. When he was seven, the head chauffeur taught him to drive a 1904 Darracq (similar to the one which played the part of 'Genevieve' in the film) up and down one of the long, straight lengths of drive on the family's estate in Kent. Although his legs were too short to reach the car's pedals, he coped manfully with the steering and made a very fair job of changing gear.

He met Segrave for the first time when the two of them were at Eton. The friendship was renewed after the war, when the Marquess went on to the reserve of officers after ten years' service in the Scots Guards. Segrave became the London general manager for Sunbeam, and the Marquess was appointed as his assistant.

Segrave went off on one speed record attempt after another, and the Marquess went, too. The final bid took them to Lake Windermere in the early summer of 1930. This time, the water speed record was the target, and the missile designed to break it was a boat powered by Rolls-Royce engines named *Miss England II.*

There were several delays. First of all, the two propellers gave trouble and had to be sent away to be modified. It was not until after Whitsuntide that they were ready. By this time a considerable number of spectators had come to the lake in the hopes of watching Segrave score another of his triumphs, but things were still not ready. Steel waistcoats had been ordered to protect the driver and the two mechanics who would be travelling with him. The firm supplying them had slipped up on their delivery, and this seemed likely to cause another delay. Lord Camden urged his friend to wait for them, but Segrave was impatient. He was particularly aware of all those people who had come to watch him, and who could obviously only remain there for a limited amount of time. He was determined that they should not be disappointed.

Presently he said that the bid must take place, steel waistcoats or no steel waistcoats. The boat was prepared, and its crew climbed aboard. Segrave sat in the middle; a mechanic from Rolls-Royce sat on his right; and the boat mechanic was on his left. Lord Camden and an expert from the firm which had manufactured the superchargers travelled some distance behind in a launch.

The first run, which was from north to south, went off perfectly well. The boat was turned round, and set off on the return trip. 'Suddenly,' Lord Camden recalls, 'we saw a large cloud of mist and spray, and we didn't know what it was. When we got up to it, we saw the boat was upside down, but even then we didn't fully realise what had happened.[1]

Meanwhile, rescue craft had come on to the scene. The boat mechanic was hauled out of the water. His body was black from bruises, but he appeared likely to survive. Segrave was obviously very badly injured, and there was no sign at all of the Rolls-Royce mechanic.

The ace was brought ashore. A farm gate was taken of its hinges to serve as a stretcher, and he was carried to a farmhouse some way up the hill. Within two and a half hours of the crash, he was dead. He had multiple injuries, the worst of which was a broken rib which had punctured one of his lungs. Had he been wearing a steel waistcoat, he might very well have survived.

Three days later, the body of the Rolls-Royce mechanic was recovered. His neck had been broken. The notepad, on which he recorded readings from the various instruments, was still strapped to his thigh, and he was hunched in a sitting position, just as he had been in the boat.

One of the great, if somewhat inaccurate, legends of motoring in the between-war years was that of 'the Bentley Boys'. The car they drove was the creation of an inventive genius named W. O. Bentley, who had found his early motoring enjoyment with motor cycles; had studied as a locomotive engineer; and had designed a rotary aero engine, which served the Royal Navy extremely well during the first world war. He had intended his car to be a beautifully built fast tourer for well-to-do young men who shared his delight in such things and who were capable of driving really well.

To what extent he succeeded is doubtful. The car was, indeed, magnificent and, if you added motor racing to the list of objectives, it was brilliantly successful. But, as a commercial enterprise, it struggled from one financial crisis to another until its take-over by Rolls-Royce in 1931. Nineteen-twenty-nine was the only year in which the company made a profit, which may be the reason why,

[1]*Miss England* had struck a partially submerged log of wood.

in a profit-orientated community, W. O. Bentley has been
so badly served by successive governments.

If quality were all, he would no doubt have been made a knight
or even a viscount. As things are, he has had to be content with
an M.B.E., which is such a small award that one can only marvel
at its insolence.

The so-called Bentley Boys were responsible for a string of
successes which Bentley's enjoyed in the Le Mans 24-Hour Race
during the latter half of the 'twenties. They were also the raw
material from which the legend was built. The public mind
shaped the story as it wished it to be, and created a team of men in
which, it was said, there were 'five millionaires'. That was rubbish.
Wolf Barnato, who became chairman of the company and was
related to a family which had made a fortune in the South African
diamond industry, was, indeed, a millionaire, but he was the only
one. Sir Henry ('Tim') Birkin was extremely wealthy, but his
fortune stopped a good distance short of the million mark.
S. C. H. Davis was a motoring writer; J. A. Benjafield was a
pathologist and a very good one, too; Jack Dunfee was a successful
business man (but not in the million class); and F. C. Clement was
a test driver.

Public imagination decreed that they had to be playboys, and
sent them off on an endless round of champagne parties accompanied by exotic mistresses. Racing, it appeared, was a glamorous
occupation which had to be fitted in among the days at Ascot,
the smart dances and receptions, the hangovers, the love affairs,
and the house parties. It was all too much like *Vile Bodies* to
be true, and very little of it was true.

A Bentley, like any other high performance car of the period,
was by no means easy to drive, and to put up a good performance
in one required a lot of skill. Furthermore, an event such as
Le Mans was extremely strenuous. Quite apart from the strain of
driving a heavy machine for long periods and at high speed, the
drivers had to carry out all their own repairs during the race—and
even fill their cars up with petrol at the refuelling halts. To do all
this, they had to be in the peak of condition and there was certainly no time for heavy socialising when racing was in the offing.

They went to parties: why not? They associated with glamorous women: most certainly (and, again, why not?) But these
men were professionals. They were dedicated to their motor

racing, and they were extremely good at it. And, on top of this, most of them made a success of their other careers.

As chairman of the Bentley company, Wolf Barnato was a shrewd business man, who went about things like a man playing a game of chess, trying, all the time, to see several moves ahead. He had to, for W. O. Bentley, the managing director, was brilliant, vague about business matters, and too shy to be a successful front man.

Of all the team, Tim Birkin was the only driver who had no other occupation. During the first world war, he had served as a pilot in the Royal Flying Corps. He was short in stature, spoke with a stammer, but was immensely tough. When racing, he always wore a blue polka-dot scarf, and he, as much as anybody, was probably responsible for inspiring the myth. Away from the circuits, he lived an extravagant life. On at least one occasion, he flew his own aircraft from the South of France to Brooklands, took part in a motor race, won it, and then flew back to the Riviera to celebrate.

He was fearless, hard on his machinery, and utterly determined. His dream was to win a grand prix. With no British car available, he eventually had to make do with a Maserati, which he used in the Tripoli race of 1933. He came third, which was creditable if not as good as he would have liked. During the event, his bare arm touched the hot exhaust pipe and was burned. At this point, it was only a very minor injury.

But Birkin was upset at the time. A romance had gone wrong, and he was submerged in the most profound gloom. He never told anybody about his burn, never went to see a doctor, but simply wrapped a piece of dirty cloth over it.

Not long afterwards, he was at a party in London. His friend and fellow driver, Dr. J. A. Benjafield, came up to him and, as was his habit, slapped him genially on the shoulder. Birkin let out a yell of pain.

'What on earth's the matter?' Benjafield asked.

'It's my arm—it's painful.'

Benjafield asked him for details, and then told him to take his coat off. The arm was horribly inflamed and swollen. On the doctor's instructions, Birkin was instantly committed to a nursing home, but it was already too late. Septicaemia set in and, in spite of Benjafield's efforts, Tim Birkin presently died.

All told, Bentley built 3,038 cars, and a further ten were assembled from the firm's components after Rolls-Royce had taken it over. Nowadays, the Rolls and the Bentley are identical in all things except their radiators. The Rolls-Royce version costs £100 more. But, with the Bentley, you also receive the image which is, unlike all but two of the 'Bentley Boys', still very much alive.

12 Under Tragic Circumstances

Mike Hawthorn was the golden boy of motor racing. In 1958, he became the first Briton to win the World Championship of Drivers: he was good looking, charming and extremely intelligent. When one regarded his smiling face in the pages of the newspapers, one might have imagined that he had not a care in the world.

But, like a thin black thread running through his life, there was a recurring theme of tragedy. His father was killed in a road accident on his way home from the racing circuit at Goodwood. His best friend, Peter Collins, died after a racing crash when Hawthorn was at the climax of his career. He himself was hounded by officials, who alleged that he had failed to do his national service. Had they read their documents more carefully, they would have seen that a kidney complaint had already caused him to fail the medical exam.

Hawthorn walked amiably through these disasters, smoking his pipe and wearing his customary bow tie, and looking the very picture of a cultivated, self-assured, English gentleman. Even when, as after a crash at Syracuse, he had to do it on crutches, there was a certain style about it. In spite of all the suffering he must have experienced, one felt that some god, somewhere, smiled upon Mike Hawthorn.

I

When, at the end of 1958, he announced that he proposed to retire from motor racing, he was only thirty years old. The news was greeted with some surprise, but many people said that it was very wise, and that a chap should know when to stop. Hawthorn said something about motor racing becoming too dangerous, and there is little doubt that Collins's death, a few months earlier, had influenced his decision. But now, it seemed, he was safe. By quitting the sport, he had left the area of hazard, and there appeared to be no reason why he should not go on living in very tolerable comfort for the remainder of a reasonably long life.

Early one afternoon in January, 1959, he set out for London from the office of the garage he owned at Farnborough in Hampshire. He was driving a Jaguar, and he was in a hurry. He drove over the Hog's Back and down on to the Guildford bypass. This is a fast road and there can be no doubt that he treated it accordingly. When, in his mirror, he saw a friend of his coming up behind in a sports car, he increased his speed. It was inevitable. That was the kind of man he was: that was how, under these circumstances, he was bound to react.

And then, suddenly, the Jaguar went out of control. It shot across the road, and ploughed into the bank on the far side. He was killed instantly.

There have since been all manner of theories about the cause of Hawthorn's final crash. One school has it that he was the first man to suffer from the fact that you cannot mix radial and cross-ply tyres on a car. Another suggests that he struck a patch of oil. But the rub of the matter is that, after all those years on the racing circuits, with far, far more driving skill than the average motorist possesses, Mike Hawthorn, World Champion racing driver, died in a common automobile accident—shortly after he had walked away from this dangerous sport on the grounds that it had become *too* perilous.

There have been other such incidents. Nino Farina, the first World Champion, survived umpteen accidents and injuries on the race tracks, but he was killed, in late middle age, when his car collided with another in the French Alps. Camille Jenatzy, that early ace whose driving was so spectacular that they called him 'The Red Devil', was shot by accident during a wild boar hunt. Alberto Ascari, having survived a crash at Monte Carlo which

might well have killed him, died a few days later when trying
out a new car on a racing circuit.

When one looks back on these tragedies, there seems to be
something inevitable about them. It is rather like a Greek play,
in which the leading character is dragged by a black providence
through act after act to a final, sacrificial, doom at the end of the
piece.

This is by no means peculiar to racing drivers. One of the sadder
figures in the restless, often chaotic, pageant of the between-war
years was an American dancer named Isadora Duncan. Miss
Duncan had many theories, and one of them was that if she and
the playwright George Bernard Shaw could produce a baby, it
might very well turn out to be the perfect human being. The idea
was that it should have her body, which was very shapely, and
Mr. Shaw's brain, which was renowned for its agility.

The sage of the British theatre, however, pointed out that nature
could not be relied upon to produce such a result. The child, he
suggested, might equally well be cursed with *his* body and *her* brain.

Perhaps the most ironical thing about this woman who wanted
so badly to communicate was that she was so often misunderstood.
When, for example, she married a young Soviet poet, her fellow
Americans immediately assumed that she must be a Russian spy.
Anybody more inadequately equipped for the role of a secret
agent would be hard to imagine, but that is what they thought.
In the end, the unfortunate poet was divorced. He returned to
Leningrad where he committed suicide.

Miss Duncan's own death was a classic example of a world in
which nothing will ever go right. She was staying at Nice, and on
Wednesday, September 14th, 1927, she was considering whether
to buy a new Bugatti. It was a touring model, a beautiful creation
which seemed to suit the flamboyance of its prospective owner.
At ten o'clock that evening, it was brought round to her hotel.
Winding a long scarf twice around her neck, Miss Duncan went
outside. The salesman explained the car to her, and then came
the inevitable 'How about a trial run?' Miss Duncan said that it
would be very agreeable.

She sat down behind the steering wheel, started up the engine,
engaged the gear, and set off along the Promenade des Anglais,
which is the wide and splendid thoroughfare that serves as a
sea front for the resort.

What she had not noticed as she moved off was that the end of her scarf was hanging over the side of the car. She had not travelled very far, before it became entangled in the rear wheel. It suddenly jerked tight. The effect was just as if Miss Duncan had mounted the scaffold. The car performed its role of hangman with horrible efficiency. She was instantly dragged out of the vehicle and, at that moment, her spinal column snapped.

People brought a great deal of unhappiness to poor Isadora Duncan; but the automobile, which can so quickly switch roles from benefactor to killer, added its contributions to the wretched score. Fourteen years before her own death, Miss Duncan had been staying at Neuilly, which is a suburb of Paris. With her were her two children (Deirdre aged six and Patrick aged three),[1] her brother Raymond, and the children's nurse—a forty-year-old Scottish expatriate whose home was at Brighton. On the afternoon of April 21st, 1913, Miss Duncan suggested that it would be nice if Nanny were to take the children on a trip to Versailles. The chauffeur, a young Frenchman named Masserand, was told to get the car ready.

At 3.30 p.m., the party set off. By the side of the road, there was a steep, grass-covered bank and, at the foot of it, the sluggish brown waters of the River Seine. About one hundred yards from the house, another street fed in traffic from the right. It was from this direction that the taxi came.

Seemingly unaware of the approaching vehicle, the taxi driver crossed its path, and Masserand had to jam on his brakes promptly to avoid a collision. The engine stalled. Muttering French blasphemies, the chauffeur climbed down on to the road, walked round to the front of the car, and seized the starting handle. One brisk turn was enough to bring the engine back to life.

In the heat of the moment, Masserand had overlooked two points. The first was that the hand throttle was set fairly far forward. The second was that he had left the vehicle in gear. Once the engine had been re-started, it shot forward, lurched across the road, and mounted the pavement on the far side. At this point, Masserand tried to climb back on board; but it was almost as if the vehicle, hell bent on destruction, elbowed him out of the way. It gave another lurch, and he was flung down on to the ground.

[1] Their fathers were the theatrical director Gordon Craig, and the American millionaire, Paris Singer, both of whom had been her lovers.

The car reached the grass bank. Increasing its speed, it lumbered down to the river which, at this point, was something between twenty and thirty feet deep. Without so much as pausing, the vehicle hurled itself into the water and instantly vanished.

A group of workmen, who were drinking on the pavement outside a nearby café, saw it all happen. One of them ran across the road and dived into the Seine. He made several attempts but could find no trace of the vehicle. The local fire brigade, which arrived soon afterwards, had no more luck, and presently a team of divers took matters in hand.

One and a half hours after the catastrophe, the car was discovered and brought ashore by the crew of a motor launch who used ropes and anchors. The bodies of the two young children were found clinging piteously to their dead nurse. The nurse's watch had stopped at 3.23. There was no sign of Masserand, who seems to have wandered around Paris in a state of shock until, several hours afterwards, he gave himself up at a police station. With what may appear as a certain lack of sensitivity, the authorities promptly charged him with culpable homicide.

It was left to Raymond Duncan to tell his sister about the tragedy.

The awful thing about motor-car crashes is the apparent lack of rhyme or reason for so many of them. Even when one has removed the debris caused by sheer bad driving, a number remain which seem to be inexplicable. Of course it is easy to theorise about them, and sometimes it is simple enough to pin matters down to a burst tyre, or something like that. But what *caused* the tyre to burst—and why was this particular puncture fatal, whilst so many take place and nobody is even bruised or scratched? Again we get this feeling of fatalism, this fearful awareness of a predetermined doom.

In the summer of 1935, King Leopold III of Belgium and his Queen, who had formerly been Princess Astrid of Sweden, were spending a holiday at a villa about two miles south of Lucerne in Switzerland. Both the King and Queen were fond of mountains and, on August 29th, they decided to spend the day climbing. Just before 9.30 a.m., the house party set off in two cars. The first was a two-seater Packard, with the King in the driving seat, Queen Astrid beside him, and the chauffeur at the back in the dicky.

The second car, which travelled some distance behind, had four members of the royal suite on board.

It had rained fairly heavily during the previous evening, but now the sun was shining and the roads had already dried out. The two cars went through Lucerne and then took the route which ran eastwards through orchards to Küssnacht and so to Lake Zug. It was a modern highway which, after Küssnacht, straightened itself out and followed the western shore of the lake. On the right-hand side there was a footpath with a concrete kerb. Beyond the path, the ground fell away steeply down a tree-clad slope leading to the lake.

The royal Packard went through a village, travelling at about 30 m.p.h., and presently reached the length of straight near the shore of the lake. Queen Astrid was reading the map. The King accelerated.

As the car gathered speed, the King was seen to point at one of the mountains. Queen Astrid looked up and nodded. Then, suddenly, the vehicle went out of control. The right-hand wheels mounted the footpath and travelled along it for about seventeen yards until it petered out to give access to a small field. At this point, the Packard turned right, raced over the grass, and plunged over the top of the bank towards the lake. About twenty yards down it struck a tree, ricocheted off it, went on for another twelve yards, hit another tree, shot over a low stone wall, and dived into the water about twelve feet below. At this point, the lake was only about two feet deep.

The time was exactly ten o'clock.

Men working in the field had seen the accident and hurried down to the car. Meanwhile, the second vehicle had pulled up, and its occupants were running down the bank. The Queen, it seemed, had been flung out when the car hit the first tree. She was alive—but only just. The impact had fractured her skull and she was clearly in a very serious condition. The King had remained on board until the vehicle hit the second tree, when he, too, was flung out. His head was injured, though not nearly so seriously as the Queen's, and one of his arms was hurt. The chauffeur had remained on board all the time. Apart from some superficial cuts on his face, caused by flying fragments of glass, he was uninjured.

The King and Queen were taken to a house in Küssnacht, and

the doctor and the parish priest were sent for. When King Leopold had been given first aid, he gently took his wife in his arms. Shortly after receiving the last sacrament from the *curé*, she died. On the following day, with Leopold in attendance, her body was taken home to Belgium in the St. Gotthard express. A detail of one officer from the Swiss Air Force and two from the Swiss Army escorted the coffin as far as the frontier. King Leopold was accompanied by the Swiss ambassador to Belgium, who happened to be on holiday in Switzerland at the time.

Villagers from Küssnacht erected a wooden cross—with a figure of Christ, painted in gold, mounted on it—at the scene of the accident. All the people from round about placed flowers at its foot.

Early attempts to raise the car from the lake failed, and, on the following day, a crane had to be used. All four tyres were punctured: the doors had been torn off and the steering column had snapped in two. However, an examination by the local authorities made it plain that there had been no fault in the steering or the brakes. The probable cause of the disaster, they concluded, had been a moment of inattention when the King pointed towards the mountain. This had caused the car to swerve. One of the wheels had struck the concrete kerb, and this brought about the first puncture. From that moment, there had been no more hope of getting the vehicle back under control.

The chauffeur in the royal car was fortunate. He had remained on board, and his injuries had been slight. In this respect, he provides an historical parallel with the chauffeur of another vehicle which, twenty-five years later, was involved in a collision on the outskirts of Paris.

Accompanied by the model named Bettina (her real name was Simone Bodin), Prince Ali Khan, playboy extraordinary, forty-eight-year-old head of the Pakistan delegation to the United Nations, and lover of horseflesh and fast cars, had been enjoying a day's racing at Longchamps. Ali Khan was now returning to Paris in his grey Ferrari. Bettina was sitting beside him, and his chauffeur was travelling at the back. They had just passed a memorial to French wartime resistance workers at Mont Valerian, when a car wearing Belgian number plates approached. The Prince's car (or was it the Belgian's? There seems to be no way of telling) went out of control. There was an almighty crash as the two vehicles collided. Ali Khan was dragged out of the debris and placed on board an ambulance. He died on the way to hospital. His skull, both his legs and his neck had been fractured. Bettina suffered a deep cut on her face, but she was allowed to go home after treatment. The chauffeur and the driver of the Belgian car only received minor injuries.

Hitler always occupied the front seat in his big Mercedes—unless he was entertaining guests. On ceremonial occasions, the raised floor at the front made him seem to be taller than he was.

Field Marshal Montgomery used a Humber, and, later, a Rolls-Royce during the war. Afterwards, he acquired a Daimler.

The chassis of this vehicle used by General Alexander in North Africa is by Ford of Canada. The body is the work of the Royal Engineers. It was rebuilt (and redesigned) after it had been dropped on the quayside at Alexandria.

Contrary to general belief, de Gaulle's Citroën was not armour plated. Nevertheless, he had several narrow escapes from assassination during the Algerian war. De Gaulle is reputed to have said that 'Only in a Citroën do I get a really comfortable ride'.

Among the cars owned by King Hussein of Jordan (second from right) has been this very fast Mercedes. The King enjoys speed— once nearly raced at Le Mans.

The chassis of this town car is that of a London taxi, but, otherwise, there are few similarities. The owner was Nubar Gulbenkian. In a later model, Mr. Gulbenkian went in for dark green and black stripes at the rear.

Originally this Rolls-Royce was the property of Earl Mountbatten. Now it is owned by Surgeon Capt. (D) D. Symmons of Oxford. The bell at the front was added by its present owner.

13   Cars for the Kings

The royal families of Europe bought cars to suit their tastes. If an ordinary motorist's preference for a certain model reflected his personality, so, to some extent, did the choice of the various monarchs reflect theirs. In 1937, for example, King Zog of Albania bought a 5·7-litre Mercedes tourer. King Gustav of Sweden, King Farouk of Egypt and King Boris III of Bulgaria, also owned Mercedes-Benz cars; but, unlike those of his colleagues in monarchy, Zog's was supercharged.

One might have expected it. Some years earlier, Ettore Bugatti had produced a car which was so manifestly intended for royalty, that it was called the Bugatti Royale. Other people, less reverently, referred to it as the 'Golden Bug'. Although the maestro had meant to build a batch of twenty-five, financial difficulties got in the way, and only six were completed. Among their owners were the King of the Belgians, King Alfonso of Spain, King Carol of Rumania, and King Zog.

This was a fantastic car which appears without fail in the *Guinness Book of Records* as the largest ever built. It was 22 feet long and had a 12·7-litre 8-cylinder engine which produced over 270 b.h.p. Top speed was about 120 m.p.h., and it cost about £18,000. By all accounts, it was an extremely difficult vehicle to drive. The brakes, especially, were open to criticism, but Bugatti paid little heed to anything that was said against them. As he told one gentleman who suggested that they might be improved: 'I build my cars to go, not to stop.' Similarly, he countered charges that it was a difficult car to start on cold mornings with a terse: 'Get a heated garage.'

King Carol's version was equipped with bullet-proof windows and machine-gun mountings at the rear. A telephone system linked the monarch's compartment with the driver up in front. Whenever the King wished to speak, he pressed a button, which was connected to a red light on the dashboard. When the light flashed it was the chauffeur's cue to pick up the phone. During the last war, the vehicle was hidden in Paris. Afterwards, it was acquired by a vintage-car enthusiast in England.

The Emperor of Japan's Big Mercedes of 1933 was also bullet-proofed. Before the imperial garage would accept it from the Stuttgart factory, it had to be tested. The vehicle was taken to a rifle range not far from the works, where officials from the Japanese government attacked it with revolvers. They fired shots at the windows and the bodywork. When it finally became clear that, had the Emperor been inside it, he would have been perfectly safe, the car was approved.

The British Royal Family, whose image was at once staid and secure, loved its Daimlers and there was no question of cladding them in armour plate. All told, four monarchs between them owned fifty cars of this make—from Edward VII's first to George VI's last. It was not until the accession of Queen Elizabeth II that the familiar, corrugated bonnet was finally ousted by the somewhat more classical style of Rolls-Royce. The bodies of all the royal cars were (and still are) painted in royal claret and black with vermilion lines. The colour scheme dates back to the days of their horse-drawn carriages.

King George V always insisted that he should be able to get into a car without having to stoop. On one occasion, his sister, Princess Victoria, went to visit him at Sandringham shortly after she had taken delivery of a new Rolls-Royce. On the way, she remarked to the chauffeur: 'Have you never driven King George?' The latter said that no—he had not. 'Would you like to?' Yes—he would like to very much indeed. 'Very well,' said the Princess, 'we shall get him into the car.'

They stopped at the sovereign's entrance to the great house

and the King himself came out to greet the Princess. She asked her brother what he thought of the new car. He murmured gruffly to the effect that yes—yes. It was quite nice. The monarch was not particularly interested in cars and his attitude made this very clear. However, after a few minutes' conversation, the Princess persuaded him to make a very short trip down to the nearest village. The journey took place in silence. When it was over and His Majesty had disembarked, Princess Victoria again asked him what he thought of it. 'It is,' he said, 'just like getting out of a rabbit hutch.'

The King liked Daimlers: he liked their high doors which made it possible for him to step inside without bending his back, and he liked the two armchairs amidships. They were level with the rear door and well forward of the back seat, in which his detectives sat totally concealed.

If the King received good service from Hooper and Daimler, these two firms were well looked after by the monarch. During the depression of 1931, he ordered several new vehicles to replace the older members of the fleet.[1] Since economy, even for royalty, was a matter of top priority, he paid for them out of his personal income. The object was to keep as many workers as possible employed during the lean months of what threatened to be a very hard winter.

Although he did not particularly care for motoring, he made a number of long journeys by car. In 1926, he was staying at Balmoral, when a stoppage by the coal miners started what was soon to become the General Strike. He felt that his presence was needed in London and so, without any more ado, he ordered one of the Daimlers to be loaded up and was driven all the way back to Buckingham Palace.

Two years later, after a serious illness, he had to make the journey from London to a house at Bognor Regis, which had been put at his disposal for convalescence. One of the Daimlers was converted into an ambulance for the occasion. During the sixty-five-mile trip, no car was allowed to overtake the royal vehicle.

This illness left the monarch in a somewhat delicate state of health. Previously, when he went out on the moors to shoot

[1]Six years later, at the coronation of his son, King George VI, it was estimated that something like 1,000 Daimlers were involved in one way or another.

grouse, he enjoyed walking. Now such activity was out of the question, and Hooper built a special six-wheeler car on a Crossley chassis for these excursions. It could travel over rough country: had two doors and a collapsible front seat which, when folded up, disappeared under the dashboard.

Queen Mary enjoyed motoring, though she disliked the smell of tobacco smoke in a car. Consequently, long before the advent of air conditioning, a somewhat rudimentary system was installed in the royal vehicle. Basically, it was an arrangement of ducts, which enabled the smoke to be extracted and fresh air to be pumped in. To make matters harder, the ducts had to be sited in such a way that they did not blow a cold draught on to the King's head. This was a point about which, in her specifications, the Queen had been most insistent.

Before being delivered the car was tested by a member of the Hooper management, who sat in the back, puffing at his pipe for all he was worth, and burning smouldering lengths of brown paper. It worked well enough, until the vehicle was taken out on to the road. When it was moving, the back pressure caused by a following wind forced the exhaust fumes through the ducts and into the rear compartment. Eventually the problem was solved by fitting a flap over the tail piece of the exhaust.

The last royal car to be built with the armchairs was completed in 1935. In that year, too, the custom of an open driving seat came to an end. Thereafter, fully enclosed vehicles were constructed.

In the following year, King George V died. He was succeeded, if only for a matter of months, by King Edward VIII. The new monarch already owned a Buick limousine, which had been delivered to him earlier that year, and which was built at the firm's Canadian factory. During his short reign, he added one new car to the stock in the Royal Mews—a 32 h.p. straight 8 Daimler limousine.

When King George VI came to the throne in December of 1936, he was the father of two young daughters and well known as a Lanchester enthusiast. At the time of his brother's abdication, he owned three of them—one of which was a sports model in which, at weekends, he used to drive his wife and the two young princesses from their London home at 145 Piccadilly to the Royal Lodge at Windsor. When, in April, 1937, his first royal Daimler was delivered to him, it contained a number of fairly substantial changes.

The armchair seats in the middle were missing. In their places there were two collapsible seats for the use of the princesses. The King and the Queen sat on the rear seat, and the detective moved up front beside the chauffeur.

But one of a sovereign's jobs is to be seen. As things had been, the King and Queen would have been completely invisible tucked away at the back. Consequently, large windows were installed on either side of the rear seat, and, to improve the illumination, a pane of glass was fitted in the roof. This was covered by a sliding panel which, initially, was hand operated. Later on, an electric mechanism did the work.

An arm rest was fitted in the centre of the back seat. It contained pencils, a note-pad and a box for cigarettes. Special reading lamps with adjustable shades were provided for use at night. In some respects, they resembled the lamps used by navigators in modern rally cars.

King George VI had always been against car radio, and he stuck to his guns for some time. Eventually, however, he yielded to family pressure, and agreed to have one installed. There were, however, reservations. It had to be fitted in such a way that nothing could be seen.

With ingenuity, a small transistor set was installed in the arm rest. Twin loudspeakers were built into the bodywork behind the driver and the aerial was fitted underneath the running board. When the Royal Family was at Balmoral or elsewhere in the Highlands, reception was a good deal less than perfect. Otherwise, it worked very well.

When one comes to think of it, a good deal of imagination was expended on the royal cars. Towards the end of his reign, King George VI had trouble with his circulation. His hands, especially, were affected, and they became very cold. To overcome it, electrically heated gloves were provided. They were plugged into the vehicle's wiring system.

For many years, the supplier of royal cars was a Mayfair firm of Daimler distributors named Stratton Instone Ltd. (later, they changed the name to Stratstone). Whenever a new one was needed, the first action was to order the chassis. Daimler invariably produced a special version for this; and, before they went out of business in 1959, it was a foregone conclusion that Hooper would build the body. The Royal Family was nothing if not loyal to its brand,

A good deal of discussion went into the planning of the body and, once the brief had been settled, Hooper used to produce scale drawings. Before the last war, it took about three months to construct a royal car. Nowadays, the period would be between five and six months—largely because of shorter working hours at the factory, and because the cars themselves are more complex. The Daimlers of King George V were extremely square in shape and, consequently, relatively undemanding. Whilst the present royal cars pay little more than lip service to streamlining, there is a greater sense of design about them. Consequently, they need rather more skill and care in construction.

The vehicles which new cars replaced were taken in by Stratstone and an allowance was made for them—just as any motorist trades in his used car. The royal insignia were removed (including the police lamp on the roof) and the bodies were supposed to be repainted in non-royal colours. A number of them were afterwards shipped out to the East (especially to India), and several were purchased for the mayors of towns in Britain. The next stage often found them in the possession of a car-hire firm and that, normally, would be about as far as anyone could trace them.

When George VI came to the throne, the tally of royal vehicles amounted to a 40/50 h.p. Daimler limousine, a 32 h.p. Daimler, a 32 h.p. car for the royal household, and a 27 h.p. Humber Pullman. There were also a Leyland Lioness lorry, two Buicks and two Ford station vans. A pair of ancient Daimlers and the Crossley six-wheeler were on the list of cars to be disposed of. Lord Willingdon bought the Daimlers when he was appointed Viceroy of India, and it was probably one of these that was discovered on the airfield at the end of the war. The six-wheeler vanished, seemingly, without trace.

It was considered that the Daimlers had about four years of useful royal life. The period for the Ford utilities, which were based on the Royal Lodge, was three years; and the six-wheeler shooting brake and the Leyland lorry had six-year lives. After these periods, they were replaced.

Whilst the Royal Family does not have to make a profit, there have to be limits to its expenditure. Consequently, a certain amount of hard bargaining went into the disposal of a car from Buckingham Palace. In many ways, a former royal vehicle was a highly desirable property, for, quite apart from its distinguished associations, it had obviously been well looked after. Queen Mary, for example, bought a Daimler in 1931. By November of 1935, it had only broken down twice. The first time was due to a stoppage in the petrol pipe. The second was when the radiator overheated on a hot summer's day.

If these cars had a fault, it was probably this tendency to overheat. Queen Mary's was one of the two bought by Lord Willingdon, and His Excellency was advised to have a special cooling system designed for warm climates fitted before taking it out to India.

In 1936, the transaction for the purchase of a royal car worked out something like this:

A special straight-8 chassis	£900
A Hooper enclosed drive limousine body	£675
	£1,575

—minus an allowance of £475 for a 30/40 Daimler, which was taken in part exchange.

Discretion has always been the keynote of commercial dealings by the royal household. Admittedly, during the previous century, the French branch of a large cocoa company produced an advertisement in which the illustration portrayed Queen Victoria and a lady-in-waiting sitting in the dining car of a train. Through the far window, you could just make out the tower of Windsor Castle. Her Majesty and her companion were both drinking what were, by strong inference, cups of the chocolate in question (though, to be fair, their expressions did not seem to suggest that they were enjoying it). Even though the manufacturers held a royal warrant, this kind of thing was strictly taboo and if the Queen ever saw a copy, she was probably very angry. Since it appeared in a French publication, however, the chances seem unlikely.

An example of how careful firms enjoying royal patronage have to be is shown by a photograph which was published in January, 1939. It showed a new royal Daimler which had just been completed, but which the King had not yet seen. His Majesty was said to be extremely annoyed at this premature release of information, and all further publication of the offending picture was stopped. Daimler's over-zealous advertising manager was put on the carpet, and it became a condition of all further orders that a written undertaking had to be produced, stating that authority to photograph the royal cars would be obtained from Buckingham Palace before any pictures were taken.

At the outbreak of war, the King stressed that no more royal cars were to be built until it was all over. However, a Lanchester limousine, which had been ordered in July of that year, was nearing completion, and His Majesty agreed that it should be delivered. A four-year-old vehicle, that had been 'used considerably by the little princesses', was accepted by Stratstone in part exchange.

In September, 1940, three of the royal cars were damaged by an anti-aircraft shell which burst outside the garage in the Royal Mews at Buckingham Palace. Their engines were unharmed, but most of the glass was broken and a number of small holes were made in the bodies. Since the insurance policy did not include war damage in its coverage, it looked as if the cost of repairs would have to come out of the King's personal income. It was, however, possible that, when the war was over, the government might make a contribution towards the bill. The vehicles were sent up to the Daimler works, where the cost was estimated at £215. The most expensive individual item was the replacement of triplex glass in the roof of the state car. This was put down at £17 18s. od.

The King of England travelled in a Daimler which was suited to pomp and ceremony and to comfort, but which was unarmed and unprotected. Other world leaders had large vehicles which were armour-plated, and in which there were hidden pockets packed with revolvers and ammunition. Field Marshal Paul von Hindenburg had a Big Mercedes tourer during his years of declining power. He acquired it in 1930. Four years later, his successor, Adolf Hitler, was provided with an even bigger version. Mussolini had one, too—and so did Joseph Stalin. Beside the royal Daimlers, these Daimler-Benz products looked huge and aggressive. Perhaps there was something symbolic about the cars owned by world leaders at this period. As I remarked at the beginning of this chapter, a man's personality is apt to influence the type of vehicle he prefers.

14 The Assassin

The man was short, with a swarthy complexion and dressed in a
cheap suit. During the past few years, he had travelled under so
many different names that he had almost forgotten his real identity.
The Czech passport in his pocket described him as Peter Keleman,
and said that his home was in Zagreb. As it turned out afterwards,
there were twenty Kelemans living in Zagreb, but not one of them
was called Peter. Nevertheless, for the time being, that would do.

His original occupation had been as a chauffeur, and it was in
this capacity that he had first served Ivan Mikhaylov, leader of
the Macedonian terrorist organisation in Yugoslavia. But he had
been smart and quick-witted and an expert shot. Mikhaylov had
noticed these talents, and promoted him. Now he was a professional
killer. He already had a number of political assassinations to his
credit. He was, you might say, experienced, but this assignment
promised to be harder than the others.

The Mauser automatic in his pocket felt heavy, and he hoped
that nobody would notice it. If he failed on this job, the penalty
was death. That had been clearly stated at the outset. '*Instant
death*' was how they had described it at the briefing session in
Paris, though it was hard to see how it could be accomplished so
quickly.

He looked down the street. Somewhere in the crowd his assistant

K

was waiting with a bomb in his pocket. That man's task was to explode it the instant Keleman (we'd better call him that) fired his first shot. The attention of the police and the spectators would be diverted, and, with luck, he might escape.

It was a glorious October day, and the city of Marseilles was gaily decked out with bunting. The big crowd seemed to be in a carnival mood, though it was difficult to see why they should be so excited about a visit from the King of Yugoslavia. What was the monarch to them? Keleman gripped the butt of the Mauser and edged carefully forward. The policemen were stationed at intervals of ten yards apart and their backs were turned to the crowd. Good. That made things very much easier.

He looked at his watch. The time was four o'clock. Now the spectators down the street were cheering, almost muffling the clip-clop of the horses on which the military escort was mounted. A minute passed, and the horsemen drew level with him. They were some distance ahead of the royal car and that, in itself, was useful. It meant that the King would be virtually unprotected.

The royal car was a D8 Delage, which had been built some time between 1930 and 1932. It was the landaulet version in which the roof at the back let down. It was down now, to give people a better view of the King and to enable him to enjoy the French sunshine. There were four people in the car: the chauffeur, a general named Alphonse Georges, the French foreign minister (an elderly gentleman named Louis Barthou), and the King. The monarch was wearing the heavily braided uniform of a Yugoslav admiral, with a stiff winged collar and a black bow tie. He was regarding the crowd through a pince-nez: his smile was vague and rather strained. He did not seem to be enjoying himself.

As the Delage drew level with him, Keleman pushed his way forward, raced across the yard or two of tarmac, and jumped on to the running board. Simultaneously he drew the Mauser out of his pocket. The lever was set at automatic.

King Alexander of Yugoslavia had sailed for Marseilles in his country's only capital ship, the light cruiser *Dubrovnic*, on October 6th, 1934. His wife, Queen Marie, who was a bad sailor, had decided to make the journey to France by the Simplon-Orient Express. She had chosen wisely, for the first day or so at sea had been rough.

As they approached the French coast on the 9th, the weather

improved. Three destroyers from the 1st Mediterranean Squadron, which was based at Toulon, came out to meet them. Later, when they had anchored in the harbour at Marseilles, Jacques Piétri, the French minister of marine, came aboard the *Dubrovnic*. His task was to escort the King ashore.

The object of the royal visit was political. King Alexander had become his country's monarch after the first world war. It was he who, in 1929, changed the nation's name from the somewhat cumbersome 'Kingdom of the Serbs, Croats and Slovenes' to Yugoslavia, which means 'South Slavia'. In that year, too, he established an absolute dictatorship. He was a short man with a likable simplicity of manner and a good deal of charm. His role was not a particularly enviable one, for the war between 1914 and 1918 had done little to achieve stability in the Balkans. In many ways, these states were just as turbulent as they had been at the time of Franz Ferdinand's assassination.

His present mission was supposed to take him to Paris for preliminary talks with the French government aimed, eventually, at improving relations between Yugoslavia and Italy and, after that, a *rapprochement* between France and Italy. Whether Mussolini, who was then in supreme command of Italian politics, was anxious for any such understanding is doubtful. According to theories which were put forward afterwards, if you linked together all the people who had been responsible for Peter Keleman's presence in Marseilles that day, the chain would ultimately lead to the Italian dictator.

King Alexander stepped ashore on the quayside, and M. Barthou came forward to greet him. They shook hands: a band struck up, and the minister ushered his royal guest towards two guards of honour which had been lined up for the occasion. One was a contingent from the 141st Regiment of Infantry: the other were colonial troops from Senegalese Tirailleurs. The two men walked solemnly down the ranks, and then climbed into the Delage. The remainder of the royal suite, which included the Yugoslav minister of foreign affairs, were accommodated in a second car.

The King and the minister sat side by side in the back of the Delage. General Georges, who was a member of France's Supreme War Council, accompanied them on a jump seat.

Slowly the small procession moved off. The bunting fluttered in the gentle autumn breeze. On all the flagstaffs, the Tricolor, the Yugoslav flag and the city flag of Marseilles flew side by side. There were enormous crowds, and King Alexander may have wondered why the French authorities had turned down his offer to provide thirty of his own top security men to reinforce the police. After the inspection, the guards of honour had been dismissed, and the policemen lining the route seemed to be spaced out rather far apart. Nor were the arrangements assisted by a party of press photographers who broke through the cordon and swarmed round the royal car.

At first there was plenty of cheering and flag waving; but, as the procession rounded the corner into the Place de la Bourse, the sounds became less friendly. A group of men began to whistle in a decidedly hostile manner, and a squad from the security forces went to investigate. But then the whistles were drowned by more cheers from the rest of the crowd.

The cars were now moving at a walking pace, with the escort well ahead of them. Suddenly, as the royal vehicle drew level with the Bourse, a man was seen to break out of the ranks of spectators, dodge through the line of policemen and leap on to the running board. Using one hand to steady himself, Keleman aimed his Mauser at the King and fired two shots at point-blank range. Barthou instantly reached out to grab the man's wrist; and Froessac, the chauffeur, one hand still busy with the steering wheel, tried to knock him off the car with the other. Both attempts failed. The terrorist wrenched his gun away and turned it on the foreign minister, wounding him in the arm. Then he attacked General Georges, who was hit in the chest and both arms.

For a few moments everything was chaos. One of the security officers, who could only partially see what was happening, assumed that the gunman was a photographer, and came forward to remove him from the car. He was promptly shot in the stomach, and died some while afterwards. Barthou, who was obviously in considerable pain, climbed out of the car and walked away as if in a daze. Bleeding profusely, he wandered round the streets for some time, before, at last, ordering a taxi to take him to hospital. And, even then, it was some while before he could receive attention, for the crowd made it necessary for the driver to make a considerable detour. By the time he got there, he had lost so much blood that his chances of survival were over. Ironically enough, his wound had not been serious. If somebody had applied a ligature early on, he might very well have survived.

At about the time that Barthou was getting out of the car, a colonel from the 141st Infantry, who had been up in front with the mounted escort, swung round with his sabre drawn. He made a couple of slashes at the man on the running board, who fell off on to the road—obviously hurt. A security official opened fire on him, but the man shot back, wounding two more policemen and a woman in the front row of the crowd.

Now the spectators were surging forward, as if intent on lynching the gunman, but the police formed a tight ring around him. One of them picked him up and carried him to a kiosk a few yards away. By the time Peter Keleman was taken to hospital, he was dead. But his work was already accomplished, for King Alexander had been hit in the liver and in the region of his heart.

When two of his suite, the foreign minister and the court chamberlain, came on board the Delage to examine their monarch, they could detect no sign of a heart-beat. After cutting open his starched collar with a penknife, they laid his small figure across the cushions on the back seat. Then they told Froessac to drive on. Travelling as fast as the crowd would allow, he took the mortally wounded monarch to the Prefecture where, presently, six doctors arrived. But all they could do was to affirm that the King of Yugoslavia was dead.

Apart from the fact that Keleman (his real name was found to be Gheorgieff) was a sophisticated professional killer and Gavrilo Princip was a callow schoolboy, there are a number of parallels between the assassination of King Alexander and that earlier victim of terrorism, Archduke Franz Ferdinand. In both cases, the plot was germinated in the turbulent Balkans; it grew out of the unrest of Serbs and Croats and Macedonians and Slavs, all of whom were seeking their own identities and who wanted, above all things, their own sovereignties. In both cases, the security arrangements left a good deal to be desired. Both men were killed during a procession and both men were travelling in cars at the time.

The British Royal Family might be able to travel securely in their Daimlers which were never armoured. But, if you came from the Balkans, it was advisable to follow the Emperor of Japan's example, and pay the fairly large sum of extra money that produced a vehicle which was safe from an assassin's bullets.

15 The Loyal Servant

The prototype twentieth-century dictator was Benito Mussolini, otherwise known as Il Duce. Mussolini came to power in 1922, ten years before Adolf Hitler and about two years before Stalin. Hitler and Stalin became, perhaps, larger figures, but Mussolini got there first.

It is difficult to discover very much about his cars. Lancia's records were destroyed during the war, and other people, who might know, are reluctant to talk. However, we have it from Enzo Ferrari that, in 1924, he owned a very fast Alfa Romeo three-seater sports car, and he enjoyed driving it. In his *Memoirs*, Ferrari recalls a journey Mussolini made from Milan to Rome in this vehicle. During the course of it, his passengers were reduced to a state of nervous exhaustion by his flat-out approach to corners. 'What is more', Ferrari wrote, 'the road was wet and the Duce . . . had several times got into a hair-raising skid.'

Two years earlier, Mussolini had owned a Lancia Asturia, which had a custom-designed body by Pinin Farina and four-wheel independent suspension. The engine was a powerful V-eight unit: there were Bosch spotlights, a rev counter, and the driver was able to control the back shock-absorbers. The rear compartment was luxuriously fitted out with an adjustable seat and arm rests, a gooseneck reading lamp, and plenty of pockets and cubby holes. Communication with the chauffeur was by means of a bell; and, if he wished, the dictator could render himself invisible to the outside world by drawing the blinds which were fitted to all the rear windows. He travelled about 10,000 miles in this vehicle.

Certainly he was addicted to speed. His personal chauffeur was a racing driver named Ercole Boratto, who won the Benghazi–Tripoli race of 1939 in an Alfa Romeo 2500 6C SS. Mussolini's son also took up motor racing. Indeed, the sport was part of the dictator's image. He was responsible for building the circuits at Monza and Tripoli, and the latter was a very fair example of mid-twentieth-century totalitarian architecture of the type which became associated with Nazi party rallies in Germany.

At one time, the Alfa Romeo team was virtually unbeatable on the tracks. To some extent this was due to the dictator's support and encouragement—though there must have been occasions when the drivers wearied of the telegrams he used to send them on the eve of big events, and the way in which he interfered with their careers. In 1935, for example, that legendary Italian driver Tazio Nuvolari decided to be independent and race a Maserati of his own. His plans had not become very far advanced when he received a brusque message from Il Duce. It instructed him to give up the notion at once, and to rejoin the Alfa Romeo team which, at the time, was being run by Ferrari. If Nuvolari had attempted to argue, he would no doubt have been told that it was all for the greater glory of Italy.

When the reign of Alfa Romeos came to an end in the mid-'thirties, it was largely due to the efforts of Hitler. Although the Führer was not personally interested in the sport, and there is no evidence that he ever watched a race, he had clearly become aware of its possibilities for enhancing national prestige. Shortly after coming to power, he offered a prize of £40,000 to the constructor of the most successful German car to compete on the circuits, and this caused Mercedes-Benz to make a dramatic come-back. At the same time, Ferdinand Porsche busied himself with the design of an extremely powerful rear-engined vehicle, which was called the Auto-Union. Between them, the Mercedes and Auto-Unions won pretty well everything in sight, and the Alfa Romeos of Italy had to be content with second place.

At about the same time as the German motor racing renaissance began, Mussolini received a present from his friend Hitler. It was, perhaps, one of the most exclusive cars ever built, for there were only four owners of the touring version: Hitler himself, Hermann Goering, Joseph Stalin, and Mussolini. This was the Grosser Mercedes, an absolute giant among cars and extremely powerful as well. Whether it provided the Duce with an compensation for the sight of the silver Mercedes out-performing his own red Alfas on the circuits is, perhaps, doubtful. But it was certainly a wonderful thing to own.

In Germany, the Nazi leaders were by no means aloof to the pleasure of personal possessions. When Hitler became Chancellor in 1933, his colleagues Joseph Goebbels, Rudolf Hess, and the construction expert Dr. Fitz Todt, all acquired Mercedes 3·8-litre drophead coupés. During his term as German ambassador in London, Joachim von Ribbentrop owned a Mercedes which was painted in black and grey, with the wheels picked out in red. Unlike its owner, it survived the aftermath of the war, and presently turned up on a bomb-site car lot in Manchester. It was sold for £900.

Heinrich Himmler had a 1938 Horch, the large Pullman saloon version, which was painted in the SS colours of black with red lining. Goering had a great many cars, and his attitude was one of striving continuously to keep up with his boss. The Grosser Mercedes was undoubtedly the star of his fleet and, just as the Führer's was armoured, so was his. The other Nazi leaders do not seem to have indulged themselves in this extravagance.

Hitler changed his cars at yearly intervals. On his fiftieth birthday in 1939, there were two automobiles among the presents. One was a prototype Volkswagen by courtesy of the factory: the other was a giant Mercedes. The Volkswagen was the tiddler of the collection and there is no knowing to what extent he used it. On the whole, as became his position, he was a Mercedes man. His cars were supplied to him by the Daimler-Benz director in Berlin, a gentleman named Jacob Werlin, who died in 1965. Werlin must have done his work well, for on his fifty-fifth birthday he received a handwritten letter of congratulations from his most important customer. In 1942, he was appointed special general inspector for the entire German motor-car industry. The terms of reference stressed, according to a contemporary newspaper report, that 'Hitler was his direct and only boss'. That, in the atmosphere of scheming and intrigue which prevailed in the Führer's headquarters, must have been an advantage.

Undoubtedly, Hitler was fond of cars, and he took a keen interest in those which were under construction for his own use. He often used to look in at the Daimler-Benz factory at Stuttgart and, according to one of the directors, 'he was interested in the technical side, and easy to talk to and to explain things to. When, in 1936, he ordered another Grosser Mercedes, he spent about two hours discussing the technical details. At the time, he was very keen on the Volkswagen idea, and he used to say that the jump from a big car to a cheap Volkswagen was comparable to that which separated the horse from the early automobile.'

Technically he was, in some ways, remarkably reactionary. He used to fly a great deal, but he always preferred his early Junkers 52 aircraft with the fixed undercarriage to the big, four-engined Condor that he used towards the end of his life. He was nervous about the efficiency of the latter's retractable landing gear.

One of his official state cars—the Mercedes 770—turned up in America after the war and was put on show as part of a fund-raising exercise. Some of the design was attributed to Hitler, who decided where the firearms should be located. As the result of this, there were compartments for pistols in the arm rests, in the driver's seat, and in the head rests, and in the sides of the rear seats. In many ways, it was like a mobile arsenal. When it had been completed, he insisted on going out on to the firing range and testing the effectiveness of the armour. Not surprisingly, he was well pleased with the result. The body was lined with half-inch sheets of steel, and there was also plating underneath the floor-boards to protect its occupants against grenades and land mines. The windows were made from quarter-inch bullet-proof glass, and there was a metal shield which could be raised up behind the rear seat by means of a cranking handle. According to one esti-mate, 400 lb of the car's total weight of 10,000 lb were accounted for by these precautions.

Hitler always used to travel in front beside the chauffeur, and the floor in this section was raised slightly to make him appear taller when he stood up. To facilitate standing, the front seat was collapsible, and there was a hand grip on top of the windscreen. Normally, eight people could be accommodated in the car.

The engine was a supercharged straight-eight which produced 155 horsepower, or 230 horsepower when the supercharger was in action (it cut in automatically when the accelerator was fully depressed). Each cylinder had two sparking plugs, and the fuel system was duplicated in such a way that if one failed the other could be brought into action. The driver was able to lubricate the chassis simply by pressing a pedal.

Although it was a giant, its length of twenty feet still left the record for size in the hands of the Bugatti Royale, though it must have broken a few other records. For example, its fuel tank could contain fifty-six gallons of petrol which was, perhaps, just as well. Although it was capable of travelling at 135 m.p.h., it only managed to squeeze between three and four miles out of a gallon of petrol. The sump accommodated 9·5 quarts of oil, the windows were raised or lowered automatically, there were twin carburettors, twin exhausts, and no fewer than forty instruments on the dashboard.

Possibly because he was so proud of them, Hitler was generous with the products of Daimler-Benz. In 1937, he sent one as a gift to King Farouk of Egypt. Admiral Horthy—the dictator of Hungary —received one, and Field Marshal Mannerheim of Finland was given a state car similar to Hitler's on his birthday. Nowadays, it is preserved in a museum at Helsinki.

By all accounts, Hitler was a difficult man to work for if you were a general or a senior official. Lower down the line, however, he was a good boss and he was certainly very amiable to his chauffeurs. His first driver was a man named Schreck, and the dictator seems to have been extremely fond of him. After Schreck's death at a comparatively early age in 1936, Hitler kept an oil painting of him on the wall of his private office at Berchtesgaden. It hung next to a portrait of his mother. Significantly, perhaps, there was no picture of Hitler's father.

On Schreck's death, the second chauffeur, a young man named Erich Kemptka took over the duties, and remained with Hitler until the latter's death. Nowadays, Kemptka is employed on the production line of the Porsche plant at Stuttgart. He is a quiet, courteous, individual with very expressive hands. Although his close association with Hitler has cost him a great deal of suffering he still remains loyal—in spirit, at any rate—to his old boss. In many ways, there is something admirable about him. His openfaced honesty commands respect, and so does his refusal to adapt his outlook to an age which has rendered it totally unacceptable. If Erich Kemptka has a fault, it is, possibly, that he is inclined to be naive. When asked, for example, about the treatment of the Jews, he will protest that this was entirely the work of Himmler, and that Hitler knew nothing about it until 1944. He will also go on record as saying that, when the news did reach the Führer, he was very angry.

Clearly Kemptka has not read his copy of *Mein Kampf* very carefully, and history has done everything in its power to prove him wrong. But the important thing is that he says this with complete conviction. It is the resolute, if somewhat narrow, outlook of a man who was, above everything else, a loyal servant.

It is, perhaps, tempting to believe that people who commit monstrous crimes conduct themselves as monsters. This, of course, is untrue. Some of the most notorious murderers have been respectable, even prudish, individuals. Lucretia Borgia may have been a poisoner, but she was none the less capable of putting on a most convincing act as a gracious hostess. As for Hitler, no less a man than Winston Churchill was once fooled by his 'agreeable manner and disarming smile'. That, of course, was several years before the smile became a snarl. For Kemptka, the magic never wore off, and he will still tell you, not without enthusiasm, that 'Hitler's eyes were speaking eyes. They were very, very great eyes. He was very kindly to people. When he talked to them, he *captured* them. He was never, *never*, angry—nor was he impulsive.'

Other people may think differently, and a German friend of mine, who was embraced by Hitler as a child, has another recollection of his eyes. She recalls that the sight of them caused her to burst into tears, and that she turned for comfort to propaganda minister Joseph Goebbels—who seems to have been the jolly uncle figure of that particular party.

Kemptka comes from a small town in the Rhineland not far from Essen. After he left school, he spent three years studying electrical engineering and a further year learning about mechanics. He then became employed as a mechanic in a garage owned by a DKW dealer in Essen.

One of the customers at the garage was a man named Terwoven, who was the town's gauleiter. Shortly before the 1932 presidential elections in Germany, he approached Kemptka and told him: 'Hitler needs a second chauffeur for his struggle—would you like to put in for the job?' Kemptka said that he would.

Soon afterwards, he was called to the Kaiserhof Hotel in Berlin. There were thirty-five candidates for the appointment, and they were all lined up in a row. Hitler inspected them, asked one or two questions, and then walked off. They were told that they would hear the verdict later. Kemptka returned to Essen.

A few days later, he received a telegram telling him to report to Rudolf Hess at the Braunhaus in Munich, which was the Nazi headquarters. He recalls that 'I was worried when I got it, for Hess was a big wheel in the SS. However, when I went there, I was told that I'd been given the job.'

Three days later, Schreck, who was the chief chauffeur and who drove the big car, became ill, and Kemptka found himself bearing the brunt of driving Hitler during the election campaign. At first, he stayed in an hotel at Munich: later, he was given an apartment in a large family house which had been converted by the Nazi party into flats.

Schreck eventually recovered, and Kemptka resumed the duties of second chauffeur until the former's death. Then he took charge of all twelve cars in the Führer's fleet. There were three of them based on Berlin, three more at Munich and a further three at Berchtesgaden, plus three more for guests. Kemptka shared the views of the Daimler-Benz director about his employer's grasp of technical matters. 'He was very interested in the engines of cars or planes,' he says, 'and he understood them. He could drive, but he never did.'

Earlier in his career, Hitler had enjoyed being driven at high speeds, and he sometimes liked to regale his entourage with stories about how Schreck had taken the car up to 100 m.p.h. After he had come to power, however, he was more cautious. In cities, he insisted that 25 m.p.h. should be the limit. On the open road, he raised it to 50 m.p.h. It was probably just as well. On journeys from Berchtesgaden to Munich, or to Berlin, there was invariably a convoy of vehicles containing Hitler's associates, and keeping the correct distance between cars, even at 50 m.p.h., was far from easy.

Kemptka recalls: 'Hitler was the best chief I know. On long journeys, he used to talk to me. It wasn't really personal talk, and he certainly never discussed his problems. He kept them inside himself, though he did sometimes discuss political matters, and he made jokes. He related anecdotes—stories about funny things that had happened to him. He was not like a big boss. He was very, very normal: very personal to people.'

Often he read on a journey. In Kemptka's experience, he never bothered with fiction, but enjoyed factual works on buildings, engines, history and medicine. He read quickly and assimilated a great deal.

They often took a record player with them in the car. After an energetic performance at a political meeting, Hitler liked to put on classical records. Beethoven and Wagner were his favourites, and Kemptka considers that they helped him to relax. 'They took his mind off politics', is how he puts it.

On a long journey, they would stop from time to time, and Kemptka was allowed to smoke a cigarette. Hitler always sat beside him in the car; one of his adjutants and his valet travelled in the back. The only variation of this arrangement would be when there was an important guest on board. On these occasions, the Führer sat in the back with the visitor.

Sometimes on a long trip, they would eat at a restaurant: often they took packed meals and flasks of coffee. If time was short and they had no opportunity to stop, Hitler passed Kemptka's food across to him. Nor was he too proud to peel a hard-boiled egg for his driver. When, later, they reached their destination, Kemptka usually became Hitler's dinner guest. It was really very democratic and, in case he needed it, Kemptka's status was guaranteed by the rank of obersturnführer[1] in the Waffen SS (Hitler's personal bodyguard).

The car which Kemptka had to drive at the time of the 1932 elections was an old six-litre supercharged Mercedes and by no means easy to handle. 'You had,' he says, 'to work the hand- and footbrakes at the same time.' The later vehicles were much more manœuvrable and even the giant, armour-plated, Grosser Mercedes presented few problems—mainly because they were fitted with special, servo-assisted, steering.

When he visited the army, Hitler invariably used a big six-wheeler, which was powered by a five-litre engine. It was a good deal slower than the rest of the fleet (top speed was about 50 m.p.h.), but it could be driven across country. During the last year of the war, Hitler mostly used a six-wheeler. Towards the

[1]The rank was equivalent to that of a senior lieutenant.

very end, however, the Allied bombing made it impossible to get any spare parts out of Stuttgart. He then used an Austro-Daimler product known as a Steyr. It must have been all of five years old, but there was a sufficiency of spares in Berlin.

Wherever his master went, Kemptka nearly always went, too. The Führer was by no means always at his ease with people, but he was happy in the company of the efficient, well-mannered chauffeur, who was not only a good driver, but who also carried out the role of his personal transport officer. The hours were sometimes hard—Kemptka often had to be on duty from 7 a.m. until two o'clock in the following morning—and the duties were exacting. One particularly difficult time was during the Olympic Games, which were held in Berlin in 1936. No doubt because they appealed to his sense of the dramatic, and building the stadium gave him an opportunity to indulge his passion for architecture, the games were one of the few occasions on which Hitler showed the slightest interest in sport. From Kemptka's point of view, however, they provided one of the worst headaches of his career. Organising the arrival of the official cars, punctually and at the correct entrances to the stadium, was, in view of the mass of spectators which swarmed in the vicinity, immensely difficult.

No doubt feats such as this brought Kemptka closer to his master. Throughout the war, he accompanied him almost everywhere. When they were in Berlin, he lived in an apartment which had been put at his disposal in an annexe to the Chancellery. Among its amenities was a small piece of garden.

The last time that Kemptka drove Hitler was on March 5th, 1945. It was a flying visit to the headquarters of forces which were holding the Oder-Dnieper line. After that, he never left Berlin, and seldom strayed very far from the Chancellery. During the last days, Hitler confined his movements to walks around the Chancellery garden, or for a short distance down the street outside. Kemptka remembers that he looked unhappy, but: 'All the problems stayed inside him. When a guest called, he came out of himself and seemed to be a little bit more cheerful.' During the final week, Hitler never went out at all.

Among the 'guests' were Albert Speer, who told Hitler that he could get away from Berlin in an aircraft: and Ribbentrop, who said that he had a car waiting and that it would be possible to escape along the last street in the city to remain open. Hitler refused both offers.

That was on April 24th, by which time something like 1,000 people had crowded into the Chancellery. All they could do was to wait in the somewhat slim chance that General Wenck's illusionary army would be able to relieve the beleagured city. According to Kemptka, 'we already knew that the war was over'.

On the night of April 28th–29th, when Hitler went through his form of marriage with Eva Braun, Kemptka was leading a party of eighty troops in an unsuccessful counter-attack against the Russians in the Potsdamerplatz. After the wedding, the Führer told his SS adjutant Guensche (the words are Kemptka's version: 'Bring 200 litres of gasoline. My wife and I go from this life. When we are dead, I want Mr. Kemptka to burn us.' 'It was,' Kemptka adds, 'a very, very personal wish.'

By six o'clock in the afternoon of April 29th, Kemptka had returned to the bunker. 'I was talking to Hitler,' he says, 'and Hitler asked: "How do you feel?" Then he asked: "What is the situation of the people?" "They all feel good," I said, "but they are waiting for Wenck." "Yes," Hitler said. "Me, too." At this time, I don't think he wanted to die, because he never mentioned the gasoline. But you couldn't tell. Always there was that poker face.'

Early in the following morning, Guensche called Kemptka and told him to send for the 200 litres of petrol. Kemptka told him he was crazy. With shells bursting all round, any attempt to move that much motor spirit would be suicidal. The only period, in Kemptka's opinion, when it would be possible was at five o'clock in the afternoon. For some reason, probably because they were relieving their forward troops, the Russians always stopped firing for a short while at this time.

But Guensche was insistent. 'Please *try*', he told Kemptka. A soldier was sent off to the fuel store and told to bring the petrol down to the bunker as quickly as possible. Then Guensche disappeared for a short while. The soldier arrived with the motor spirit, and Kemptka went off to look for the missing adjutant. Presently, the latter came out of Hitler's room.

'I still think you're a bit crazy,' Kemptka told him. 'What do you want this 200 litres of gasoline for?'

Guensche said simply: 'The chief is dead.'

Kemptka couldn't believe him. 'But I talked to him last night at six o'clock,' he protested.

'Come and see for yourself,' Guensche said. He ushered him into Hitler's room.

'He was dead,' Kemptka recalls. 'He had shot himself with a revolver in his mouth. I asked Guensche: "Where's Miss Braun?" "She's beside him," he told me. I looked round, for I hadn't noticed her, and there she was.'

Kemptka went out and helped the driver to take the petrol into the Chancellery garden. Then he returned to the bunker. Presently Hitler's valet, Linge, and one of Hitler's doctors came out of the room carrying the Führer's body on a stretcher. They were followed by Martin Bormann, who was carrying Eva Braun in his arms. Kemptka went up to Bormann and took Miss Braun from him. It was a fair way down to the garden and presently Kemptka's arms became tired. He felt Miss Braun gradually slipping away from him. Fortunately, Guensche came up and relieved him of his burden.

As they went into the garden, the Russian artillery and mortar fire intensified. Some of the shells were falling dangerously close. The two bodies were laid side by side, and Kemptka and Linge splashed the petrol over them. It soon became clear that 200 litres were not enough. To do the job properly, Kemptka decided a thousand litres would be needed. The soldier was sent back again to the fuel store.

At this point there occurred one of those snags which can turn an apparently heroic situation into pure bathos. Hitler's idea of a splendid funeral pyre nearly collapsed simply because, when it came to the crunch, nobody had any matches to set the corpses alight. Luckily, shortly after this disconcerting discovery was made, Goebbels came out into the garden. He was a heavy smoker, and he was able to supply the missing light.

From time to time throughout the evening, Kemptka returned to the scene to make sure that the fire was still burning. Eventually, he says, soldiers came and took away all that remained of Adolf Hitler and Eva Braun, and carried them to his own apartment, where they were buried in the garden.

After Kemptka had set fire to the corpses, he fell into conversation with Goebbels and they were presently joined by the propaganda minister's wife. She was crying. 'I don't know what has happened to us all,' she said.

He told her that he had two cars available. If she liked, they could be used in an attempt to get herself and the six Goebbels children away from the Chancellery.

'It will be very dangerous,' he told her. 'The best I can do is to get you from the bunker to another part of Berlin. There, we might be able to get hold of a bigger car.'

Goebbels himself replied: 'I'll wait for news, and then I'll know what to do.'

Some while later, when it was clear even to the optimistic propaganda minister that General Wenck's army was not going to get through to them, he told Kemptka: 'What else can I do? I'll do the same as Hitler, because I am a soldier.'

Mrs. Goebbels said: 'What my husband does—I do the same.'

'But what about the children?' Kemptka asked.

'I have talked to our doctor,' she said. 'The situation is very, very negative for us. He must give them an injection.'

The children were aged between six and twelve. At some point, Mrs. Goebbels seems to have asked their eldest daughter: 'When Germany breaks down, do you want to live or be dead?' It seems a strange question to put to a twelve-year-old; but perhaps her answer was even stranger. She said that she would prefer to be dead.

At first the doctor refused to inject the children. 'No,' he said, 'I won't do that. I'm the grandfather of many children myself.' But Mrs. Goebbels insisted. 'If you won't do it, I'll do it myself.'

At this point, one of Kemptka's drivers brought his girl friend, who had been wounded, into the bunker. They desperately wanted to get married, but there was nobody qualified to carry out the ceremony. Kemptka set off to find the competent official. By the time he got back, the Goebbels children were dead.

Goebbels and his wife were still alive. The latter took him by the hand. 'I wish you all good things in the future,' she said, 'and good luck for all the people who want to escape. See my son by my first marriage.[1] Tell him about us and how I am dead.' Then she paused, and Kemptka had the impression that her mind

[1]Harald Quandt, who had been taken prisoner by the British during the campaign in Abyssinia. He was killed in 1967, when his private aeroplane crashed.

L

suddenly succumbed to the fearful strain which had been imposed upon it, for she added: 'He must look after the children.'

That was the last he saw of them. Later he heard that Goebbels had shot himself and that his wife had taken a pill. But there was no more time to bother about such things. The Russians were outside the bunker, and this was the final chance to escape.

With Guensche, Linge, and some soldiers, he left the Chancellery and made his way along tunnels in the Berlin underground railway system as far as the Friedrichstrasse station. As they came out into the street, an army officer told them that there was now no way out of the city. Fighting was going on round about, and Russian troops had occupied a number of buildings. There were several dead civilians lying on the pavement. Presently they were joined by Martin Bormann.

'What's the matter here?' Bormann asked.

Kemptka shrugged his shoulders. 'Look around you,' he said.

'Listen,' Bormann said. 'I need a tank quickly. I must get out of here—it's very important. I have an appointment outside Berlin.'

Erich Kemptka refrained from telling his superior officer that, just then, there were no doubt a great many people who would have liked to keep appointments outside Berlin. At that moment, by a quite remarkable coincidence, three German tanks clattered down the street. Kemptka stopped the first one, and the commander told him that they were all that remained of a large armoured division.

Bormann came up and was about to commandeer the vehicle when Russian shells began to fall perilously close. They took shelter behind the tank, with Bormann on the left, then Guensche, then Kemptka, and then Linge. Within what seemed to be a matter of seconds, a Russian anti-tank weapon scored a direct hit on the vehicle. Kemptka was wounded in the shoulder: Guensche and Linge seemed to be all right, but of Bormann there was no sign.

It is, of course, possible that he ran off, but the timing does not seem to fit. One second he was seen to be there: the next, no Bormann. Kemptka insists that he must have been blown to smithereens by the shell which hit the forward end of the tank.

He admits that he was blinded by the explosion, but this can only have been momentarily. Shortly afterwards, he had reached the comparative safety of a house, had found a set of civilian clothes and had changed into them. He had also sufficiently charmed a girl into helping his escape by pretending that he was her husband. These actions do not suggest a man whose eyesight had been affected by the explosion. Of course, Bormann might have escaped unnoticed in the ensuing chaos, but Kemptka swears he did not. He eventually went to the extent of committing his convictions to print, when he wrote *Ich habe Adolf Hitler Verbrannt* ('I burnt Adolf Hitler'), which was published in 1950.

From Bormann's point of view, if he did survive, it would no doubt be convenient for such an impression to be circulated. But he was one of the least popular members of Hitler's entourage and few people would have felt inclined to do him a favour. Nor would such an act accord with the impression one gets of Erich Kemptka. Although loyal to his dead boss, and still of the opinion that, though the war was a terrible mistake, Nazism itself was 'for the best social good of the workers', he is not the type of man to tell such a flagrant lie.

Unlike Guensche and Linge, who were captured by the Russians, he eventually made his escape from Berlin. Some time later, he was picked up by the Americans. He was one of the witnesses at the Nuremburg Trials after the war, but his own reputation came through without any blemishes. Nevertheless, it was a long time before he could find anyone to employ him. 'In the eyes of the people,' he says—not without bitterness, 'I was a gangster of war.' It is hard to imagine this slender, precise-speaking man, with his eloquent hands and his dapper suit, in such a role, but the reputation took a long time to die. It was not until 1954 that he finally got a job as a driver. At the time of writing, he is in charge of the last control on one of the Porsche finishing lines.

16 Naval and Military

James Bond (alias '007'), who was Britain's secret weapon in the early 'sixties, is in danger of being misrepresented in automobile history as the owner of an Aston Martin. This is due to a member of that distinguished marque which was once issued to him, and which exploited his licence to kill as well as his licence to drive. At a stated cost of £8,000 it was modified in such a way that it contained an ejector seat for unwelcome passengers, knives which came out of the hub caps to slash the tyres of the opposition's vehicles, an exhaust system which could also put down a smoke-screen, and goodness knows what else. When it appeared in the film *Goldfinger*, it was extravagantly publicised, and it has been known ever since as the 'James Bond Aston Martin'.

This serves to show how misleading the residual facts left for posterity can be. Bond was not an Aston Martin man. Like an earlier super-hero named Hugh Drummond ('Bulldog' Drummond to his readers), he preferred a Bentley. It has all been set down, perfectly clearly, in *On Her Majesty's Secret Service*. At the beginning of chapter two we read that: 'James Bond had been nursing his car, the old Continental Bentley—the "R"-type chassis with the big 6 engine and a 13:40 back-axle ratio.' And, a few pages later: 'He leaned forward and flicked down the red switch. The moan of the blower died away and there was silence in the car as he motored along, easing his tense muscles. He wondered if the supercharger had damaged the engine. Against the solemn warning of Rolls-Royce, he had had fitted, by his pet expert at the Headquarters' motor pool, an Arnott supercharger controlled by a magnetic clutch. Rolls-Royce had said that the crankshaft bearings wouldn't take the extra load and, when he confessed to them what he had done, they regretfully but firmly withdrew their guarantees and washed their hands of their bastardised child. This was the first time he had notched 125 and the rev. counter had hovered dangerously over the red area at 4,500. But the temperature and oil were OK and there were no expensive noises. And, by God, it had been fun!'

The Aston Martin never belonged to Bond. It was issued to him by the quartermaster for the 'Goldfinger' assignment, and was only used once. Ian Fleming, Bond's creator, owned a Thunderbird, which cost him £3,000 and which was paid for from the sale of *Casino Royal* (the first James Bond novel) screen rights. It was equipped with Fordomatic transmission, and had a power output of 190 h.p. According to his biographer, John Pearson, 'Predictably, Fleming was a cautious, extremely tidy driver with a marked dislike of unnecessary risk. He always treated his cars with great respect, and while he much enjoyed the sensation when the "two extra barrels of the four-barrel carburettor came in, at around 3,000 revs, with a real thump in the back", he was never a man who went speeding for the fun of it.'

If Ian Fleming created James Bond in his own image (or in what he would have liked that image to have been), John Buchan's spy-story hero, Richard Hannay, is said to have been based on Field Marshal Lord Ironside, one-time Chief of the Imperial General Staff, former commandant of the Staff College at Camberley, and a man of many adventures.

On one early assignment (or so the story goes) he was sent to German East Africa, where he assumed the disguise of a German corporal. Towards the end of the operation, he was cornered by a couple of Africans, who threatened to give him away. In addition to being a brilliant linguist, Ironside was immensely strong. He was six feet four inches tall and weighed twenty-three stone. Although he was unarmed at the time, he made short work of the two men by, literally, squashing the lives out of them.

Later, as commander of the British expedition to Archangel

in 1918, he was giving a lecture in a small hall when a Bolshevik marksman tried to take a shot at him through the window. A member of the audience, one Count Constantine Ossipor, spotted the man in time, drew a revolver and killed him with one bullet. As a mark of his gratitude, Ironside insisted that the Count should accompany him back to England.

General Ironside's chauffeur, Mr. Percy G. Parker, lives in a small country house overlooking a village green a few miles from Camberley. He recalls that his master, just for the hell of it, once took two two-foot tyre levers and bent them in half. And, whenever he travelled in a touring car, he never bothered to open the door. He preferred to climb in over the side.

Percy Parker had served in France with the Army Service Corps during the first world war. Afterwards, he was posted to the Staff College as chauffeur to the reigning commandant— a somewhat irascible senior officer named Hastings Anderson. Anderson's personal car was a Standard Twelve which, for some publicity stunt or other, had once been driven down the steps of the Crystal Palace in London. For his military duties, he had a Crossley. Whenever the General was about to set out on a journey, Parker had to parade with the car ten minutes before the scheduled time of departure. The object was to give his master time to inspect the vehicle. Since there was a great deal of brasswork, cleaning it was a difficult business; but Parker prided himself that, once he had polished it, 'you could see your face in the fittings'. No doubt it had to be this way, for Anderson once discovered the merest trace of metal polish underneath one of the front door handles.

'This car's filthy,' he barked. 'Take it back and clean it.'

When General Ironside took over command of the Staff College, Parker's lot was very much more agreeable. His new boss was a delightful man to work for: he always addressed his driver as 'Boy' and, when they went on long journeys together, he insisted that they should take their meals at the same table.

Under Ironside's regime at Camberley, the Crossley was replaced by a 23/60 Vauxhall. It was a powerful car which gave very little trouble—unlike the General's own vehicle which was a rare beast known as a Magnetic. It was only in production for about five years, and the interesting feature (which gave it its name) was the transmission. Powered by two large batteries bolted on to the running board, it functioned rather like the armature in an electric motor. It was not, apparently, very reliable, for the electrical contacts were apt to corrode, and there were very few people who knew how to put it right. Once, when it broke down in North Wales, a mechanic had to be summoned all the way from London.

The flow of petrol from the fuel tank to the carburettor had to be started off by means of a hand pump. Provided that, thereafter, the vacuum remained, there was no problem. On a tour across Europe, however, something went wrong with the system in France. Ironside never even considered the idea of turning back. From that point, as he described things afterwards, he 'pumped' himself across the continent.

Loyalty between a general and his driver was a two-way affair. If Percy Parker enjoyed driving Ironside, the latter appreciated his services just as much. There was, perhaps, an understanding between the two men, and they certainly shared some amusing moments. Parker once picked up his master in London to take him to a levée at St. James's Palace. As was his habit, the General was wearing civilian clothes. On the way they had to visit his tailor where, in a small back room (as, again, was his custom), he would change into uniform. Time was short and at one point the road was blocked by a woman driving a very old Austin Seven. She was letting in the clutch too rapidly, not giving the engine sufficient throttle, and stalling at every attempt to get it going. Eventually the delay became too much for the General. He climbed out of the car, walked over to the Austin Seven, and pushed it out of the way.

After Lord Ironside had left the Staff College, Percy Parker went on to the reserve. For the next ten years, he was employed as chauffeur to King George V's sister, Princess Victoria. On one occasion, the Princess, who possessed a driving licence, conceived the notion that she would like to drive home from an engagement. The start of the trip was unfortunate. The engine was functioning perfectly, but the car refused to go. Parker hunted down the trouble and presently had to suggest that Her Royal Highness might like to take the handbrake off.

After that, things went splendidly until the Princess was faced with the problem of stopping the vehicle. Fortunately, they had just turned into the drive of her house in Buckinghamshire, and were only travelling at about six or seven miles an hour. Suddenly she said: 'How do you stop this thing, Parker?' Before he had time to explain, they left the track and eventually came to an undignified standstill on a rosebed outside her equerry's house.

Shortly after the outbreak of the second war, Percy Parker, who had rejoined the colours, was posted to France. For a while, he was employed as chauffeur to Lord Gort, the Commander-in-Chief of the British Expeditionary Force. Lord Gort's car was an absolutely standard Humber Pullman. His passengers were rather less run-of-the-mill. On one occasion, he was driving Lord Gort and the French Premier, M. Paul Reynaud, along a stretch of highway between St. Pol and Arras. It was a bitterly cold winter's day with ice on the road. The car was preceded by two outriders on motor cycles. At some point, they hit a patch of ice. Their machines slipped sideways, throwing the riders down on to the tarmac.

Parker was in a dilemma. If he jammed on the brakes, the car would go out of control. If, on the other hand, he did nothing, he stood a very fair chance of running over the soldiers. With masterly skill, he reduced speed by changing gear, and the two men got out of the way in time.

M. Reynaud was quick to show his approval. He turned to Lord Gort and smiled: '*Quel conducteur—eh!*'

After the evacuation from Dunkirk, Parker was summoned by Lord Ironside to the War Office, and once again became that great man's driver. When, in 1941, Lord Alanbrooke took over the duties of C.I.G.S., he more or less inherited Parker. The two men were old acquaintances. When Ironside had been commandant of the Staff College, Alanbrooke had been one of the instructors. They were building the Royal Tank Corps depot at Bovington, Dorset, at the time, and officers from the Staff College had formed a habit of driving down there at weekends to inspect the progress of the buildings.

These trips became competitive. The nearest town to Bovington was a small place named Wool, and the idea was to see who could make the fastest time from the Staff College gates to the centre of Wool. Ironside got it down to two hours ten minutes, and then clipped a further minute off his own record. One Monday morning, however, Alanbrooke (he was Colonel Alan Brooke at that time)

STAR CARS. Above:
Gary Cooper.
Below: *Errol Flynn.*
In post-war years,
both owned Mercedes
cars. Mr. Cooper
had a 300S. Mr.
Flynn a 300
Cabriolet.

The first car to be owned by a Pope was a Graham-Paige. In 1930, Pius XI added this Mercedes 'Nurburg' to the Vatican's collection. Below: Pope John XXIII at the consecration of a new Mercedes in Rome on December 17th, 1960.

JOURNEYS INTO THE PAST. Above: *King George VI took a ride in a Daimler very much like the one his grandfather owned, when he visited the Daimler works in the late 'thirties. Below: Fifty years after he had built it, Henry Ford took his quadricycle out for a little exercise.*

The first of the
'Docker Daimlers' was
exhibited at the 1951
London Motor Show.
The interior was an
exercise in luxury
pushed almost to its
limits. Outside, the
sides of the body
shone with 7,000
gold stars, and all
the fittings were
sprayed with gold
leaf. It may have
been a little ostenta-
tious, but it attracted
enormous attention.

reported that he had done the journey in two minutes under the two hours. That, even allowing for the fact that he drove a Bentley, was really flying.

His rivals assumed that speed alone had not been enough to account for such a quick trip, and that he must have found a new route. Tragically, however, that was the last round of the contest. Some days later, Alanbrooke failed to report at the Staff College. On the previous evening he had been travelling from Reading to Maidenhead with his wife. A woman backed out on to the road without watching what she was doing. There was a crash, and his wife was killed.

As chauffeur to the C.I.G.S., Parker drove many famous people. On one occasion, shortly before 'D' Day, he was taking General Eisenhower through the East End of London to an urgent appointment. They must have been doing about 50 or 60 m.p.h. when a traffic policeman stopped the car. Evidently, he had not noticed its illustrious passenger, for he accused Parker of exceeding the speed limit. The situation was remedied when Eisenhower poked his head out of a rear window and explained to the officer that 'Nobody ever won a war at 30 m.p.h.'.

Winston Churchill was among his passengers on several trips, and at least two of them might have had disastrous consequences. Once, while travelling to a military establishment on Salisbury Plain with Alanbrooke and Churchill in the back, he came to a narrow stretch of road. On one side, there was a water trough: on the other, a drive leading up to a large house. Ahead of them, an old man was making heavy going of it on a bicycle.

Suddenly, without making any signals, the aged cyclist swerved across the road towards the drive. To pull up would have been impossible. Parker did the only thing he could. Wrenching the steering wheel hard over, he swung the car round to the right and swept into the drive yards ahead of the cyclist. After suitable recriminations, he turned the vehicle round and the journey continued.

Later in the war, he was taking Churchill and Alanbrooke to witness the testing of a new weapon at a range somewhere in the Midlands. It was another of those cold winter days, and the last mile or so of the trip was along a very narrow country road. As they slithered up a hill, Parker suddenly had to bring the vehicle to a halt as the way ahead was blocked by a gun limber.

He waited for a few seconds and then to his alarm he saw that the limber was starting to slide towards them out of control.

It was a large vehicle and it was rapidly gaining speed. Unless he took swift action, it would crash into the waiting car, crushing it to bits and killing everyone on board. Parker let off the brake and went down the hill backwards ahead of the sliding juggernaut. To retain some measure of control, he engaged bottom gear. Presently, he reached the bottom, rounded a corner and got out of harm's way.

Churchill could be a difficult passenger. Parker is a man blessed with considerable self-control, but on one trip it broke down after a good deal of nagging from his very important passenger. They were making for the Prime Minister's country house at Chequers. Part of the journey was along a country road: it was a pitch-black night, and the puny light afforded by the partially blacked-out headlamps gave little help. All the while, Churchill seemed to be saying: 'Can't you go any faster?' Parker knew that this was impossible, but he didn't like to say so. Presently he hit upon an idea which ought, he decided, to bring peace with honour. By changing down into a lower gear, he produced an effect by which the car *seemed* to be going more quickly without actually doing so.

It was all too convincing. Suddenly the familiar fruity voice growled: 'Do you want to break our bloody necks?' Parker muttered something about how the hell can you please *some* people, but did so a little too audibly. Happily, the outcome was entirely satisfactory. On the following morning, he was summoned to Churchill's study, given a brief and almost amiable dressing down, and sent away with a cigar to show that there was no ill feeling.

Normally on these journeys an A.D.C. travelled in front to read the maps. In wartime Britain, where all the signposts had been removed (the idea had been to thwart any German parachutists who might have landed and hadn't got any maps), this assistance was almost essential.

Once, when Churchill and Alanbrooke were inspecting coastal defences down in Kent, the former received an urgent message which caused him to cut his visit short and make a rapid return to London. There was no A.D.C. on board and Parker had to muddle through with the navigation as best he could.

As they were wriggling through a labyrinth of by-roads, Churchill accused: 'You don't know where you are!' Parker pointed out that, whilst he might not be able to give their precise position, he knew very well that they were going in the right direction. 'How can you?' Churchill asked. Parker explained that it had to do with something he had learned at school, and which had obligingly remained in his mind. According to this piece of Post Office folklore, all the cups on telegraph poles are mounted on the side nearest to the capital. There must have been something in it, for they reached London safely and without undue delay.

These were days of long journeys and not a great deal of sleep. Once, when travelling with Alanbrooke, Parker had made a grand tour of the south of England. They had visited military establishments in Kent, Sussex, Hampshire and Somerset and had at last reached Exeter. Something like 400 miles had been covered at what should have been the end of the day's work. But Alanbrooke received a message recalling him urgently to London. An R.A.F. aircraft was waiting at the town's aerodrome to take him there. 'Can you bring the car back to the War Office as fast as possible?' he asked Parker. Another 170 miles were added to the score; but, as Parker points out, the car (a Rolls-Royce) was not tiring to drive and there was hardly any traffic on the roads. 'It really wasn't much of a problem,' he told me.

The car in question has become commonly known as 'Monty's Rolls' in much the same way that, years later, the fictitious James Bond gave his name to a mythological Aston Martin. In the days following the war, it was frequently exhibited and became well known for its windscreen, which sloped inwards rather than outwards.

In fact, during his famous campaign in North Africa, Field Marshal Montgomery had used a four-litre Humber Super Snipe, which was affectionately called 'Old Faithful' and is now at the Montagu Motor Museum in Hampshire. It was the 1941 military version, with a six-cylinder engine and four-wheel hydraulic brakes. Five people could be seated in relative comfort. It was a touring model, with a collapsible windscreen fitted to the backs of the front seats, and large pockets for maps on the insides of the doors.

The so-called 'Montgomery' Rolls-Royce was a much more imposing vehicle. It had been custom built in 1939 for the de Havilland Aircraft Company's chairman, A. S. Butler. Before finally deciding on its appearance, Mr. Butler's revolutionary notions about the windscreen were tested in a wind tunnel.

They turned out, in spite of the unorthodox look, to be entirely sound aerodynamically. Indeed, the wind resistance was reduced by something like 15 per cent, and the principle was afterwards incorporated in a de Havilland aeroplane. Moreover, it reduced the dazzle from oncoming headlights at night, and stood up better to driving in the rain. Since there was not enough petrol to run a Rolls-Royce in wartime, Mr. Butler loaned his car to the Army, and it was earmarked for the C.I.G.S.

Another Rolls-Royce, which might be more appropriately called the 'Monty Rolls' was the one he used after he had relinquished his command in Italy and taken over 21 Army Group just before the invasion of France. It had been damaged during an air raid in 1941. Afterwards, the owner returned it to Rolls-Royce for repairs, and then loaned it to the War Office. In 1944, the Army bought it and allocated it to Montgomery. When it was put ashore on a beach in Normandy on June 6th, 1944, it had the distinction of being the first staff car to land. The Field Marshal continued to use it when he took over the duties of C.I.G.S. from Lord Alanbrooke in 1946. Nowadays, it is housed in the museum of the Army School of Transport at Borden in Hampshire.

One of the most unorthodox staff cars ever built was a vehicle used by Field Marshal Lord Alexander during the North African campaign. It was a station wagon made by Ford of Canada, and, at the start of its life, it was entirely normal. When it was being offloaded at Alexandria, however, it was dropped on to the quay and badly damaged. The wreck was handed over to the Royal Engineers, who designed and constructed an entirely new body. There were no doors, which may have been a disadvantage. On the other hand, the engineers equipped it magnificently for its work in the desert by building a lavish assortment of racks around the rear end—to store jerry cans and great fat sand tyres.

On the other side, Field Marshal Erwin Rommel was using a Horch as his command vehicle. After 1939, only thirty of these cars were produced, and they were, without exception, supplied to the German General Staff. Rommel's had sockets to carry map boards fitted to the body on either side of the rear seats. It was equipped with two twenty-gallon petrol tanks: had two gearboxes (providing eight forward speeds and two reverse), and did ten miles to the gallon. Each wheel was fitted with an independent hydraulic jack.

General Sikorski, commander-in-chief of the Polish Army and Prime Minister of the Polish government in exile, went about his business in a Rolls-Royce. It was the only Phantom III ever built as a true two-seater.[1] In 1938, the manufacturers had delivered it to the General in Warsaw. After the German conquest of Poland, he drove it to Paris and, when France fell, he brought it to England.

Late one night in the middle of the war, Percy Parker was on his way back from Chequers to London with Field Marshal Lord Alanbrooke and the Chief of Naval Staff, Admiral Sir Dudley Pound, in the back. Both senior officers were asleep as they sped along the fast lane on a stretch of dual carriageway in the outer suburbs. The sky was clear, there was a full moon, and they had the road entirely to themselves.

The car was drawing level with Northolt Aerodrome when there was a 'swishing noise'—'as if', as Parker recalls it, 'something was coming up fast from behind'. Suddenly, there was a deafening explosion as a bomb exploded a few yards away. The car was picked up by the blast and deposited on the grass of the central reservation. Fortunately the only damage was to the electric clock.

Sir Dudley Pound awoke, nudged Alanbrooke and asked in a sleepy voice: 'Who's rocked the boat?'

The Admiral was fond of fast motoring. One of his first cars was a Model-T Ford, which he shared with a parson. The clergyman had the use of it on Tuesdays, Wednesdays and Thursdays, whilst Pound had it on Fridays, Saturdays and Sundays. So that everything should be scrupulously fair, they took it in turns to drive it on Mondays.

At the outbreak of war, he persuaded the Director of Stores at the Admiralty to buy a one-year-old Bentley. A leading seaman was seconded to him as chauffeur, though he much preferred to do the driving himself. According to the officer who was his secretary at the time, 'He used to do the trip to Chequers from the Admiralty in forty-five minutes! I used to be scared stiff coming down the Finchley Road' (in north-west London) 'with the priority sign in action and crossing all the red lights! Scotland Yard were very kind to him—never a summons.'

[1] i.e. there were no dicky seats.

His son, George Pound, confirms that travelling with the Admiral was a somewhat unnerving experience. He writes: 'My father always drove himself and a trip home was something that my brother and I never relished, as his thoughts were always elsewhere. He drove like Jehu and his habit of "coming to" at the last minute was quite unnerving. However, he really was a first-class driver—a fact which even the Alexandria police' (when he was Commander-in-Chief, Mediterranean) 'would admit—even though they *did* leave their road-junction pedestals when they saw the V8 Ford with the Admiral's flag approaching.'

The tendency of the Admiral's thoughts to be 'elsewhere' once nearly had serious consequences. It was latish one evening after a long meeting of the Chiefs of Staff Committee. Sir Dudley's car was waiting for him near the entrance to the War Cabinet offices. He placed his brief-case, which contained 'Top Secret' papers, on the roof, unlocked the door, and drove off to take dinner at a restaurant. When he had parked the car, he suddenly noticed that the brief-case was missing. Then he remembered: he had left in on the roof. In about as near as a very senior naval officer can ever be to panic, he hurriedly drove back to the Cabinet offices. The missing brief-case was lying in the gutter, untouched, at the place where it had quietly landed when its owner drove off.

It would be safe to say that the most famous naval officer of the second world war was Admiral of the Fleet Earl Mountbatten of Burma. In 1920, the late Earl of Medina had taken delivery of an eight-cylinder vehicle known as a 'King' (the firm was American and various models were produced between 1910 and 1924). The Earl and Lord Louis[1] both had a passion for innovations and gadgets. This particular 'King' was treated by its owner to just about every refinement under the sun. The instrumentation, particularly, was affected.

In addition to the usual collection of dials and switches, he equipped it with an air-speed indicator; a device for testing the sparking plugs; a switch for dimming the headlamps (very ingeniously, it instantly re-wired them from series to parallel or vice versa); a tachometer; a vacuummeter—which supplied

[1]Earl Mountbatten of Burma was Lord Louis Mountbatten until 1946, when he was awarded the title of Viscount Mountbatten of Burma. An earldom was granted in 1947, when he also became Baron Romsey.

such statistics as the total fuel consumed, the fuel consumed per trip, and the amount of fuel remaining in the tank; and an incredibly clever gadget which he called a 'mileometer'. In some respects, it foresaw the 'moving maps' which, nowadays, are used for navigational purposes on supersonic fighter aircraft.

The map was contained on a spool. A drive from one of the front wheels unrolled it as the car went along, and an arrow in a small window indicated the position at any given time. There was also room for special instructions, or notes about places of interest, to be printed.

It is, perhaps, hardly surprising that, after brilliant service as a gunnery officer in the Royal Navy, the Earl embarked on a no less successful career with a firm of gyroscope manufacturers.

Lord Mountbatten was very much a Rolls-Royce man. His first was a wedding present from his wife, when they were married in 1922. This was followed, in 1924, by another which was quite unlike any other Rolls-Royce of the period, and which gave ample evidence of its owner's flair for re-thinking. With the help of his father's old chauffeur, he equipped it with dipping headlamps. The method involved moving the whole bracket by means of a counter balance weight—instead of, simply, dipping the mirror. In this respect, it may not have been ideal, but it can fairly be described as the first car ever to be equipped with such a refinement.

But the modifications went a good deal further than this. Mountbatten's ideas encompassed the very appearance of the car and that, in the staid world of Rolls-Royce, was little short of heresy. For some time, he had held the opinion that their conception of a bonnet had a flaw to it. It did not produce that unity of design, that feeling of inevitablity which is such an important characteristic of a beautiful thing. Instead of seeming to grow out of the body, it looked as if it had been added as an afterthought.

With assistance from the coachbuilding firm of Barker, he determined to do something about it. He produced a design in which the bonnet was virtually an extension of the rest of the car. It even, and this is saying a lot when one remembers that the year was 1924, created the effect of streamlining. The management of Rolls-Royce were horrified. At first, they tried to cancel the order. But they were told by Barkers that it had already been paid for, and there was nothing they could do—except to waive the warranty. For the next twelve months there was a runnning battle about the legality of the design and then, suddenly, the manufacturers capitulated. Indeed, they did a good deal more than that, It was as if the wind of truth had suddenly blown through the offices. Not content with withdrawing all objections to Mountbatten's ideas, they re-examined their own policy. From then onwards, as you might say, all Rolls-Royces followed the Mountbatten bonnet line.

His next innovation came about in 1926, and was inspired by his experiences when riding a motor bicycle. How much better it would be, he decided, if the headlamps of cars could follow the precise direction of the front wheels. Barkers had a Rolls-Royce on order for him, and they agreed to try the idea out. Thus swivelling headlamps came about, and a great success they were, too. They did not interfere with the steering, nor make it any heavier, and they were an enormous improvement when driving along winding country roads at night.

Having turned a theory into practice, Mountbatten set about trying to patent the idea. Considerably to his surprise, he discovered that there was a law against it. Whilst it was permissible for spotlights to be fitted to a vehicle, the regulations required that all headlamps should be fixed. He had to give up all notions of popularising his invention, and thought little more about it until some forty years later, when Citroën announced their 'eyeball' headlamps. These were connected to the front wheels and, according to their manufacturers, moved 'sharply in the same direction, lighting up the road immediately ahead'. If the law had not been an ass, a British manufacturer might very well have got there first.

Mountbatten's delight in powerful cars was shared by his wife. In 1923, she took delivery of one of the first 20 h.p. two-seater Rolls-Royces ever made, and three years later, on the advice of King Alfonso XIII of Spain, she bought an Hispano-Suiza. It had an aluminium body and travelled very quickly indeed. According to one source, 'its exhaust sounded like a subdued diesel'. Another has it that 'the engine sounded like an old-fashioned Singer sewing machine'. Her husband had once driven the seventy-odd miles from his London home to Portsmouth in one hour and thirty-two minutes (in *The Life and Times of Lord Mountbatten* by John Terraine he is quoted as pointing out that this 'was long before motorways and when four-wheel brakes were scarcely known!'). Lady Mountbatten was also well able to handle a big car at high speed.

Before the Mountbattens inherited Broadlands at Romsey in Hampshire, they owned an estate down in Sussex at a place named Adsdean. Whenever His Lordship arrived by car, he used to toot the Morse code signal for 'L' (· – · ·) on his horn. This was the cue for the gates to be opened. At Broadlands, the code was changed to '7' (– – · · ·) and that is still in use today. In its own way, the registration number of his 1936 Rolls-Royce was also a code. It was 'LM 0246'. You could read it in two ways. Either the 'LM' could be isolated to stand for 'Louis Mountbatten', or you could take the whole of it, and translate it as 'London Mayfair 0246', which was his ex-directory London telephone number.

Of his four pre-war Rolls-Royces, two survive. The 1924 car eventually passed into the hands of Major R. F. Crossman, a well-known brewer, who took it over to France in 1946. Seventeen years later, it was discovered in the Dordogne area, bearing French number plates and in a singularly run-down condition. It was brought back to England, where it was purchased by Surgeon Captain (D) R. Symmons, v.d.r., r.n.r., who spent £2,500 on its restoration. When the TV series 'The Life and Times of Lord Mountbatten' was produced a year or so ago, His Lordship was very anxious that it should appear in one of the episodes. Captain Symmons brought it down to Broadlands and, after an elapse of forty years, Mountbatten climbed into the driving seat. Followed by a film crew on a Land-Rover, he took it up and down the drive. Unfortunately, the public were never able to see the results, for the footage in question was left abandoned on the cutting-room floor.

However, this fine old car finally made it on TV. It was used in the BBC's production of 'The Forsyte Saga' as the vehicle in which Fleur Forsyte drove to her wedding.

The 1930 Rolls is at present in the possession of an enthusiast living in Lincoln.

During the war years, Earl Mountbatten had two narrow escapes when travelling in a vehicle. Shortly after the invasion of Sicily in 1943, he was travelling along a narrow road on the island in company with Field Marshal Montgomery. They were using a jeep and were approaching a fork. Suddenly a marauding Messer-

M

schmitt pilot noticed them and went into the attack. Fortunately, the jeep driver took one of the roads, whilst the Messerschmitt pilot followed the other. During the attack, Mountbatten recalls, he and the driver ducked right down, whilst Montgomery, with supreme indifference, remained sitting bolt upright as if nothing untoward were happening!

Later, when he was Supreme Allied Commander in the Far East, Mountbatten was driving his own jeep back from a visit to the American front line in Burma. At one point, a front wheel travelled over a bamboo stump, which flew up and hit him in the left eye. When, presently, he arrived at an American field hospital, it seemed as if he would lose the sight of it.

In *The Life and Times of Lord Mountbatten*, he recalled: 'The accident could hardly have come at a worse time. I had to spend five days in the American forward hospital with both eyes bandaged in complete blindness. And just at that moment the Japanese attacked again. . . .

'I persuaded the doctor to unbandage my eyes and let me out of hospital. I immediately flew to Army Air H.Q. and there took one of the most serious decisions of my whole time as Supreme Commander.'

Diplomacy takes many forms, and this is just as true in war as it is in peacetime. One day towards the end of hostilities, Winston Churchill and President Roosevelt paid a visit to King Ibn Saud, who was then the ruler of Saudi Arabia. The British Prime Minister had considered it appropriate to take with him a gift for the monarch, and his luggage included a fine set of cutlery. He was about to produce it, when he became aware of his American colleague saying: 'Your Majesty, I should like to present you with an aircraft.'

Confronted by the prospect of fearful loss of face, Churchill forgot all about the knives and forks, and extemporised brilliantly with: 'Your Majesty, *I* should like to present you with a Rolls-Royce.'

The Foreign Office was alerted and given urgent instructions to produce a suitable car. This was very much more easily said than done. For the past five years, the firm's output had been devoted exclusively to war production, and not one Rolls-Royce chassis had been built.

After frantic enquiries, an unsold Phantom III of 1938 vintage was run to earth at a firm of dealers in Huddersfield. The existing body was scrapped and a new one built in its place. In accordance with instructions, a silver washbasin was fitted in the rear of one of the front seats. Following advice that the sovereign preferred to sit cross-legged on the floor, the orthodox back seat was replaced by a semi-circular one which occupied nearly all the compartment.

Presently the car, looking magnificent in the Saudi-Arabian royal colours, was put on display in what was Hooper's London showroom. Prince Faisal (now King Faisal), the monarch's son, who was then employed as his country's foreign minister, came to Britain to take delivery of it.

He was impressed—there was no doubt about that. But could he see how the washbasin worked? It was filled with water, and then the plug was removed. Unfortunately, what was all very well for the open road was less than good for the showroom carpet.

And there was one other snag. His Majesty had contracted severe rheumatism, and this compelled him to give up his custom of sitting cross-legged on the floor. Was it possible that the semi-circular seat could be removed, and a more conventional one put in its place?

Hooper's reacted with praiseworthy speed and the car was shipped out to Saudi Arabia. It is still there—somewhere. As proof of his more austere way of life, the present monarch uses a Chevrolet.

17 Show Business on Wheels

Can anyone remember Fred Karno? Or Tom Mix? Or Jackie Coogan? Or Clara Bow? Possibly not, and yet these are names which entertained hundreds of thousands of people. In their time, they commanded huge rewards for their labours. They lived their lives on a level of luxury comparable to that of the rajahs. And some of them had nearly as many wives.

During the second world war, soldiers in the British Army used to sing a ditty to the effect that 'We are Fred Karno's Army . . .' Like elderly officers and some of the early equipment, it had been dug out from the relics of earlier battles. They sang it with a good deal of gusto, though it is doubtful whether many of them knew, who, precisely, this Mr. Karno was.

He was a comic: a professional funny man, who used to pack the Empires and the Hippodromes and the other 'palaces of variety', and cause the audiences to gasp for air as they chortled at his jokes. It was obviously a trade which paid him well, for, in 1921, we find him taking delivery of a Rolls-Royce.

Mr. Karno had to be patient. The demand for Rolls-Royces was so great in the years immediately after the first world war, that he had to wait two years for the chassis, and another five months before Fountain's Auto Carriage Works at Horsham completed the coachwork, Mind you, they made a beautiful job of it.

The roof was black, and the rest of the body was painted in 'cobalt violet'. Pale fawn cloth (with a subtle mauve tint) was used for the upholstery. Up front, there were two sliding seats, and there was room for an extra one—which could be folded up, or set up in such a way that the occupant sat sideways, or it could be taken out of the car and used for picnics. The windows could be raised or lowered 'by turning a small handle on the inside', which may be unworthy of comment nowadays, but was sufficiently remarkable in 1921.

Some years earlier, that fine Shakespearean actor, Sir Johnson Forbes Robertson, had become the first member of the entertainment industry to order a Rolls-Royce. It had a landaulet body, and was delivered to his London home on May 16th, 1912. In 1914, that great Scottish entertainer, Sir Harry Lauder, bought a Model-T Ford. It cost him 550 dollars.

Over in Hollywood, the stars of the silent screen were accumulating vast stables of cars. A somewhat precocious child performer named Jackie Coogan (they even manufactured 'Jackie Coogan' biscuits in his image) was striking it really rich. While still a long way from twenty-one, he owned two Rolls-Royces, and his father had the first agency for this make of car in southern California.

Tom Mix was almost the prototype cowboy star.[1] He had fought the Chinese in the Boxer Rebellion of 1900; had served as a Texas Ranger; and had made his entry into motion pictures as an armed guard to protect film crews during the making of wild-animal films. In the sombre company of James Dean, Belinda Lee, and Jayne Mansfield, he became one of Hollywood's car casualties.

It happened in 1940. Mix had spent the previous night drinking with friends, and was on his way back to Hollywood. As he approached the small town of Florence in Arizona, he failed to see a detour sign. As a result, he spun off the road, and the car turned over. Luggage, which he had stacked on the rear seat, was flung forward. It struck him hard on the back of the neck, and he was killed instantly.

Clara Bow, the 'It' girl of Hollywood, died of a heart attack in 1965, though there must have been some very dangerous

[1]In spite of Tom Mix's undoubted fondness for cars, another performer, Hoot Gibson, became the first man to lasso a steer from a motor vehicle.

moments during the wilder escapades of her motoring life. Miss Bow was a tragic figure. She had been born in Brooklyn, the daughter of a part-time waiter and a mother who became insane. As a young girl, she won a beauty contest in which the prize was a screen test. For some reason, the news of her victory brought a violent reaction from her mother, who attacked her with a carving knife. From that moment, Clara Bow became a chronic insomniac.

She threw wild parties, and these invariably ended up in hell-raising drives around the motion picture capital. On one occasion, she drove an open car at full speed down Hollywood Boulevard with the whole of the 'Thundering Herd' football team on board.

Rudolf Valentino owned a number of fast cars, and liked to make the most of their impressive performances. Among his stable were an Isotta-Fraschini and a Voisin. He never raced in the way that James Garner (who caught the bug during the making of 'Grand Prix') and Steve McQueen have done, but he cared a great deal for his vehicles and, in spite of anything his film image may have suggested to the contrary, was a very capable mechanic.

When the Model-A Ford succeeded the Model-T, America rejoiced. The end of the Model-T, which had been in production for the better part of eighteen years, seemed like the finish of an epoch. It had brought motoring within the means of millions of people, and it had provided employment for a huge labour force. When the news came out that it was to cease production, America began to worry. Surely the golden age of Ford was not to die without either a bang or a whimper?

It didn't die. The Model-A appeared, and there were church services in many parts of the United States in which hundreds of thousands of people went down on their knees and said thank you for its coming.

Hollywood clutched the new car to its fat bosom and loved it. When one reads reports of its reception there, one has the impression of a very effective, possibly slightly over-played, public relations campaign. But Ford deny this. In a car world which was inhabited by many much more exotic vehicles, the film stars and producers bought their Model-As and shared in the national whoopee.

Dolores del Rio bought one. Cecil B. de Mille had one. And

Douglas Fairbanks and his wife, Mary Pickford, drove one down Hollywood Boulevard from their house 'Pickfair'.

Among the cars owned by Clark Gable were a couple of early Jensens, at least one Mercedes, and a 1935 Duesenberg with a specially built short chassis. Only two short-chassis two-seaters were built in that year. The other went to Gary Cooper. After the war, Cooper bought a Mercedes 300S roadster, and so did Bing Crosby.

Al Jolson owned a 1928 Mercedes; Emil Jannings had a 1927 Lincoln and a 1930 30/200 PS Mercedes tourer; Jean Harlow had a V12 Cadillac finished in black and a Rolls-Royce painted in white; Gloria Swanson and Johnny Weissmuller (the original Tarzan) were among other Cadillac owners; and, many years later, Warren Beatty and Faye Dunaway, playing the roles of Bonnie and Clyde, drove to their final gun battle with the law in a 1951 Plymouth.

Meanwhile: back in Britain . . .

If you stand outside a house in London's Regent's Park for long enough, you may be rewarded by the sight of a famous actor, dressed in a crash helmet and an old overcoat, wheeling a 750 c.c. Norton Atlas out on to the road. He kicks the engine to life, and sets off on a few circuits of the park.

The motor-cyclist is Sir Ralph Richardson, who has always had a very strong sympathy for machinery. As he told me: 'Like most people, I find enjoyment in the sensation of moving faster than I can run. Physical momentum attracts me for its own sake. I enjoy bicycles and motor cars and aircraft; but the progenitor of superhuman movement, the horse, I do not enjoy.

'I never venture on a horse except from professional necessity, and then I am always nervous. I have noticed that those who like horses are mostly very nice people, though they are inclined to regard machines as being vulgar, whilst for me machines can be beautiful.

'In the papers, there are pictures of these very nice people, princesses sometimes, upon horses; but often they look extremely nervous.

'Sometimes, horses can be less dangerous than motor cycles, but I always suspect that a horse would like to throw you off its back.

'I know that a motor bicycle can throw you off without any

provocation or warning when it decides to go into a speed wobble.
I have had this happen to me at a speed that no horse ever attains
—that is 85 m.p.h. Then, I was badly hurt and taken to the nearest
hospital, which was a lunatic asylum, and there I was nursed for
several weeks with loving care and kindness.

'But then, on another occasion, an aircraft that I was flying
suddenly discarded its engine valves; and, in the uncongenial
landing that followed, it was smashed and took fire. All that
happened to me was a nick in my trousers.'

Sir Ralph told me that he has always been fond of motor cars.
It is an interest that he used to share with Sir Cedric Hardwicke.

'I took Cedric out in a twelve-cylinder, 1936, Phantom Rolls-
Royce—a car of which I was particularly proud,' he said, 'and in
the quiet of Regent's Park I slipped into neutral and asked him to
drive. He said: "This is amazing, you cannot hear the engine
at all." I said: "It is very beautiful." Cedric went into gear and
de-clutched, but nothing happened. All that while, the engine
had been stalled!

'Many years ago, Laurence Olivier and I used to drive about
together. One day, he drove me straight over the Croydon–
Brighton crossroads at 40 m.p.h. I was appalled. I said: "I will
never forgive you for that, Laurence." Later, he brought a new
model back from America and he invited me to drive it. I was
crazy enough to take him down Piccadilly at ninety. Laurence
never said a word.

'I do not pilot an aircraft any more, and I do not enjoy motoring
for its own sake as I did in the past, but I have kept my youth's
fondness for the motor bike. I do not drive it quite as often as I
might, because sometimes I cannot get it to start.'

The only two things that Ralph Richardson and the late James Dean
can have had in common were their professions and a fondness
for machinery. Beyond that, there was no similarity. Richardson
is the epitome of an English gentleman. He wears tweeds, smokes
a pipe, enjoys painting pictures, smiles easily, and is extremely
courteous. James Dean made three films, built a rapid reputation
as a rebel (with or without a cause—it doesn't matter), and died
violently at the wheel of a Porsche. Afterwards, presumably
through the devices of an ingenious press agent (these things don't
just *happen*), he became the subject of a rather horrible death

cult. To the average person, he may appear to have been a not very likable young man.

But the truth, thank God, is seldom so simple, and no judgement can ever be absolute. Living in Stuttgart, there is a German mechanic named Rolf Whetherich who probably knows more about Dean than many people did. After one has talked to him for a while, a somewhat different impression begins to form.

As a youngster, Whetherich was dragooned into the Hitler youth movement and was taught to fly a glider. He enjoyed it. Later, he served with the Luftwaffe as a parachutist and discovered that 'jumping was beautiful'. After the war, he returned to Stuttgart with the intention of working in aviation. Germany, at the time, was not allowed to manufacture aeroplanes, and the industry was dead. Instead, he went to the Daimler-Benz plant at Unterturkheim to study as a car mechanic. In 1950, he transferred his services to Porsche. The plant was turning out one car a week and there were fifty-one other people on the staff. Now they employ 3,500 workers and produce ninety cars a day. But, even then, the factory's list of customers included such people as the Shah of Persia and King Farouk of Egypt.

The supreme commander was still Professor Ferdinand Porsche, who, in Whetherich's opinion, never really grew old. He treated the mechanics well, but was less tolerant of his engineers. In many ways, he was temperamental, especially if anybody made a bad mistake. On these occasions, he was apt to throw his hat on the ground and jump on it. 'But,' Whetherich recalls, 'his rage never lasted long.'

Whetherich himself was in a rather unsettled frame of mind at this period. It was understandable. As a youngster, every means of propaganda had been used for the express purpose of proving that Germany was the greatest nation on earth; that Germany was invincible; that the German people were a master race; and so on.

The war had shown that this was not entirely true. All the beliefs, which had been so carefully built up in his mind, crumbled. The fundamental teaching of childhood had turned out to be false, so what, in all this wretched world, was true? Perhaps, although for an entirely different reason, he already had points of contact with the man who was to have such a large effect on his life, cinema star James Dean.

He wanted very badly to fly, but that was impossible. And so he turned to motor sport as a substitute, and he did reasonably well at it. 'We were,' he recalls, 'hungry and poor. The poorest drivers of all began on motor cycles, and these were the hottest. But I was afraid of motor cycles. I used to have one, but I forgot to make the footrests high enough. Once I took it out on a wartime airfield in the Black Forest. I raced down the runway, but at the end I had to make a 180 degree turn and I came off. There was blood all down my side—like a peeled potato.'

In 1954 he was sent by Porsche to Los Angeles. An ex-patriate German named Newman was setting up a Porsche franchise over there and opening up distributorships all down the west coast. Whetherich's job was to train mechanics in Porsche practice.

At about this time, the United States were beginning to take a rather wider interest in motor racing. Old airports were being converted into circuits, and new tracks were being built. Riverside, Bakersfield, Fresno, one by one they came on to the map. And, among the names which were emerging from the general mass of motor-racing enthusiasts were Dan Gurney, Phil Hill, Richie Ginther, Masten Gregory—and James Dean. Gurney, who was working for Lockheed, drove to work in the export model Porsche 1500 Speedster. In the evenings and at weekends, he raced it in the stock-car events, and this was tough on the Porsche. The time eventually came when it needed new pistons and cylinder linings, but he had no money with which to buy them. Whetherich, somehow, helped him out.

There was talk—masses of talk. Gurney once said: 'In ten years, Rolf, I'm sure I'll be driving for Ferrari.' In fact, he made it in five. With one exception, they all wanted to become professional drivers and, with that exception, they all achieved their ambitions. The odd man out was James Dean.

Whetherich had met Dean at a Porsche dealer's showroom. The original export car had been built from Volkswagen components, and it was by no means easy to handle. It had a good deal of oversteer and rather too much horsepower for the brakes. Dean had one and he now wanted the later model.

He was a quiet young man, moody and inclined to be reserved. At parties, he drank little and spent most of the time watching people. In Whetherich's opinion, it was his way of learning how to act.

'It needed a long time to get to know him,' he recalls. 'In a country where it was usually "Hi—Rolf boy!" at first sight, it was six, or maybe eight, weeks before he said: "I'm Jimmy, you're Rolf." He was very, very reserved to everybody. He had a hunger to see Europe, but he never made it. He used to ask me about Heidelberg and Mozart and what was Hitler really like. But, all the time, there was a fire burning inside him. Above everything, he wanted to be a *great* movie actor.

'Like me, he was hungry for the sports car. As a driver, he had talent. He learned a circuit quicker than the others did. He learned easily, and that was good. His eyesight was good and so were his concentration and reactions. But he had no eyes for the rev. counter and no ears for the engine. He was hard on his cars.'

The directors of Lockheed may not have worried about what Dan Gurney did with his leisure, but James Dean was too valuable to his employers. When M.G.M. teamed him up with Elizabeth Taylor for *Giant*, they inserted a clause in his contract to the effect that there was to be no motor racing while the film was in production. This made Dean angry and, perhaps as an act of defiance, he promptly ordered one of the 1500 four-cam RAK1500 Porsche Spiders. It was one of the first to be delivered to the United States.

By the end of September, 1955, *Giant* was finished. Between them Dean and Whetherich studied the motor-sport calendar and saw that there was a race scheduled to take place at Fresno on October 1st. With no further picture planned for M.G.M., the young actor could afford to take a holiday. He was immensely proud of his new car, which had cost 10,000 dollars, and he asked Whetherich to get it ready for the Fresno race.

A number of other enthusiasts from Los Angeles were planning to take part, and most of them intended to take their cars to the circuit on transporters. Dean, on the other hand, decided to drive there. The engine had barely been run in and a further 200 miles on the clock could do nothing but good.

They set off on September 30th, accompanied by a few friends in another car which was being used to carry spare parts. Whetherich and Dean were alone in the Spider.

Part of the route from Los Angeles to Fresno is across the desert. Near Bakersfield, there is a filling station and café known as the Black Corner Snack Bar. It is the last refuelling point before the

road takes to the desert. Some way further on, there is a junction
at which traffic coming from the direction of Fresno can branch
off to Sacramento.

At four-thirty in the afternoon, James Dean and his party
stopped at the Black Corner Snack Bar. It was intensely hot,
and they spent about an hour consuming soft drinks. By a coincidence, Barbara Hutton's son, Lance Reventlow, was also there.
He was on his way to the race with a very fast Mercedes.

Presently, with their tanks topped up with petrol, they set off
again. The sun was behind them and Dean and Reventlow were
both driving very quickly. The road was dead straight, and they
had the right of way at the fork to Sacramento.

It took them about fifteen minutes, with James Dean in the
lead, to reach the road junction. Coming towards them was a
young student in an old Chevrolet. Without making a signal,
he swung across the road at the precise moment that Dean arrived
at the fork. In the ensuing collision, the young man escaped with
superficial face injuries. Dean was killed instantly. Whetherich
was thrown out of the car. He was unconscious for four days,
and had to remain in hospital for several months.

Afterwards, the student said that he had never seen Dean's
car approaching him. He blamed the fact that it was painted
silver grey, and this, coupled with the heat haze on the road,
had rendered it invisible. If one adds the fact that he had the
sun in his eyes, one is bound to feel that he was speaking the
truth.

But that did little to restore Rolf Whetherich's health, and
nothing could bring back James Dean.

According to his agent, Peter Sellers has owned 105 cars. They
have included a number of Rolls-Royces, at least one Ferrari,
Rovers, Renaults, Sunbeams, Jaguars, a Morgan, and a Mercedes
or two. One of the Rolls-Royces was formerly the property of
that famous horse-racing jockey, Sir Gordon Richards. But,
amid this passing stream of automobile splendour, Mr. Sellers
has been faithful after his fashion to one car. It is, you might say,
a kind of domestic pet. The vehicle in question is a 1932 Austin
12/4.

The Sellers style in motoring matters takes several different
forms. There is, for example, the way he words advertisements

when one or another of the tribe comes up for re-sale. Let us consider two examples:

'Fred' (which is a name he dislikes) 'offers very clean little 1958 Silver Cloud, speedometer as new, real little sparkler, not a bit wavy, good runner, a car for the konisewer.

'A snip at five and a quarter (thou) to clear. A Fred car is a good car. Get one today and really go motoring.'

Or:

'Titled motor car wishes to dispose of owner. 1958 Rolls-Royce Silver Cloud seeks new owner of distinction after small, meticulous, but non-U mileage. Rather tired of being conducted by professional funny man and his chauffeur, neither of whom appear in *Debrett*. Deliverance: £5,250.'

The sale of this particular model was to make room in the stable for the forty-eighth Sellers car—a Bentley Continental priced at £7,000 and fitted with two-way radio telephone.

From time to time, Sellers has been quoted as saying 'I just adore cars' and 'I never seem able to keep a car for long'. Before his marriage to Britt Ekland, he presented her with a £1,500 Lotus. It was painted in red, capable of 115 m.p.h., and made a very pleasant companion to the ring of emeralds, diamonds and rubies which adorned the third finger of Miss Ekland's left hand.

But the man who has everything in the motoring line should also have a racing car. Although, to the best of my knowledge, he never took part in events as a driver, Sellers had several. In 1965, partnered by his agent, Theo Cowan, he formed Peter Sellers Racing Ltd. It was based on a garage in Ilford, and the tangible assets included a racing driver, a Lotus 23B and a 1,000 c.c. Lotus As explained at the outset of the venture, the object was to break into Formula 1 racing 'in two or three years' time'. In fact, they never got that far. The reason, Theo Cowan told me, was 'partly due to economics, but mainly to Mr. Sellers's programme of filming abroad'.

Perhaps the most disappointing event in the motoring life of any performer was that which befell a member of the Monkee's pop group. One of the young gentlemen had just spent £3,640 on a very, very special Mini. It was, if reports published at the time are to be believed, the most expensive Mini in the world. Having collected the car from the small factory where basic products are rendered exotic beyond comparison, he took it to the nearest motorway, and there proceeded to belt the living daylights out of it. This was, perhaps, understandable. When you have paid several thousands of pounds for something which, in a more raw condition, costs only a few hundred quid, you do not expect to have to undergo such earthy ordeals as running the blessed thing in. But that, alas, is what is necessary. The Monkee's engine seized up after a few miles and . . . Well, anyway, one couldn't help feeling sorry for him.

The Beatles, before they broke up, became bashful about their personal possessions, and declined to discuss their cars. A search through a newspaper library, however, was sufficient to discover that Mr. McCartney had owned such expensive merchandise as a 1924 Hispano Suiza (done up in a psychedelic colour scheme in which the body was a comparatively austere navy blue, but the upholstery was on fire with a 'rainbow' colour scheme), a 1967 Mini Cooper-S, a 1969 Bentley and an Aston Martin. The Mini appears to have been involved in one of the world's more bizarre traffic accidents.

They were all going to a party given by the Beatles' one-time manager, the late Brian Epstein. Among those on the invitation list was Paul McCartney's chauffeur, a gentleman by the name of Mohammd. It was agreed that Mr. Mohammd should travel separately, driving the Mini. He climbed into the car and shut the door, unaware that one of the safety belts was hanging out. All went perfectly well until he reached a traffic jam at one of the western approaches to London. Here, by some remarkable trick of fate, the dangling safety belt hooked itself around the bumper of another car. When the parade got moving again, the other vehicle (which had now become a kind of parent ship) caused the luckless Mini to swing round and damage its side.

However, as Mr. McCartney observed philosophically after-wards, it was nothing that insurance could not put right.

In February, 1970, Mr. John Lennon moved into a new Mercedes. It was 22 nearly feet long, weighed two tons, and the seven seats were done up in black velour. To keep its occupants happy, it was equipped with a refrigerator, a two-way telephone, television, radio, a record player, a tape recorder, push-button windows, a sunshine roof, and an electric point in which to plug a teamaker. The cost, according to the popular press, was £14,200. Mr.

Lennon's other rather more domestic automobile possessions have included a Rolls-Royce with a bed in the back.

I cannot find out very much about *what* the other Beatles have owned except that George Harrison had a 1929 maroon and grey Rolls-Royce which, I think, was given the psychedelic treatment by a firm of bodybuilders, who took 157 hours to carry the work out. They charged 22s. 6d. an hour, which was a bargain. The normal rate was 32s. 6d.

Nowadays, the trend among the younger and more eminent members of show business is to have the rear windows of their cars manufactured in black glass. In this respect, they resemble the purdah wagons that some of the rajahs owned, though the motive is not quite the same. So far as I can gather, the object is to protect the occupants from the eyes of inquisitive bystanders and (if such a contradiction is possible) to attract attention at the same time. No doubt the very fact that the owner should feel any *need* to obscure the interior from prying eyes suggests that he must be a very important person. Richard Harris has a P5 Rolls-Royce which has been given this treatment. And a pop singer has a similarly doctored Daimler.

18 Status Symbols

If you live in Singapore or Kuala Lumpur, and you have a thirst for status, you can, in return for a comparatively modest fee, rent a police motor-cycle escort. Or if you have the income of a certain young prince from a Middle Eastern sheikdom, you can walk into the offices of a firm of London coachbuilders, place the bright new shirt you have just bought on the managing director's desk, and say: 'I want a Mini done up in this pattern.'

Indeed, if one looks at the prospectus of the firm in question, one is quite amazed at what can be done to make a humble Mini stand out from the crowd. When all is done, the bill may easily add up to £4,000, but what does it matter? In this horribly anonymous world, one has at least stamped one's personality on to one's car.

Of course, the Mini itself will be a great deal more comfortable after the experience. The seats will have been hand made; there will be wall-to-wall carpets in 'best quality wool'; there will certainly be a sunshine roof, and enough wood panelling to cover a Jacobean hall. So that you can have music wherever you go, you may order a five-push-button radio *and* an eight-track stereo player complete with speakers. Television is not provided, but a dictating machine is available.

Less affluent seekers after automobile status may prefer to

follow the example of a certain gentleman in Liverpool. Clearly very gifted mechanically, he has built a device with which he can start the engine of his car by remote control before getting out of bed in the mornings. The idea is that it warms up while he shaves and has his breakfast. Perhaps he has at last produced a mechanical chauffeur. For, in its original French, the word means stoker, or fireman—in other words, a warming-upper.

Refrigerators in high-level motor cars are by no means rare, though they do have the effect of putting the price up. When, in 1967, Aristotle Onassis bought a Rolls-Royce with a built-in refrigerator, the total bill came to £20,000. Had he wanted the car to be armour-plated as well, it would have added another £50,000. Rolls-Royce have never needed to consider where, in their armouring service, they should draw the line. Presumably, a man would have to be very sincere and highly vulnerable and, therefore, very powerful, not to be put off by the price.

Another firm did, once, receive an enquiry for an armour-plated Mini, but they had to decline the contract. With all the extra weight, the little car would have been unable to move.

One rather charming account of individualism in car design comes from West Germany. A young resident of the town of Wuppertal has covered his sports car with fur. He claims that it stands up better to such things as rain, flying stones and minor bumps. Cleaning, of course, is very much easier—he just runs a vacuum cleaner over it.

In 1966, a petrol-tanker driver in Carlisle lined the interior of his car with fur, and one cannot help wondering whether he was not inspired by a quip Lady Docker made to newsmen at the 1955 London Motor Show. She was referring to a vehicle on the Daimler stand which had real zebra-skin upholstery. At first, she said, her idea had been to do it in mink—but that had turned out to be too hot to sit on.

Later, she protested that it had just been a joke and that, in any case, zebra was by far the most practical skin for a car seat. All the others were liable to moult.

Lady Docker was to post-war motoring as Salvador Dali was to between-war painting: she outraged and, at the same time, delighted. You may have considered her 'Docker Daimlers' as the most beautiful things that ever shone from a motor-show stand, or you may have regarded them as a tasteless waste of money.

N

Whichever way it was, you could not possibly have ignored them, and you had to admit that there was much which was admirable in her determination to attract publicity.

In those days, the Daimler company was a subsidiary of the Birmingham Small Arms Group of which her husband, Sir Bernard Docker, was chairman. When she married Sir Bernard, she discovered (as she says in her book *Norah*) that 'the Daimler car was in danger of becoming a relic'. Whenever they went abroad, their own Daimler was admired, but the compliment was spoilt by a tiresome habit people (who ought to have known better) had of referring to it as a Delahaye. Why on earth, Lady Docker wondered, should the name be so wretchedly mangled and mispronounced? She came to the conclusion that, outside the British Royal Family, far too few people knew about the car.

Lady Docker's father had been connected with the motor trade, and she had grown up among cars. Consequently, it was not altogether unreasonable that she should become appointed to the board of another B.S.A. adjunct, Hooper and Co. (Coachbuilders) Ltd. She had a special responsibility for Daimler designs. Before very long, a drawing table was added to the furniture of her Mayfair home.

Her object was to get Daimler's talked about, and she succeeded. She believed the firm ought to be producing 'a small, popular, Daimler car, aimed at the mass market by its competitive price and still containing the same standard of workmanship to be found in any royal or V.I.P. model', but she used as her platform a series of one-off models which were so un-mass market it was hardly true. There was something brilliant about the sheer arrogance of the idea, and it may very well have worked. Certainly after her five-year reign at the drawing board was over, there were very few people who could not say 'Daimler'.

One even suspects that, in France, there were motorists who, admiring their friends' Delahayes, called them by some other name.

The first of the Docker Daimlers appeared at the 1951 Motor Show. It was purely a show car, and it attracted a great deal of attention—not least because all the fittings seemed to have been manufactured from solid gold. In fact, the explanation is rather more pedestrian. Chrome at the time was very difficult to obtain, and so a substitute had to be found for the bumpers, wing mirrors, and so on. Brass was out of the question because too much time would have been spent cleaning it. Eventually, an assistant in the Hooper drawing office suggested that gold leaf might be a good idea. It was well received and all the fittings, including the exhaust pipe and the petrol cap, were sprayed with it.

Lady Docker took her inspiration wherever she could find it. Once, on a cruise in their yacht *Shemara*, she was wearing a cocktail dress in black with gold stars. One of the guests admired it and said, by way of a joke, 'Why don't you cover your car with gold stars?' Lady Docker took a more serious view of the suggestion. She liked it, and gold stars were added to the décor. Her original idea had been to have them all over the car; but, on the more sober advice of Hooper's chief designer, they were eventually limited to the doors and the sides of the bonnet. Nevertheless, an heraldic artist, who had been hired to do the job, had to paint 7,000 of them.

Inside the car, all was ankle-deep in luxury. The upholstery was in gold brocade, the folding tables were made from Australian camphor wood, there was a cocktail bar, a tea cabinet, a sliding glass sunlight roof panel, and radio (in the royal manner) embedded in the arm rests. All told, £8,500 was spent on the production. Throughout the period of construction, strict security was maintained at the Hooper works, for fear lest some rival organisation might pirate the idea. It would seem to have been unlikely, but, one supposes, you cannot be too careful.

At the following year's Motor Show, there was another Lady Docker 'special'. This time, the theme was referred to as 'Blue Clover'. The dashboard, steering wheel and upholstery were all done up in lizard skin. The outside of the car, which was a sports model, was painted in powder blue, 'dappled', as Lady Docker has described it, 'with clover leaves'.

And so it went on, through 'Stardust' in 1953 (silver stars on dark blue bodywork, chromium fittings and a crocodile interior), 'Silver Flash' in 1954 (dark green exterior: the interior trim in scarlet crocodile), to 'Golden Zebra' in 1955. This was Her Ladyship's last aesthetic coup, and she really let herself go. The basis was a cream and gold fixed-head sports car. The dashboard was made from real ivory: there was the inevitable cocktail cabinet, a vanity box, a built-in picnic basket, and a collapsible umbrella with an ivory handle. Lady Docker's initials were painted in gold on the door: the upholstery was genuine zebra skin, and there was a gold model of a zebra on the bonnet.

Altogether, it was a magnificent finale to the series, and well worthy of the evening dress which, that year, its creator had worn at a New Year's Eve ball. Costing £1,000, it took three weeks to make and had all the Daimler cars, drawn to scale, embroidered on it.

If the Docker Daimlers attracted attention, the motor vehicles of Nubar Gulbenkian were scarcely less spectacular. Mr. Gulbenkian has been described by the director of a coachwork firm with whom he did business as 'one of the world's gentlemen. He was not so much a hard bargainer as someone who wanted a fair return on his money. You named the price: if he agreed to it, that was that. There was no question about right or wrong.'

He himself once told a B.B.C. interviewer that 'I like to act naturally; it's so much easier than putting on an act. I am an Armenian, you know.' The observation was made after the broadcaster had asked him why he always wore an orchid in his buttonhole when he went hunting.

Between them, Mr. Gulbenkian and his wife owned a succession of Rolls-Royces, and at least one of them produced a designer's nightmare. It had a sedanca de ville body (i.e. a sliding roof over the chauffeur's compartment), which was all very well until somebody—Mr. Gulbenkian—had the idea that it would be nice if the roof could be opened and closed at the touch of a switch. In the end, using a complex system of electric motors and after goodness knows how many problems, Panelcraft (the firm of coachbuilders entrusted with the job) made it work. 'But,' as one of their partners told me, 'I don't think we'd ever take on another electrically operated sedanca roof. It involved so much work and was very difficult.'

Far more famous than his Rolls-Royces, however, were the Gulbenkian taxis. The idea stemmed from his dissatisfaction with the London cab services, which he found uneconomical and uncomfortable. Consequently, he decided to have one of his own. The basic idea was to take an ordinary London cab and to have it transformed, as nearly as possible, into the kind of vehicle that Rolls-Royce might have built.

The original drawings were produced by that doyen of London

Rolls-Royce dealers, Jack Barclay, who was also charged with the task of procuring a suitable cab to work on. This was not easy, for Gulbenkian insisted that it should have a petrol engine (on the grounds that it was quieter than the diesel version) and, if possible, an automatic gear change.

Eventually, a petrol-engine cab was located, though the automatic gearbox was impossible. It was handed over to Panelcraft, where the existing body was removed, and the painstaking task of building the new, and rather more luxurious, version began. Unlike any orthodox London taxi, it had twin headlamps, an entirely new radiator and wings, and a most elegant body done up in basketwork at the rear. Carriage lamps, which also served as parking lights, were fitted to the sides. The sedanca roof was manually operated, but all the windows and the division between front and rear compartments went up and down electrically. The interior featured black woodwork with a brass inlay at the back. There was no car radio.

The first of the Gulbenkian taxis was commissioned in 1957, and was eventually sold to a man in Chicago who runs a replica of an English pub. It was good, he said, for publicising the business.

In 1965, Panelcraft built a second Gulbenkian taxi. It was very much like the first, except that it had a raised windscreen and, instead of basketwork, the body at the rear was done up in dark green and black stripes.

All told, Panelcraft produced three of these vehicles. The third was commissioned by a visiting American woman, who had seen Gulbenkian's parked in the street and wanted to possess one like it.

The great, the *classical*, millionaires of the Scott Fitzgerald period liked their wives' diamonds to be as big as the Ritz, their homes as huge and well furnished as palaces, and their cars to be sumptuous conveyances for their expensively nourished bodies. Whether the chief executive of today has similar views is, perhaps, doubtful. In an egalitarian society they cannot, or dare not, any longer flaunt their possessions, and it seems to be almost a mark of shame to own a Rolls-Royce.

Of course Howard Hughes had his own Boeing 707 aircraft; and Hugh Hefner, the circular-bed-bound monarch of *Playboy*, owns a DC–9; and Conrad Hilton commutes from one of his hotels to another in a £430,000 Hawker Siddeley HS 125; and

Bernie Cornfeld has (or had—I am not sure about the current form) a BAC 1-11. Oh yes. Indeed. But what goes for these gentlemen does not necessarily go for the heads of public corporations. It is, as a matter of fact, rather difficult to find out what, precisely, *does* go for them. During the research for this book, I mailed a questionnaire to the heads of some of the world's largest companies, asking for a few details about their cars and their motoring likes and dislikes. A number never replied at all. Several sent in polite refusals signed by their public relations officers, and five of them provided the information that I asked for.

Some of the refusals were interesting. A spokesman for a tobacco company told me that he doubted whether his chief executive was interested in motoring at all, which was, perhaps, understandable. One could not help, on the other hand, being a little surprised to learn that the head of a giant oil company 'has no special interest in motoring'. Nor was I entirely satisfied with the letter from a large firm of chain stores, in which an executive told me: 'I am sure you will appreciate that we do receive a very great number of similar requests concerning members of our Board.' This I felt inclined to doubt.

However, I can report that Sir David Barran, head of Shell Transport and Trading, uses a 1969 Daimler limousine in which he covers about 10,000 miles in an average year. The most memorable car he has ever driven was a 1930 MG belonging to a friend at Cambridge ('I found myself doing 92 m.p.h. and have been frightened of the thought ever since'), and he considers that the greatest virtue a chauffeur can possess is patience ('not pushing into traffic in an offensive manner because he is driving an important person in a big car. Sense of humour. Tolerance of other car drivers').

Mr. R. P. Dobson, chairman of British-American Tobacco Co. Ltd., uses a Jaguar Mk VIII for business—has a Jaguar XJ6 and a Mini-Clubman for domestic purposes, and enjoys driving. He learnt the art back in 1928, using a Clément-Bayard of 1913 vintage, and does not employ a personal chauffeur.

Hugh Hefner began his motoring in a second-hand Studebaker and now owns a 300 SL Mercedes and a Mercedes-Benz 600 Limousine. It gives him satisfaction to possess examples of the finest cars in the world, but, he says, 'much less than the satisfaction of owning the world's finest private aeroplane'. He never makes long journeys by automobile and rarely drives himself.

Mr. Edwin R. Nixon is managing director of I.B.M. United Kingdom Ltd. For business, he uses a chauffeur-driven Jaguar 420G (1970 model). For domestic motoring he owns a Jaguar 420 (1968 vintage) and his wife has a Triumph Herald 13/60. He drives himself to and from his London office, enjoys it, and likes listening to classical music on the radio. He considers that, under present-day conditions, travelling by car is an added strain to anyone responsible for running a large company, and believes that a chauffeur should be a 'good driver; have an intimate knowledge of London; be a good map reader; be a presentable, timely and reliable person; and must be acceptable to his employer's wife and family'.

Finally: Professor Lotz, head of Volkswagen. Predictably, all the vehicles he drives come from his own factory; he does not use them for long journeys; and he does not enjoy the sensation of speed (a point on which Sir David Barran of Shell agrees with him. Sir David wrote: 'I like to get quickly to my destination, but dislike feeling that it is being done fast').

On, admittedly, rather slender evidence, one came to the conclusion that heads of industries mostly use their firms' cars, just as some of them use their firms' aeroplanes, and that a personal Rolls-Royce is a relative rarity. Indeed, one informant told me that 'if you *must* have something like that, it is better to have a Bentley. It is less ostentatious.' Lord Cole, who is chairman of Rolls-Royce (1971) Ltd., uses one of his cars, but then you might expect him to. Perhaps the rot, at any rate in Britain, really began during the 1956 crisis in the Middle East. As the result of the closure of the Suez Canal, petrol rationing had to be introduced in the U.K. To reduce the consumption of motor spirit, quite a number of exalted business men kept their big cars in their garages, and used small things such as the Austin A30. Several of them enjoyed the experience so much, that they continued to use them after the trouble was over.

Certainly I could find no examples of car love on the scale of that experienced, many years ago, by the head of a German export-import firm. The gentleman was named Wilhelm Eilers and his business was at Bremen. In the summer of 1939, he bought one of the last Maybachs ever to be built. When war broke out, he realised that the German Army was about to requisition all such vehicles for use as staff cars. Herr Eilers, although he was no doubt a patriotic German, just couldn't bear the idea of being parted from his new acquisition, and so he had the vehicle walled-up in his factory. It remained there until 1949. Afterwards, he used it for touring southern Germany, Austria and Switzerland. In 1963, it was sold to the well-known German motoring writer Richard von Frankenberg. Nowadays, it can be seen in a motoring museum at Langenburg.

From the profane to the sacred in motoring is less distance than it is in many other activities. The first Pope to have a car was Pius XI. Sometime during the mid-'twenties he bought a Graham-Paige which remained in service at the Vatican until 1930. It was replaced by an Isotta Fraschini; and, in that year, a Fiat 525 and a Mercedes were also acquired. Another Mercedes was purchased in 1937, and subsequent Holy Fathers have been driven in Cadillacs, Chryslers, an Alfa Romeo, Lincolns, a Citroën DS 19, a Fiat 1800, and more Mercedes.

The Mercedes of 1930 was painted in purple, which gave it a rather pleasing suggestion of antiquity. The Pope's seat, as in all later Vatican cars, was an armchair mounted in the centre of the rear compartment. A special roof was fitted to enable His Holiness to get in and out of the car without having to bend down. By no means the least of the design problems was that of coping with his voluminous robes.

Nowadays, the Pope normally uses a Mercedes 300/SEL, though he also has a Mercedes 300/SE and a Mercedes 600 available. They are all drophead coupés and feature the central armchair at the back. The rear compartments are also fitted with revolving seats, which are usually facing His Holiness and on which members of his staff travel.

The Pope seldom makes long journeys by car. During an average year he only travels about 800 miles by this method. Indeed, the longest motor trip ever made by the present Pope was on Christmas Eve, 1966, when he went to Florence and back without an overnight stop. The distance was 344 miles. The Mercedes 300/SEL was used and the Pope was accompanied by his chauffeur, his special secretary, and the head of the Vatican transport office—who also performed the function of a courier.

Above: *President Kennedy at the moment of his assassination.*
Below: *seconds later, as Mrs. Kennedy leans over her husband and a member of the Secret Service detail climbs on board.*

Famous between-wars hurdler, the Marquess of Exeter, has replaced the 'winged lady' on his Rolls-Royce with an artificial hip-joint. The joint, in a more functional capacity, served His Lordship faithfully for many years. Photo by courtesy Jon Whitbourne. Photo by courtesy Jon Whitbourne.

Princess Anne received her Scimitar as a joint Christmas and 20th birthday present from her parents and the Prince of Wales.

H.M. the Queen and Prince Philip on one of their less formal motoring occasions. The Passenger on the rear seat is a detective.

After over fifty years of Daimlers, the present Royal Family went over to Rolls-Royces. This picture was taken during a state visit to Ethiopia in 1965. For her private motoring, the Queen uses a 3·5-litre Rover.

The car of the United States President is a specially constructed Lincoln Continental Executive Limousine. Platform at the back is for members of the President's Secret Service detail. The centre section of the roof is hinged and can be folded back. It enables the occupants of the passenger compartment to stand up during parades.

All told, the Vatican's present fleet of vehicles amounts to 147. It includes fifty-four cars, twenty-six mail vans, twenty-three lorries, sixteen buses and so on down to two mobile cranes and one road-sweeping truck.

No Pope has been able to drive, though the present incumbent enjoys motoring and, when he was a Cardinal in Milan back in 1955, he once attended a motor race.

The Citroën DS 19 in the Vatican garage was a present from the French car manufacturers to Pope John XXIII on his seventy-eighth birthday. It was painted in what its makers describe as 'prestige black'. Other celebrated Citroën owners include the President of Algeria (who has had one since 1964), the President of Madagascar (in May, 1970, a shooting brake-type ambulance was flown out for his personal use after an operation), and the King of Morocco (he bought a 1970 5 DA–21 'Pallas').

The late Dr. Duvalier, former President of Haiti, was also a Citroën owner. In an attempt to ensure that the only menace to his life was his somewhat imperfect health, the government ordered an armour-plated version. The manufacturers were compelled to reply that, if this were done, the extra weight would reduce the car's top speed to 25 m.p.h. In the end, they compromised. The car was *not* armour-plated, but it was fitted with bullet-proof tyres, and a special radio was installed.

Contrary to a number of rumours, President de Gaulle's Citroën (it is now used by his successor) was not armoured—possibly for the same reason that Dr. Duvallier's had to forgo this precaution—or perhaps because de Gaulle, who never suffered from an inferiority complex, believed himself to be indestructible. At all events, it was a stretched version of the DS 21, painted in grey and silver, air-conditioned, and fitted with radio and an internal telephone system between the front and rear compartments. The windows were all electrically operated, and the radio aerial went up or down by the same method.

The chauffeur and an aide travelled in front. The seat at the rear was normally used to accommodate two, though the arm rest could be raised to fit three in. There was a jump seat for an interpreter, which was used when the late President entertained a foreign guest.

But perhaps the finest feature of the presidential Citroën was its stopping power. Once, when driving through a storm at night, the headlamps suddenly picked up a large tree which had been blown across the road. The driver jammed on his brakes, and the car came to a rapid and obedient halt. The President lived to make another speech, and the much vaunted road-holding ability of this fine car was seen to be every bit as good as its manufacturers had said it was.

19 Top People

One day during the declining years of the last century, the Hon. John Scott-Montagu, who was Member of Parliament for the New Forest, arrived at the House of Commons in his electric carriage. Members were in the habit of parking their coaches and horses in the palace yard, and Scott-Montagu saw no reason why he should not leave his automobile there. The policeman on duty, however, thought differently. Uncompromising as a 'no waiting' sign, stolid as only a law enforcement agent can be, he blocked the way.

'I'm sorry, sir,' he said. 'You can't bring that thing in here.'

The Hon. John Scott-Montagu was not to be put off so easily. Obviously argument with the policeman would get him nowhere, and so he sought the help of the Speaker of the House. After a good deal of discussion, he was allowed to bring his vehicle into the yard. A precedent was established, but it shows how suspiciously motor cars were regarded in those days.

When Parliament is in session nowadays, the palace yard is packed with cars, and members have their own motor club. For a modest sum of money, anyone belonging to the House of Commons Motor Club can purchase a red perspex badge to mount on his windscreen, a key fob and a tie. The present chairman is Sir Gerald Nabarro, Conservative M.P. for Worcestershire

South, resident of a picturesque village in the Cotswolds, and owner of the most luxuriant handlebar moustache to have been seen in the mother of Parliaments for many a year.

One of Sir Gerald's hobbies is collecting number-plates for his cars. About eighteen years ago, he noticed that several new vehicles were appearing in the town of Kidderminster with the letters LAB on their plates.

'Electorates,' he told me, 'being notoriously fickle and, in many instances, shallow, and, in some cases, highly unintelligent, I observed to my political agent that all the LAB cars running around might prompt people to believe that Labour was going to win the next election, and that it had more support among the electorate than the Conservatives did.

'He laughed and shrugged it off; but, going home that night, I kept thinking to myself: "Well, if it is LAB now, it must be MAB soon, and, after that, it must be NAB. So I rang up the chairman of my Conservatives in Kidderminster, and I said to him: "Is it true that NAB is going to come on to the scene soon?", and he said: "Yes—I should think in about four or five months from now." So I said: "Well—could you please get NAB1 for myself and NAB2 for my wife?" He said: "Yes—I will indeed, but you will have to place an order for two new motor cars." As I was about to replace my own car and my wife's, I ordered an Armstrong Siddley Sapphire and a Morris 8, and these were duly numbered NAB1 and NAB2.'

Nowadays, Sir Gerald has NAB1 to NAB8 inclusive and also NAB10. NAB9 is missing. It used to be on a moped but, as he told me, 'some damn fool tore up the registration book ten or twelve years ago'.

The House of Commons Motor Club looks after its members' interests. For countless years Members of Parliament have received first-class rail warrants for commuting between their homes and Parliament. If they preferred to travel by car, that was their affair. No allowances were provided for this purpose.

But when, in an attempt to make Britain's railways more profitable, a number of lines were closed down, members became increasingly dependent on their vehicles, and it seemed only reasonable that they should have some sort of a mileage allowance.

When it was introduced in 1963, it was established at $4\frac{1}{2}$d. a mile, which was better than nothing but certainly not generous.

When Sir Gerald became chairman of the club in 1966, one of his first actions was to campaign for an improvement. It took him three years, but eventually, in 1969, it was raised to 6d. a mile. This was better, but still unrealistic. In the following year, with some figures provided by the Automobile Association to help him, he managed to raise it to one shilling a mile. This, according to the A.A.'s statistics, was the cost of running a Mini.

Among the club's other services is that of advising on taxation allowances in so far as they affect its members' motoring, and to secure bulk insurance for their cars. The club is run in conjunction with the R.A.C., which provides a treasurer. Out of the 630 members of the House of Commons, about 400 belong to it.

When David Lloyd George was Prime Minister of Britain during the first world war, he went about the nation's business in a Rolls-Royce. Afterwards, he seems to have remained loyal to the brand, for one of his later vehicles was a Phantom III, built in 1930. Among the special features was a stool, which could be raised from the floor, and a drinks cabinet. Perhaps the two were interconnected, for the purpose of the stool was to support the famous politician's leg when he was suffering from one of his attacks of gout.

Sir Winston Churchill owned many cars. Latterly, they included a 1964 Morris Oxford, a 1955 Humber Hawk shooting brake, and an Austin 10. The last of these had been purchased new in 1938 for £172 10s. od, and Sir Winston seems to have been particularly fond of it. In 1948, when he was away from home, Lady Churchill sold it and bought a Hillman in its place. When he heard the news, he was upset and asked his wife whether she would try to buy it back. She succeeded, but only after she had agreed to pay double the price she had received for it. When, after Sir Winston's death, it was put up for sale at Sotheby's, it fetched £1,350.

The cars of present-day cabinet ministers are provided by the Government Car Service, which comes under the Department of the Environment. The Prime Minister has a 3½-litre Rover allocated to him. The department's chief transport officer told me that 'there is a tendency to avoid ostentation in a Prime Minister's car. He must have something good and solid—something out of which you get your money's worth. It is, after all, paid for by the government and comes out of taxes.'

All members of the Cabinet with the exception of the Home Secretary (who is driven by a policeman) and the Defence Secretary (who has an Army driver), have vehicles and chauffeurs allocated by the car service for their exclusive use. They are only available for public duties, and cannot be used for campaigning purposes during a general election. The Prime Minister is allowed to use his for private motoring, but he must pay for it at the rate of so much a mile.

When Harold Wilson was Premier, his driver was a man named William Housden. Mr Housden had originally been allocated to Mr. Wilson in 1947, when the latter was President of the Board of Trade. When the Conservatives were returned to power, he drove Harold Macmillan during his period as Minister of Housing and, afterwards, throughout his seven years as Premier. He re-joined Mr. Wilson in 1964, after a short spell with Selwyn Lloyd, who was Lord Privy Seal at the time.

It is by no means uncommon for a minister to ask for a particular individual as his driver. As Mr. Housden told me: 'If he has had somebody in a previous existence, he sometimes asks: "Can I have that man who drove me before?" A driver gets to know what his boss's likes and dislikes are. He gets to know whether he's punctual or not, and so on. He gets to know the foibles of a minister.'

The Prime Minister's car is, in most respects, pretty standard. It has a white recognition light mounted up front, but, otherwise, it would be difficult to tell it from any other $3\frac{1}{2}$-litre Rover. Nor is it accorded any privileges by the police. If a driver contravenes the traffic regulations he is, as Housden put it, 'on his own'. Similarly, if he cannot find a parking meter free in a big town, he has to do the best he can—even if it means leaving the car five miles down the road.

But there does seem to be some sort of special relationship between a minister and his chauffeur. The latter must know what action to take under any given set of circumstances. If, for example, the minister is liable to be late for a meeting—should he speed up, or won't it matter if they are five minutes behind schedule?

'You have,' Housden told me, 'to be a psychologist. You have to know when he likes to talk, and when he wants to be quiet. He never tells you—you just have to sense it. This awareness comes with time. It's really a sort of sixth sense.'

Do they ever discuss politics? 'Once or twice,' he said, 'I've given my opinion. I've said: "I don't quite understand why this or that is being done." You become interested in politics. Twenty-four years ago, when I first joined the car service, I knew nothing about them. Now I think I'm something of an authority. After all, if *I* don't understand something, the chances are that millions of others won't. I suppose in a way we sometimes act as a sounding board—a sort of guinea-pig.'

The Prime Minister's car used to rely on the Automobile Association's radio network for urgent messages, but nowadays the vehicle is equipped with a radio telephone. It also has an ordinary wireless set. Prime Ministers, according to Housden, 'are great ones for the news. Mr. Macmillan liked music on a journey and Mr. Wilson was fond of it, too. But they didn't want any chat. They became annoyed when the disc jockeys broke in.'

Wilson liked to sit in the back. His detective[1] sat beside the driver, and the other seat at the rear was usually occupied either by Mrs. Wilson, or else by his secretary. Macmillan, on the other hand, preferred to sit in front once they were out of London, and the Scotland Yard man sat on the back seat.

There are times when a good deal of highly confidential conversation is conducted at the back. A Prime Minister's chauffeur must, above everything, be discreet, but this doesn't seem to pose any great problem. As Housden said: 'You don't hear what's said in the back unless you want to. Most of us agree that the less we know, the better it is. In any case, you have to concentrate on your driving. Once or twice, someone has said "Bill . . . Bill!", but I haven't heard a thing. You have to concentrate one hundred per cent.'

The Prime Minister's driver has a room at his disposal at Number Ten Downing Street and another at the official country house at Chequers in Buckinghamshire (it was presented to the nation by Lord and Lady Lee in 1917 as a country seat for premiers. Along with the house went an endowment fund of £100,000 for its upkeep). The journey from London to Chequers gives the Prime Minister a chance to unwind, an opportunity to shed the stress of office for a few hours until the inevitable red boxes containing official documents arrive. He seems to be at his most

[1] The Foreign Secretary and the Home Secretary are the only other cabinet ministers to be provided with a detective.

relaxed on these occasions, glad to get away, even if very briefly, from the nation's business.

For the driver, there is less relaxation. He is responsible for cleaning his vehicle, inside and out: for ensuring that it is serviced regularly, and for carrying out daily inspections of the tyres and the oil and water levels. In the car service's new establishment in central London, an automatic wash is provided, but the vehicle still has to be leathered off afterwards.

Thanks, no doubt, to high standards of maintenance, William Housden's twenty-four years of driving the high and the mighty have been extremely free from trouble. The score of disaster adds up to two punctures and a battery failure. The latter occurred outside an hotel in London at 9.45 one evening. Mr. Macmillan had been at some function or other and had to be back in the House of Commons at 10.00 for a division. Housden was waiting outside to collect him when, without any warning, the battery packed up. The Premier had to take a taxi back to the House. To make sure that such a situation should never recur, the Prime Minister's car has since been equipped with a reserve battery. A trickle charger is incorporated in the system to keep the second battery charged up. An auxiliary petrol pump has also been installed.

They used to say that no man was a hero to his valet. Whilst the feelings of Prime Ministers' chauffeurs may stop some way short of the fanatical devotion that Hitler's man felt for his master, it seems to be a pleasant relationship based on mutual respect. William Housden served Harold Macmillan for twelve and a half years, which is the longest period that any driver has ever been with one particular minister. Afterwards, he was rewarded with an M.B.E.

When Harold Wilson's premiership came to an end, he presented Housden with a pair of superb tobacco pipes. That, perhaps, was not surprising. William Housden enjoys a pipe and, outside the Chamber of the House (where smoking is forbidden), Mr. Wilson smokes one almost incessantly. When he was Prime Minister, his car was equipped with a specially large ashtray to cope with the voluminous amount of ash.

The cars for the defence ministers and the heads of the services are supplied by 20 Squadron of the Royal Transport Corps, which is accommodated in an old barracks, dating back to the Crimean War, in north-west London. As with the Government Car Service, there is a system of priorities. The heads of staff and the defence ministers have what are known as 'allocated' cars and drivers. In other words, each one has a particular vehicle and an individual chauffeur set aside permanently for his use. Slightly lesser mortals have what are known as 'first call' cars. This means that they can have a vehicle at any time, though it may not always be the same one, and the driver will be whoever is available. Below this level, officers in need of transport have to trust their luck.

The lists are drawn up by the Permanent Under-Secretary at the ministry and, I was told, 'You have to put up a jolly good case to get on to them.'

A system of grading is also applied to the cars. Grade I vehicles are restricted to the heads of services and the ministers. The former have Daimlers and the latter used to have them. When Harold Wilson adopted the 3½-litre Rover as the chief executive's car, however, it produced complications. Clearly it would have been wrong for two of his ministers to travel around in what might have been regarded as superior vehicles. Consequently they, too, were issued with Rovers—which, in the automobile hierarchy of 20 Squadron, is really a Grade II car (as supplied to 'three-star' ranks such as lieutenant-generals, air marshals and vice-admirals).

When the late Admiral Sir Michael Le Fanu was Chief of Naval Staff at the Admiralty, he, too, used a Rover; but that was because Lady Le Fanu was disabled, and found it difficult to get in and out of the Daimler.

In any case, the Admiralty is, in some respects, a world of its own. Whilst the senior officers of the Army and Air Force are driven by sergeants (or, at a pinch, by corporals), the senior naval officers are piloted by civilian drivers. This dates back to the years before the Army took over responsibility for the transport of all three services in 1967, and when each made its own arrangements. Indeed, the Admiralty is rather reactionary in this respect. Traditionally, the First Sea Lord's car was always numbered 0001 RN. Under the more recent set-up, it became 543G19, but this was not acceptable to their Lordships. Consequently, it still carries 0001 RN on the outside, whilst its official number

o

plate is fitted underneath the bonnet. It once produced a delicate situation when the car was stopped by the police on a journey back from Windsor. The trouble, according to the law—which had not been told about this fine example of inter-service diplomacy— was that no such vehicle existed.

Like senior politicians, the heads of the services prefer to stick to one driver. As an officer of 20 Squadron told me: 'Normally, there is a tremendous rapport between senior officers and their drivers. So much depends on their characters. When a driver leaves, it's a problem finding a replacement. It's a question of temperament. It's no use leaving the general unhappy and having an unhappy driver on your hands. Driving a general needs a cer- tain approach, a lot of maturity. The driver must be pleasant and take a great pride in his job.'

And: 'The senior officers' drivers are mostly long-serving soldiers. It's a special job—in a way, they're an élite. They must be extremely good drivers, with high personal standards of turn- out and cleanliness at all times. They must have good manners and they must speak well.'

To earn its keep economically, an 'allocated' car ought to cover at least 1,000 miles a month. On the other hand, it can only be used on official business. Nor may money be spent on extra fittings to suit its user's taste.

'Whether or not it is in order to introduce modifications to a new car,' I was told, 'depends upon what's wanted. A reading lamp in the back is generally considered to be O.K. But if the officer wanted a cocktail cabinet installed behind the front seat, he'd be told, very politely, that he would have to pay for it himself. Everything has to be approved, even if it only amounts to drilling a hole in the body. Radios are generally considered to be reason- able; but, even here, it is better to stress the need to hear the news, than to say that you like listening to "Housewife's Choice". Cars are not fitted with radio sets as a matter of course: they have to be applied for.'

20 Squadron R.T.C. is also responsible for the Royal Baggage Train, which consists of half a dozen 25 cwt vans. They are normally employed on military duties, but are sometimes used to move the royal baggage when the Queen goes from one of her homes to another.

King George VI was the last British sovereign to order a Daimler. Nowadays, the royal fleet of cars is headed by four Rolls-Royces. Rolls-Royce I and Rolls-Royce II, which are used for state occasions, are known as the 'Canberras'. Or, when the roofs have been taken off, and the Queen is enclosed in a case of moulded Perspex, as the 'bubble-cars'. They are fitted with fluorescent lighting inside, have radio sets in the arm rests, and are powered by big V8 engines. During a procession, they mostly travel in second gear.

The Queen always sits behind the chauffeur on the right: a detective occupies the passenger seat in front. When the Queen is not on board, all the Rolls-Royces have conventional Rolls mascots. When she is travelling, she carries her personal mascot, which is made of silver and depicts a naked St. George riding a horse with a dead dragon at its feet. A version made from sugar was mounted on top of Her Majesty's wedding cake.

Rolls-Royce III is a landaulet which was acquired by the Queen in 1954, and Rolls-Royce IV is a Phantom IV limousine built by Mulliner. It was a wedding present from the Royal Air Force in 1950.

In addition to these very senior cars, the royal fleet includes two Austin Princesses, which are used on semi-formal occasions— such as visits to the theatre—four estate cars, two Land-Rovers and the Royal Family's personal cars. For ten years, the Queen had a dark green 3-litre Rover, which she had bought in March, 1961. In February, 1971, she replaced this with a new, 3½-litre Rover. Prince Philip has a dark green 1961 3-litre Alvis coupé. It replaced a Lagonda that he had purchased in 1954. Prince Charles has an Aston Martin DB9; and Princess Anne received a Reliant Scimitar as a joint Christmas and twentieth birthday present from her parents and the Prince of Wales.

The royal transport needs are handled with quiet efficiency by the staff of the Royal Mews at Buckingham Palace. In addition to the cars, this establishment is also responsible for the 30 carriage horses. The Crown Equerry, Lieutenant-Colonel J. M. Miller, c.v.o., d.s.o., m.c., who was formerly in the Welsh Guards, is in charge of the mews, which also houses fifty families. Among the staff, there are ten civilian drivers.

Normally, the head chauffeur or his deputy drives the Queen. They receive their instructions from programmes which are prepared by the private secretaries, and which are circulated to all the people concerned.

When making a trip, the Queen prefers to inconvenience people as little as possible. If a strict programme has to be followed —as, for example, on a journey to London Airport—Scotland Yard is warned beforehand. The traffic lights are adjusted to give the royal car a clear run through, and dangerous crossroads are manned by policemen. But, even on these occasions, over-zealous officers, who hold up the traffic for five minutes or so before the car is due, are frowned upon. There are no police outriders, no blaring sirens, and no question of indulging in such small motoring weaknesses as jumping the traffic lights.

When the Queen goes abroad, the host country normally provides transport. On visits to the Commonwealth, however, either Rolls-Royce I or Rolls-Royce II is usually taken. By removing the bumpers, the car can be accommodated in a special garage on board the Royal Yacht.

On the summer royal migration to Balmoral, the cars are driven up. A special train takes the staff and the luggage, and it was once considered whether, perhaps, to send the cars up by motor rail. It turned out to be expensive (the royal household keeps a tight rein on its budget) and, in any case, there was a possibility that the paintwork might become chipped.

The cars do relatively low mileages, and are kept for as long as possible. Running maintenance is carried out at the Royal Mews. Servicing and repairs are undertaken by the manufacturers. The vehicles are washed daily, and the rule is strictly that of the bucket and leather. Anything more violent might mar the pristine beauty of the paintwork.

For rougher and readier purposes, there are the two Land-Rovers, the two Ford Zodiac and two Vauxhall estate cars. One of the Land-Rovers is equipped for shooting: six guns can be carried on either side and there are ammunition boxes fitted up front. When it goes up on to the grouse moor, the loaders travel on board it. Prince Philip usually follows in the other.

These vehicles contrast strongly with the Daimler shooting brake which was ordered in 1936 and now lives in retirement in the Royal Mews. The metal was painted and grained until it looked like wood. There was room for six guns on the partition between the driver and the spacious rear compartment—and, at the back, there was a table which could be let down for meals on occasions when it was too wet to eat outside.

The shooting brakes bought by the royal household are standard models whenever possible. Sometimes, however, there isn't a large enough version available, and one gathers that this presents problems. They have to carry large loads of luggage, plus a chauffeur, plus a police officer, and it isn't easy to find one which is large enough and yet not too big.

At least twice, firms have produced special estate cars in attempts to suit the royal needs, and have offered them to the Queen. One filled the bill admirably. Another was fitted with a body which was too heavy for the engine.

Many of the facts about the Royal Family's motoring are predictable. Nevertheless, one comes away from the Royal Mews feeling faintly surprised. The establishment is conducted rather like a well-run business. Costs are take into consideration, and economies considered. Everything is carefully programmed: there is no fuss and not a great deal of ceremony. Heaven knows what one expects—but, whatever it is, it is not quite this.

20 The Presidential Passenger

According to legend, the only President of the United States of America to have been given a speeding ticket was Ulysses S. Grant. He cannot have been going very fast, for it happened in the early 1870's, and he was driving some sort of horse-drawn conveyance at the time.

Assuming that Grant did break the law, subsequent Presidents have had little opportunity to repeat the offence. John F. Kennedy, admittedly, drove himself occasionally when he and his family went down to their weekend retreat in Virginia, and Lyndon B. Johnson sometimes took the wheel when he was at his place in Texas. He may even have ventured on to public roads, driving from one ranch to another. But these excursions were made in remote areas and have little significance. As a general rule, the President never, ever, drives himself. That function is performed by a member of the United States Secret Service. Nor, even on a short trip, is the President's transport confined to one car. There is always a second, back-up vehicle, with Secret Service men on board for the protection of (as they call him) 'the Boss'.

The Secret Service became responsible for the President's safety after one of the first journeys (possibly *the* first) ever made by a First Citizen in an automobile. The date was September 6th, 1901. President McKinley was visiting the Pan American

Exposition at Buffalo, New York, when a man named Leon Czolgosz came up to shake him by the hand. What nobody knew was that Czolgosz had a .32 Iver Johnson revolver concealed beneath a handkerchief.

As McKinley held out his hand, Czolgosz shot the President dead. His body was taken to the Temple of Music, and thence, in an electrically driven ambulance, to a hospital in Buffalo.

McKinley was the third President to meet death at gunpoint. In 1865, the actor, John Wilkes Booth, shot Lincoln in his box at Ford's Theatre, Washington; and, in 1881, an embittered lawyer and unsuccessful politician named Charles J. Guiteau killed President James A. Garfield with a .44 calibre revolver.

After McKinley's assassination, seventeen bills concerning the protection of the President were put before Congress, but none of them was passed. Nevertheless, his successor, Theodore Roosevelt, was given a protective detail from the Secret Service (founded in 1865 to combat the counterfeiting of banknotes, which, at the time, accounted for about one-third of all the money in circulation).

McKinley was dead when he made that trip in an electric ambulance. Theodore Roosevelt was very much alive when, in 1907, he purchased a White steamer. This was probably the first car to be owned by a President of the United States—just as one of the last animals to be quartered in the White House stables was a mare belonging to Mrs. Roosevelt.

In 1909, William Howard Taft took over the presidency, and Taft was an automobile enthusiast. He seems to have inherited the White steamer, in which he was driven by his chauffeur, George Robinson. According to a contemporary report, 'he enjoyed settling back against the cushions and watching the landscape glide by. He enjoyed high speeds.' 'High speeds,' in this instance, were in the region of 40 m.p.h.

Taft presently bought a new White steamer and added a couple of Pierce-Arrows and a Baker electric to the White House fleet. In 1911, a new garage was built and all the cars plus, improbably, the White House cow (an amiable animal named Pauline, which Mrs. Taft purchased) were moved into it.

The Pierce-Arrow was the leading American 'prestige' car, and it provided the backbone of Woodrow Wilson's collection and that of his successor, Warren G. Harding. On his last birthday, which took place on December 28th, 1923, Wilson was given a Rolls-Royce. By then he was out of office, and cannot have made much use of it, for he died about six weeks later. Nevertheless, he should go on record as the only President of the United States, in or out of office, who has owned one of these vehicles.

Nowadays, the President uses a Lincoln, and there are all manner of theories about why this make ousted the Pierce-Arrow as the presidential car. According to some, the latter had outlived its usefulness. Certainly, it had been an excellent vehicle to get into if you happened to be wearing a top hat, and it was extremely comfortable. In 1923, however, sales began to decline, and the company had to re-think its policies. Even so, these fine cars were used by United States embassies overseas and by the heads of government departments in Washington—long after the President himself had switched over to the luxury product of the Ford plant.

Possibly it was a mixture of circumstances, and there were plenty to choose from. The Lincoln Motor Company had been founded in 1920 by Henry M. Leland who, seventeen years earlier, had designed the first Cadillac. By 1922, it was in financial difficulties, and a sitting duck for a take-over by Henry Ford and his son, Edsel.

Meanwhile, there had been a move to put up Henry Ford for President in the 1923 elections. At first, the automobile emperor wanted no part of it. But the idea developed rapidly, and even he could not ignore its potency. At one point *Collier's* magazine published the results of a poll which estimated that, if he stood for the presidency, he could expect an 8:5 lead over the reigning incumbent, Warren Gamaliel Harding. A New York insurance company offered a 400,000-dollar policy against Ford's election; business and professional men at Dearborn (the Ford headquarters) formed a 'Ford for President' organisation; and placards with the message 'We Want Henry' were printed. Hatbands bearing the same message were on sale at one dollar each.

Presently word got out that, if Henry Ford were elected, he would run the nation in much the manner in which he ran the Ford plant. One of his methods, it appeared, would be to go from department to department, finding out what everyone was up to.

And then, on August 2nd, 1923, Harding died. Vice-President Calvin Coolidge succeeded him automatically, and Ford pulled out of the fight. Indeed, he went further than that: he promised Coolidge his full support in the coming battle for votes.

Henry Ford and Calvin Coolidge were old friends. On a holiday in 1918, Ford and some of his closer acquaintances had called on Coolidge at his home in Plymouth, Vermont, and the politician had presented the automobile manufacturer with a four-gallon maple sap bucket, which had been manufactured by one of his ancestors in 1780.

In their book *Ford: Expansion and Challenge* (Charles Scribner's Sons), Allan Nevins and Frank Ernest Hill recall an occasion when Ford, Harvey Firestone, Thomas Edison and Calvin Coolidge went out for a drive. At some point, a noise developed in the front end of the car, and they stopped at a small-town garage. At first, the mechanic diagnosed a piston. But: 'No— I'm Henry Ford, and it isn't due to motor trouble.' He then suggested that it might be an ill-fitting tyre. 'No,' said the next voice, 'I'm Harvey Firestone, and the tyres are all right.' The mechanic then wondered whether it might be due to faulty wiring, but 'No,' said the third voice, 'I'm Thomas Edison, and the electric system is working fine.' 'Hmmm,' said the mechanic (according to one version of the story) 'Ford, Firestone, Edison! And I suppose you'll tell me that that little shrimp in the back is Calvin Coolidge!'

For whatever reason, Coolidge bought a Lincoln in 1923, and Lincolns have been the transport of most subsequent Presidents. Not that the Pierce Arrow went entirely out of favour: at the 1929 inauguration, Hoover and Coolidge were seen to be riding in a 1926 model.

Before coming to power, the Presidents shopped around for their cars. Eisenhower was something of a Cadillac fancier. Harry S. Truman bought a Chrysler Royal Club Coupé in 1940, and used it a great deal before he took office on the death of F. D. Roosevelt.

Mr. Truman's first car was a red 1910 Stafford convertible, which he purchased in 1913. He was always interested in motoring and when he became a member of the Jackson County, Missouri, Court (this is an administrative, not a judicial, appointment) he took a militant interest in better highways. One of his achieve-

P

ments was to float a large bond issue to build new roads for the county. In 1926, he became president of the National Old Roads Association.

Perhaps because of his particular interest in this subject, Truman is the only President who is known to have taken a trip in a member of that very fast, and no less exotic, family of Cords, Auburns and Duesenbergs. The year was 1960, and he was on a visit to a college at Lexington, Virginia. He was met at the railway station by a 1940 Duesenberg with an unusual history.

The car had originally been built for a German painter. The chassis was dispatched to Munich, where the body was to be built. Owing to the outbreak of war and his anti-Nazi feelings, the artist had to make a hurried exit from Germany. With admirable presence of mind and ingenuity, for it cannot have been easy, he managed to take the Duesenberg chassis with him.

Eventually, the two of them arrived in New York. The artist designed a highly individualistic body for the vehicle and the work was entrusted to a firm of coachbuilders. But the Duesenberg's frustrations were still far from over. The firm ran into a series of financial troubles, and two years went by before the job was finally completed.

Nowadays, the presidential cars are armoured and the drivers are provided by the Secret Service. Roosevelt was the last President to employ his own man—a veteran driver named Snyder, who had been in his master's employment when the latter was Governor of New York.

The first example of an armour-plated presidential car was probably an olive-grey Ford, which was put at Roosevelt's disposal when he, Churchill and Stalin met at Teheran in 1943. The idea that it might be a good idea to bullet-proof it appears to have occurred rather late in the day. The task was given to a young second lieutenant in the United States Army, who was stationed at Camp Mirabar. He had, his commanding officer told him, forty-eight hours in which to carry it out.

They worked day and night, and presently the car was ready. When they drove it to the airport to meet the President, however, they made a serious discovery. The body of the vehicle might be proof enough against bullets, but nothing had been done to equip the springs to cope with all the extra weight.

But everything was all right in the end. The President and an

207 The Presidential Passenger

aide sat in the back; the car completed its journey in good order; and nobody complained of any discomfort.

Deploying the presidential fleet of cars over the face of North America and, sometimes, the world; ensuring that, wherever he may be, there, too, will be his transport; all this is a substantial endeavour. Within the United States, the cars used to travel from one appointment to another by road. Since the President himself usually made the journey between cities by air, a lot of driving was involved and some of the schedules were very tight indeed.

And then the director of the United States Secret Service, James J. Rowley, read that a pair of Greyhound coaches had been transported by aircraft to the South Pole. If that was possible, he decided, there was certainly no reason why the more illustrious but very much smaller, presidential cars should not also hop from one assignment to another by this method.

When, after the last war, Winston Churchill went to Fulton, Missouri, with President Truman to deliver the speech in which he gave the world the expression 'Iron Curtain', he and the President travelled in a Lincoln which was known as 'the Sunshine Special'. It had been built for President Roosevelt in 1939 and was in use for eleven years. During this period, it covered about 55,000 miles. It was taken to many different parts of the world and, according to its manufacturers, 'probably carried more celebrities than any other car'. When it was retired from service in 1950, it was only because of its outdated appearance. Mechanically, it was still perfect.

At the same time as 'the Sunshine Special' was replaced, a number of other vehicles in the fleet also went on to the pension list. They were replaced by a series of oversized 1950 Lincolns. Among them was one which, in 1954, was returned to Dearborn to have its roof drastically altered.

The idea was President Eisenhower's. Convertibles were all very well in fine weather, but when it rained, and the roof had to be put up, the President was rendered almost invisible. To overcome this snag, Eisenhower had the notion that a plexiglass roof should be fitted.

As a result of this transformation, the car became known as the 'Bubbletop'. Before it was taken off the active list in March, 1961, it logged over 100,000 driving miles, travelled about

50,000 by air, and nobody knows how many by ship. It was called back into service temporarily for President Kennedy's European tour of 1963. Among those who travelled in it were the Queen and Prince Philip, Nikita Khrushchev, Charles de Gaulle and Winston Churchill.

In the spring of 1961, a new Lincoln was delivered to the White House. It was finished in navy blue, and, like the 'Bubble-top', had a plexi-glass enclosure over the rear compartment. It was equipped with hydraulically operated running boards which, at the flick of a switch on the dashboard, could be swung down to enable Secret Service men to travel on the sides. According to William Manchester in his *The Death of a President* (Michael Joseph Ltd.), the 'design of them was faulty. Jutting out, they became lethal; they would have turned bystanders into casualties, so they were never used'.

It was this car which, on November 21st, 1963, came to Dallas, Texas, and in which, at 1.30 p.m. on the following day, President John F. Kennedy was sitting when, from a warehouse overlooking the motorcade's route, Lee Harvey Oswald regarded the President through a telescopic sight and shot him dead.

After the assassination, the car was entirely rebuilt on President Johnson's instructions. It is still in the White House fleet, and, on the last reckoning, had covered 50,000 miles on land and had been flown over one million miles. It is still in good condition.

The latest presidential Lincoln was handed over to the White House towards the end of 1968. It was developed jointly by the Secret Service, the Lincoln Mercury engineers, and the custom car building firm, Lehmann-Peterson Inc. The engine is a 4½-litre V8 unit, producing 340 h.p.: it is 21½ feet long, seats six comfortably in the back, has a glass enclosure over the passenger compartment, and is packed with refinements for the security and greater comfort of its occupants.

For example, there are: separate heating and air-conditioning units for the front and rear compartments; twin two-way communication systems; a detachable black vinyl cover that can be fitted over the glass roof; a public-address system; a centre section of the roof which is hinged, and can be opened—thereby enabling people in the rear compartment to stand up during parades; a radio set built into the right arm rest at the back; a radio telephone; reading lamps; a 40-watt flourescent light; reflective aluminium fabric covers, which can be placed over the glass roof when the car is standing and which, therefore, prevent the rear compartment from becoming too hot; seats covered in a silver-grey pinstripe cloth, and a silver 'mouton' carpet; a special compressor for the air-conditioning system, which ensures that it works efficiently at low speeds; armour-plating and bullet-proof glass; and a rear bumper which folds down to serve as a platform for Secret Service agents, *plus* an hydraulically adjustable handrail at the rear of the car to enable them to hang on. When the President is travelling in it, he flies the flag of the United States from the right fender and the President's standard from the left. At night, both flags are illuminated by three miniature searchlights mounted on each fender.

According to the blurb about it, 'the basic vehicle is essentially the same as the Lincoln Continental executive limousine built by Lehmann-Peterson Inc. from regular production Lincoln Continental four-door sedans'. The resemblance certainly does not go any further.

The headquarters of the United States Secret Service is located in a large office block in mid-town Washington. It is situated on the eighth floor, and is one of a number of firms and government agencies which inhabit the building. Perhaps the most surprising thing about it is that it seems to be so *un*-secret. There is no difficulty in finding it: its name is up on the board in the lobby, just like those of its less security-minded neighbours. The reception area is pleasantly furnished: there is thick carpet on the floor, subdued lighting and rather elegant furniture. Admittedly the receptionist, who sits at a desk flanked on either side by the flag of the United States, looks as if he could eat broken glass for breakfast without suffering dyspeptic twinges, but he is amiable and politely asks you to be seated.

In the hinterland, the place seems to be inhabited by nice, friendly people, who are very helpful. They ask you to forgive the overcrowded offices and say that everything will be all right— once they've finished reorganising. They drink a great many cups of coffee, and discuss their work with animation and a good deal of pride.

Perhaps the first thing one has to remember is that the Secret Service, in spite of its name, is not a cloak-and-dagger organisation So far as the United States are concerned, that role is played by the C.I.A. and the Defence Intelligence Agency. The original task of the Secret Service was to contain the alarming amount of counterfeit currency which was making a mockery of the American money market. This accounts for the fact that it is a department of the U.S. Treasury, and it is still one of the service's prime functions. The other is the safety of the United States Presidents.

Members of the White House staff do not receive protection from the Secret Service; but, nevertheless, the list of responsibilities is formidable. Apart from the President and his family, it includes the Vice-President, past Presidents—their widows (unless they re-marry) and their children under the age of sixteen and, since the assassination of Senator Robert Kennedy in 1968, major presidential and vice-presidential candidates at elections. The safety of the Secretary of the Treasury is also their concern, but no other cabinet minister is included on the list. They are, however, responsible for the protection of foreign dignitaries when they visit the U.S.A.

The job of providing this security is continuous. The agents work three shifts in every twenty-four hours, and they move round a shift each week. For example, a man might be employed on the 4 p.m. to midnight detail one week. The next, he will come on duty at midnight; and, on the third week, his duties will begin at 8 a.m.

The agents detailed to guard the President have received special training, but this doesn't mean to say they are not employed on the service's other duties. It is perfectly possible for a man to be tracking down a counterfeit bond ring in week 'A', and to be checking in for duty at the White House at the start of week 'B'. They are, you might say, interchangeable.

According to a recruiting pamphlet, a candidate for the job of a special agent needs to be at least twenty-one. He must 'have successfully completed four years of college-level study in any major field. However, courses in police science, police administration, criminology, and law enforcement are desirable.' He must be able to pass a reasonably tough medical exam: must have at least 20/20 distant vision in one eye and no less than 20/30 in the other, and his weight must be in proportion to his height. Among other factors on which he will be rated are his 'ability to speak logically and effectively' and 'to adapt easily to group situations'.

The pay is adequate but not sensational: free uniform is provided, and a clothing allowance compensates for any damage incurred in the line of duty. 'The agents,' I was told, 'dress in clothes commensurate with the function. If it's a black tie occasion, they will wear that, and so on.' The allowance, I gathered, is intended to reimburse them against the ravages of flying eggs and ripped cloth, and not to set them up with new wardrobes. On the other hand, an assistant to the director told me, 'if they have to rent a tuxedo, they are reimbursed'.

Many of the agents have college degrees and, in theory, it would be possible to join the service after graduating. In practice, few do. Some have worked in one of the other federal law-enforcement agencies. A number have been in one or another of the armed forces, and a few are lawyers. They receive 'on the job' instruction, plus courses at various schools including six weeks at the Secret Service's own college. 'It takes,' I was told, 'three years to train an agent to work completely on his own in all facets.'

Responsibility for the President's cars comes under the transportation section, and a number of agents receive special training in all branches of driving. To evaluate the skills of these men, the Ford Motor Company's Highway Systems Research produced a special test vehicle, which measures such factors as driver performance and stress, and then works out how the one affects the other.

The car is driven by the agents on busy, fast-moving, expressways. Instruments record movements of the steering wheel, the brake pedal and the accelerator, and the driver's heartbeat is also measured.

Afterwards, a computer relates the findings, and the agent is given an assessment of his performance and how he compares with other drivers. All this enables him to correct his mistakes and improve his technique. It is particularly valuable since, being on twenty-four-hour call, the agents do not have time to go back to driving school for refresher courses.

According to one driver, the biggest hazards are 'other drivers. We label them inexperienced drivers, inattentive drivers, and those with a poor safety aptitude. Also we believe that many vehicles are in poor, unsafe condition. And many highways are not engineered for the amount of traffic they carry.'

In addition to this, there are such occupational hazards as the occasion when somebody threw paint at the presidential car. It completely covered the windscreen and reduced visibility to the barest minimum.

There is, of course, more to training than, simply, practising the handling of a vehicle. Security exercises used to be carried out at a national park on the edge of Washington. Now, the Secret Service has its own centre, where live ammunition can be used.

Ideally, the protective details like to plan their assignments well ahead of an event. One of the first actions is to send off an advance guard to arrange accommodation for the agents. Then, working as a team, they plan what they describe as 'protection in depth'.

Sometimes, they have two weeks—or even longer—to spend on preparations. At others, it may be considerably less. One of their more difficult assignments is that of protecting the President at a funeral. The time available for the reconnaissance is cut to a minimum. 'Death,' as one agent said to me, 'has no announcement.'

Within the United States, this part of the operation is assisted by the service's sixty-five field officers who are located in major cities and have a wealth of local knowledge. The scale of operations naturally varies, and 'security must be placed in accordance with the situation. For example, a stadium packed with 23,000 people is very different from a game of golf.' But every assignment has its problems, from escorting the President through the crowded streets of Washington to a cabinet meeting, to the infinite complexity of an overseas tour.

Although the President frequently flies in a Boeing 707 owned by the United States Air Force, whatever U.S.A.F. plane is carrying him has the title of 'Air Force 1'. It could be a Piper Cub or even a helicopter. When he flies to Europe, a number of cars go, too. In many respects, the handling of them is like a game of chess. One car, say, has to be in Germany while another is waiting in Britain. Once the German part of the visit has been completed, that car is shifted to (let us say) Ireland—to be ready for the President once he has finished his stay in the United Kingdom. It is all extremely complex, and it says a good deal for the medical side of the service that so few agents suffer from stress complaints (though one of them told William Manchester: 'At forty, a man on this detail is *old*').

Some heads of state, of course, prefer the President to travel in their own vehicles, and there is never any objection to this. The Secret Service men say that 'most foreign cars are well constructed from a security point of view'. And, even if they were not, one suspects that the good manners of diplomacy would prevail.

An important part of the security equipment is the follow-up car, which is also a Lincoln and which has a specially prepared engine, tyres, brakes and other systems to suit it for the job. Among the unusual features of the body are half-doors, which enable the agents to get in and out quickly. When a mêlée of spectators packs the street, and threatens to squeeze in on the presidential car, the agents can jump down on to the road, run alongside it until the hazard is over, and then re-embark in the follow-up car.

Fortunately for their peace of mind, ticker-tape processions are out of fashion—at any rate in America. In other countries, they occur occasionally, and every item in the deluge has to be scanned on its downward path in case it conceals some kind of missile. Bouquets, too, are suspect. They may hide rocks or eggs (a favourite with demonstrators). These have to be fielded by the agents. 'Sometimes,' a Secret Service man told me ruefully, 'they field them on the sides of their heads!'

At indoor functions, such as receptions, the agents tend to melt into the background, though this must not be overdone. At all times, they must be able to see what is happening. If you are talking to one of them (quite possibly not knowing who he is) and the President seems to be getting out of range, you will soon find that his attention is wandering.

Presidents vary in their attitudes to this business of being protected. President Roosevelt, who had a highly developed sense of humour, used to enjoy playing a game of hide and seek with his security men. By the very nature of the job, all Presidents must be exposed to the public view, and this makes the agents' task more difficult. Somehow, there has to be a compromise.

As the Commission on the Assassination of President Kennedy reported to President Johnson on September 24th, 1964: 'Under our system, measures must be sought to afford security without impeding the President's performance of his many functions. The protection of the President must be thorough but inconspicuous to avoid even the suggestion of a garrison state. The rights of private individuals must not be infringed.

'The degree of security that can be afforded the President of the United States is dependent to a considerable extent upon the degree of contact with the general public desired by the President. Absolute security is neither practical nor possible.'

And yet there is always the grim awareness that four Presidents have died from assassins' bullets: Lincoln, Garfield, McKinley and, latterly, Kennedy. According to Secret Service reckoning, 'about one out of every five Presidents since 1865 have been assassinated and there have been attempts on the lives of one out of every three'. At a political rally in Miami on February 15th, 1933, President-elect Roosevelt was sitting on the top of the rear seat of his car, addressing the crowd through a small microphone which he held in his hand. By sheer good fortune, he slipped down from his perch fractions of a second before a stone-mason named Giuseppe Zangara fired five rounds at him from a .32 revolver at a range of thirty feet. Four people in the crowd were wounded and the Mayor of Chicago, who was present, was killed.

On November 1st, 1950, President Harry S. Truman was staying at Blair House in Washington.[1] During the night, when the President was asleep, two Puerto Rican Nationalists, armed with automatic pistols, tried to force their way inside. In a gun battle with the would-be assassins, a White House policeman was killed: one of the Puerto Ricans and two White House policemen were wounded.

As the Secret Service agents know only too well, it is not only the 'majority' which is 'silent'. Murderers don't advertise. They strike when the moment is opportune, and a motorcade is sometimes an invitation to kill. As history had made painfully clear, the hazards of the road are not the only perils that some of the mighty have to face when they go motoring.

[1]Blair House is an historic building which, nowadays, is used as a guest house for distinguished foreign visitors. President Truman lived in it from 1948 to 1952, when the White House was being rebuilt and repainted.

Index

Adlers, 30, 37
Afghanistan, King of, 53
Alanbrooke, Field Marshal Lord, 156–9, 160, 161
Albert, Prince, 24
Albion, 72–3
Alexander, Field Marshal Lord, 160
Alexander I, King of Yugoslavia, 134–7
Alexandra, Queen, 21, 25
Alfa Romeo, 138, 139, 140, 188
Alfonso XIII, of Spain, 21, 28–9, 36, 38, 125, 164
Algeria, President of, 189
Ali Khan, 123–4
Allen, Captain C. P., 100
Alvis, 199
Anderson, Hastings, 154
Anglesey, 5th Marquess of, 15, 16, 40
Anglesey, 7th Marquess of, 16
Anne, Princess, 199
armoured cars, 50, 66, 95
Ascari, Antonio, 110, 118–19
Aston Martins, 152, 153, 159, 178, 199
Astrid, Queen of the Belgians, 121–3
Augusta, Grand Duchess of Mecklenburg-Strelitz, 28
Augustus Wilhelm, Prince, 35
Austin, 66, 155, 176, 187, 199
Automobile Association, 18, 50, 193, 195
Automobile Club de France, 102
Auto-Union, 139

Bahawalpur, Rajah of, 92
Barclay, Jack, 185
Barker coachbuilders, 60, 83, 163–4
Barnato, Wolf, 114, 115
Baroda, Gaekwar of, 84, 86
Barran, Sir David, 186, 187
Barthou, Louis, 134, 135, 136–7

Beatles, 178–9
Beatty, Warren, 171
Benjafield, J. A., 114, 115–16
Bennett, J. Gordon, 5, 38, 103
Bentley, W. O., 113, 114, 115, 116
Bentley Boys, 113–16
Bentleys, 88, 89, 113–16, 152, 161, 177, 178, 187
Benz, Karl, 2, 3, 5
Benz cars, 3, 4, 5, 29, 31, 37, 52
Berlin, 146–51
Bettina (Simone Bodin), 123–4
Bikaner, Maharajah of, 82
Birkin, Sir Henry ('Tim'), 114, 115–16
Bluebird, 110
Bollée, 72
Bombay, 84, 86, 87, 88
Bombay, Governor of, 20
Boos-Waldeck, Count, 43, 44, 45, 48
Booth, John Wilkes, 203
Boratto, Ercole, 139
Boris III, King of Bulgaria, 125
Bormann, Martin, 148, 150, 151
Bow, Clara, 168, 169–70
Braun, Eva, 147–8
Brooklands, 102, 105, 115
Brough, George, 96, 97, 100
Buchan, John, 153
Bugatti, Ettore, 125–6
Bugatti Royale, 125–6, 142
Buick, 128, 130
Burrell, Billy, 71–2
Bute, Marquess of, 19
Butler, A. S., 159–60
Buzzard, Sir Farquhar, 99
Bwalpur, Rajah of, 93

Cabrinovic, 45, 48
Cadillacs, 171, 188, 204
Cairns, H. W. B., 99

Camden, Lord, 102, 111, 112
Campbell, Sir Malcolm, 110
Caracciola, Rudolf, 38–9
Carnegie, Andrew, 19
Carol, King of Rumania, 125, 126
Carrié, Countess de, 16
Caters, Baron de, 102, 103
Catherine the Great, Empress of Russia, 65
Cavan, Earl of, 57–8
Cavan, Lady, 58
Chaika, 68
Charles, Prince, 199
Chasseloup-Laubat, Marquess de, 102
chauffeurs, 69–80, 139, 142–51, 194–9, 200
Chevrolet, 167, 176
Chiron, Louis, 52
Chittys, 108
Chryslers, 188, 205
Churchill, Lord Edward, 17
Churchill, Sir Winston, 17, 143, 157–9, 166, 193, 206, 207, 208
Churchill, Lady, 193
Citroëns, 164, 188, 189–90
Clement, F. C., 114
Clément-Bayard, 186
coachbuilding, 9, 15, 60
Coatalen, Louis, 105, 111
Cole, Lord, 187
Collins, Peter, 111, 117, 118
Columbia, 25
Connaught, Duke of, 32
Coogan, Jackie, 168, 169
Coolidge, Calvin, 205
Cooper, Gary, 171
Cornfeld, Bernie, 186
Cowan, Theo, 177
Craig, Gordon, 120
Crosby, Bing, 171
Crossley, 128, 130, 154
Crossman, Major R. F., 165
Curtis, Lionel, 97
Curzon, Lord, 84, 85
Czolgosz, Leon, 203

Daimler, Gottlieb, 2, 3, 4–5
Daimler-Benz company, 38, 40, 68, 132, 140, 141, 142, 173
Daimlers, 3, 4, 5, 6, 9, 12, 13, 21, 22, 23–4, 26, 27, 29, 31, 32, 36, 39, 52, 88, 89, 90, 91, 126, 127, 128–32, 137, 179, 181–4, 186, 197, 199, 200
Dallas assassination, 208
Darracq, 71, 86, 105, 112
Davis, S. C. H. (Sammy), 103, 107, 108, 109, 111, 114
Davnay, Major Hugh, 51
Daytona (World Land Speed Record, 1911), 52
Dean, James, 169, 172–6
Decauville, 18
Delage, 134, 135, 137
Delaunay-Bellevilles, 50–1, 54, 60–1, 72
Delhi, 83–4, 86, 92
Dietrich, de, 32
Dion, Count Albert de, 102
Dion, de, 12, 71, 86
Dion-Bouton, 102
Diviak, Carlo, 43–4, 45, 46, 47, 48, 49

Dobson, R. P., 186
Docker, Sir Bernard, 182
Docker, Lady, 181–3
Docker Daimlers, 89, 181–4
Doyle, Sir Arthur Conan, 32
Duesenbergs, 171, 206
Dunaway, Faye, 171
Duncan, Isadora, 19, 119–20
Duncan, Raymond, 121
Dunfee, Jack, 114
Dunn, Reginald, 57
Duvallier, Dr., 189
Dybenko, 64

Edison, Thomas, 206
Edmunds, Henry, 18, 19
Edward VII, 21–8, 32, 35, 38, 83, 126
Eilers, Wilhelm, 187–8
Eisenhower, General, 157, 205, 207
Ekland, Britt, 177
electric cars, 7–8, 21, 25, 27, 72
Elizabeth, the Queen Mother, 129
Elizabeth II, 126, 193, 198, 199, 200, 201, 208
Ellis, Hon. Evelyn, 12, 22
Epstein, Brian, 178
Exeter, Marquess of, 101–2

Fairbanks, Douglas, 171
Faisal, King, 167
Fanu, Admiral Sir Michael Le, 197
Fanu, Lady Le, 197
Faridkot, Rajah of, 92
Farina, Nino, 118
Farina, Pinin, 138
Farouk, King of Egypt, 125, 142, 173
Ferrari, 111, 123, 139, 174, 176
Ferrari, Enzo, 138
Fiats, 36, 72, 188
Firestone, Harvey, 205
Foch, Marshal, 51, 52
Forbes Robertson, Sir Johnson, 169
Ford, Edsel, 204
Ford, Henry, 19–20, 67–8, 204–5
Fords, 68, 90, 95, 130, 160, 161, 169, 170–1, 200, 204, 206, 211 (*see also* Lincolns)
Francis, Prince of Teck, 27, 32
Frankenberg, Richard von, 188
Franz Ferdinand, Archduke of Austria, 41–2, 43, 44–8, 135, 137
Frederick of Saxony, King, 21
French, Field Marshal Sir John, 52
French Grand Prix, 108–9, 111
Froessac, M., 136, 137

Gable, Clark, 171
Gandhi, Mahatma, 95
Garfield, James A., 204, 214
Garner, James, 170
Garnett, David, 98
Gaulle, Charles de, 189–90, 208
George, David Lloyd, 53, 193
George V, 27–8, 32, 52, 53, 88, 91, 126–8, 130, 155
George VI, 126, 127, 128–9, 130, 131–2, 199
Georges, General Alphonse, 134, 135, 136
Gibson, Hoot, 169
Ginther, Richie, 174

Goebbels, Joseph, 140, 148–50
Goebbels, Frau, 149–50
Goering, Hermann, 68, 140
Gorky, 67
Gort, Lord, 156
Gräf and Stift touring car, 43
Graham-Paige, 188
Grant, Ulysses S., 202
Gregory, Masten, 174
Guensche, 147, 148, 150, 151
Guinness, Algernon, 103–4, 105
Guinness, Kenelm (Bill), 103, 104–6, 107
Guinness, Nigel Lee, 103, 106
Guiteau, Charles J., 203
Gulbenkian, Nubar, 184–5
Gurney, Dan, 174, 175
Gustav, King of Sweden, 125

Haig, Field Marshal Sir Douglas, 54
Haldane, Viscount, 26
Harding, Warren G., 203, 204, 205
Hardwicke, Sir Cedric, 172
Harlow, Jean, 171
Harmsworth, Alfred (later Lord Northcliffe), 2, 9, 12–15, 19, 67
Harrach, Count Franz von, 43, 44, 46, 47
Harris, Richard, 179
Harrison, George, 179
Hawthorn, Mike, 117–18
Hefner, Hugh, 185, 186–7
Henry, Prince of Prussia, 21, 29–30, 31, 32
Herkomer, Professor Hubert von, 30
Hess, Rudolf, 140, 144
Hesse, Grand Duke of, 31
Hill, Frank Ernest, 205
Hill, Phil, 174
Hillman, 193
Hilton, Conrad, 185
Himmler, Heinrich, 140
Hindenburg, Field Marshal Paul von, 52, 132
Hirohito, Emperor of Japan, 126, 137
Hispano-Suiza, 29, 164, 178
Hitler, Adolf, 68, 132, 138, 139, 140–51, 175, 196
Hollywood, 169–71
Hooper coachbuilders, 60, 89, 90, 91, 127, 128, 129–30, 131, 167, 182, 183
Hoover, Herbert, 205
Hope Gosse, Dr., 99
Horch, 37, 140, 160
Horthy, Admiral, 142
Housden, William, 194–6
House of Commons Motor Club, 191, 192–3
Howe, Earl, 102
Hughes, Howard, 185
Hugnet, General, 52
Humber, 130, 156, 159, 193
Hutton, Barbara, 176
Hyderabad, Nizam of, 90, 92

Ibn Saud, King, 166
Imperial Automobile Club, 31
India, motoring in, 81–93
Ironside, Field Marshal Lord, 153–6
Isotta-Fraschini, 170, 188
Italian Grand Prix, Monza (1924), 109–10
Italy, motor car in, 61

Jaguars, 176, 186, 187
Jaipur, Maharajah of, 82
Jannings, Emil, 171
Jarrott, Charles, 103
Jellinek, Emile, 4–5, 51
Jellinek, Maja, 5
Jellinek, Mercedes, 4, 5
Jenatzy, Camille, 118
Jensens, 171
Jind, Maharajah of, 92
John XXIII, Pope, 189
Johnson, Lyndon B., 202, 208, 213
Jolson, Al, 171

Karno, Fred, 168
Keiser, 17, 18
Keleman, Peter, 133–4, 135, 136, 137
Kellner, 60
Kemptka, Erich, 142–51
Kenelm, Algernon, 103
Kennedy, John F., 202, 208, 213, 214
Kennedy, Robert, 210
Kerensky, Alexander, 62–6
Khrushchev, Nikita, 208
Kipling, Rudyard, 20
Kitchener, Lord, 53, 54, 56, 58, 84
Knyff, Chevalier René de, 102
Korff, Baron Nicolas, 60
Küssnacht, 122, 123

La Turbie, 106–7, 109, 110
Lagonda, 199
Lanchester, 20, 128, 132
Lancia, 138–9
Land speed record bids, 103–4, 105, 108, 110, 111, 112
Land-Rovers, 93, 165, 199, 200
Langtry, Lily, 26–7
Lauder, Sir Harry, 169
Lawrence, T. E., 94–100
Le Mans 24-Hour Race, 4, 38, 111, 114
Lee, Belinda, 169
Lee, Lord and Lady, 195
Leland, Henry M., 204
Lenin, 61, 62, 65, 66–7
Lennon, John, 178–9
Leopold II of Belgium, 21
Leopold III of Belgium, 121–3
Letzer, Sydney, 24
Levassor, 12
Leycester, Lieutenant-Commander W. R., 59
Leyland, 130
Lincoln, Abraham, 203, 214
Lincolns, 171, 188, 204, 205, 207–9, 213
Linge, 148, 150, 151
Lloyd, Selwyn, 194
Lonsdale, Earl of, 17–18
Lotus, 177
Lotz, Professor, 187
Lucas, 79
Ludwig I of Bavaria, 21

McCartney, Paul, 178
McKinley, President, 202–3, 214
Macmillan, Harold, 194, 195, 196
McQueen, Steve, 170
Madagascar, President of, 189
Magnus, Sir Philip, 26
Manchester, William, 208, 212

Mannerheim, Field Marshal, 142
Mansfield, Jayne, 169
Manuel II of Portugal, 21
March, Earl of (later the Duke of
    Richmond and Gordon), 102
Maria Pia, Queen of Portugal, 21
Marie, Queen of Yugoslavia, 134
Marie Fedorovna, Dowager Empress of
    Russia, 59
Marseilles, 134–7
Mary, Queen, 27, 28, 32, 52, 53, 91,
    128, 131
Maserati, 115, 139
Masserand, M., 120–1
Matthewson, R. N., 90–1
Maudslay 30 h.p., 52–3
Maybach, Wilhelm, 5
Maybachs, 187–8
Medina, Earl of, 162
Mercedes, 4–5, 6, 13, 17, 18, 35, 36, 37,
    40, 52, 68, 72, 106, 108, 109, 110,
    125, 126, 132, 139, 140, 141, 145, 171,
    176, 178, 186, 188
Mikhaylov, Ivan, 133
Mille, Cecil B. de, 170
Miller, Lieutenant J. M., 199
Minis, 177–8, 180, 181, 186, 193
Miss England II, 112–13
Mix, Tom, 168, 169
Monkees, 177–8
Montagu, 3rd Lord, 6, 9
Montagu Motor Museum, 25, 159
Montaignée, Marquess de, 102
Montgomery, Field Marshal Lord,
    159–60, 165–6
Monza, 109–10, 139
Moore, George, 20
Morgan, 176
Morgan, John Pierpont, 19
Morris, 192, 193
Mors, 15, 40, 72
Moscow, 59, 60, 62, 66, 68
Moseley, Sir Oswald, 19
motor cycles, 92–3, 96–100
motor racing and the aristocracy,
    102–16
Motor Show, 182, 183
Motor Union, 18, 84–7
Mountbatten, Lord, 92, 162–6
Mountbatten, Lady, 163
Mulliner, 19
Mussolini, Benito, 61, 68, 132, 138–9,
    140

Nabarro, Sir Gerald, 191–2, 193
Nabha, Maharajah of, 20
naval and military motoring, 153–67,
    197–8
Nevins, Allan, 205
Newcastle, 7th Duke of, 73
Nixon, Edwin R., 187
Nobel, Alfred Bernhard, 20
Northumberland, Duke of, 19
Nuvolari, Tazio, 139

Oban, 79
Odessa, 59
Olivier, Lord, 172
Onassis, Aristotle, 181
Opels, 30, 37
Ossipor, Count Constantine, 154

O'Sullivan, Joseph, 57
Oswald, Lee Harvey, 208
Owen, Professor O. Wyn, 108

Packhard, 121, 122
Paine, David A., 108
Panhard, 12, 13, 28, 86
Paris, 51, 120, 133
Paris World Fair (1889), 3
Parker, Percy G., 154, 155–9, 161
Patiald, Maharajah of, 51
Paul I, Tsar of Russia, 65
Paul, Pope, 188, 189
Pearson, John, 153
Persia, Shah of, 25, 173
Pétain, Marshal, 52
Philip, Prince, 199, 200, 209
Pickford, Mary, 171
Pierce-Arrows, 63, 64, 79, 203, 204, 205
Piétri, Jacques, 135
Pius XI, Pope, 188
Pollange, Baron de, 107
Porsche, 142, 151, 172, 173, 174, 175
Porsche, Ferdinand, 29, 109, 139, 173
Pound, Admiral Sir Dudley, 161–2
Pound, George, 162
presidential passengers, 202–14
Prince Henry Trial, 31, 32–3
Princip, Gavrilo, 41, 42, 47, 48, 137
Pskov, 63
Pudukotal, Rajah of, 86
Pulitzer, Joseph, 20

Quandt, Harald, 149
Quincey, Mrs. de, 20

R.A.C.: 1,000-mile trial to Edinburgh
    (1900), 14; patronised by Edward
    VII, 27, 32; takes Prince Henry Cup,
    33; competitions committee, 102;
    and the House of Commons Motor
    Club, 193
rajahs and their cars, 82–3, 88–93
Reliant, 199
Renault, Louis, 71–2
Renaults, 13, 16, 51, 176
Reventlow, Lance, 176
Reynaud, Paul, 156
Ribbentrop, Joachim von, 140, 146
Richards, Sir Gordon, 176
Richardson, Sir Ralph, 171–2
Rio, Dolores del, 170
Robertson, Sir William, 54–5
Robinson, George, 204
Rolls, Charles Stewart, 6, 18, 19
Rolls, S. C., 6, 95, 96
Rolls-Royce: Silver Ghost, 9, 19; first
    models (1904), 9; early owners, 13;
    birth of, 19; in First World War,
    51–2, 53–4, 55, 56, 57–8; in Russia,
    59–60, 61, 66–7, 68, 72; in India, 82,
    83, 88, 89, 90; in Pakistan, 91–2;
    engines power *Miss England II*, 112;
    takes over Bentley, 113; royal
    owners, 126, 199, 200; Monty's,
    159–60; General Sikorski's, 161;
    Phantom III, 161, 167, 193;
    Mountbatten's, 163–5; Churchill's
    gift to Ibn Saud, 166–7; in show
    business, 168–9, 171, 172, 176, 177;
    Silver Cloud, 177, 179; Aristotle

Rolls-Royce—*cont.*
  Onassis's, 181; Gulbenkian's, 184;
  Lord Cole's, 187; Lloyd George's, 193;
  Phantom IV, 199; President Wilson's,
  204
Rome, 61
Rommel, Field Marshal Erwin, 160
Roosevelt, Franklin Delano, 166, 205,
  206–7, 213
Roosevelt, Theodore, 203
Rothschild, Charles, 3, 4
Rothschild, Baron Henri de, 3, 4
Rothschild, Miriam, 4
Rothschild, Philippe de, 3–4
Rothschild, Baron Robert de, 52
Rover, 176, 193, 194, 197, 199–200
Rowley, James J., 207
Royal Family's motoring, 199–201
royalty and the motor car, 21–33,
  34–40, 125–32, 199–201
Royce, Henry, 5, 14, 18–19
Russia, Tsar of (Nicholas II), 21, 38,
  59, 60–1, 62, 64, 67
Russia and the motor car, 59–68
Russian Revolution, 59, 62–6

Sachsen-Mainigen, Princess of, 31
St. Petersburg, 51, 60, 62–6
Salomons, Sir David, 9–11
San Sebastian, 28, 104
Sarajevo assassination (1914), 41–9
Saxony, King of, 35
Schreck, 142, 144
Schroeder, 38, 39
Scindia, Maharaja of, 86
Scotland, motoring in, 79
Scott-Montagu, Hon. John (later 2nd
  Lord Montagu of Beaulieu), 6, 7, 8, 19,
  22–3, 191
Segrave, Sir Henry, 28, 110–11, 112–13
Sellers, Peter, 176–7
Serpollet, M., 25–6
Serpollet steamer, 9, 13, 25, 86
Shaw, G. B., 96, 119
show business on wheels, 168–79
Shrewsbury, Lord, 28
Sikorski, General, 161
Simms, F. R., 22
Singer, Paris E., 19, 120
Snyder, 206
Sophie, Duchess of Austria, 42, 43, 44,
  45, 47
Soumarakoff, Count, 60
Spanish Grand Prix, 28, 111
Speer, Albert, 146
Spencer, Earl, 52
Stafford convertible, 205
Stalin, Joseph, 64, 68, 132, 138, 140,
  206
Standard, 154
Stanton, Oliver, 23–4
status symbols, motor cars as, 180–90
steam cars, 6, 8, 72
Steyr, 146
Studebaker, 186
Sunbeam, 105, 111, 112, 176
Swanson, Gloria, 171
Symmons, Captain R., 165

Taft, William Howard, 203
Targa Florio (1924), 38
taxis, 184–5
Taylor, Elizabeth, 175
Terraine, John, 164
Thomas, Parry, 108
Thrupp and Maberley, 20
Thunderbird, 153
Todt, Dr. Fitz, 140
top people's motoring, 191–201
Tourist Trophy Races, Isle of Man, 103
tragedies, motoring, 117–24, 169
Tripoli race (1933), 115; circuit, 139
Triumph: motor cycle, 96; Herald, 187
Truman, Harry S., 205–6, 207, 214

United States and the motor car, 63,
  67, 68, 202–14

Valentino, Rudolf, 170
Vanderbilt, A. G., 20
Vanderbilt, W. K., 5
Vauxhall: Prince Henry car, 29, 58;
  Motor Company's Russian contract,
  51; at the Staff College, 154–5, 200
Victoria, Princess, 126–7, 155–6
Victoria, Queen, 12, 22, 28, 29, 32, 103,
  131
Victoria Eugenia, Queen of Spain, 29
Vinner, N. V., 64, 65
Voisin, 170
Volkswagen, 140, 141, 174, 187

war and the motor car: (1914–18),
  50–8, 69–70; in Lawrence's desert
  campaign, 95–6; (1939–45), 156–62
Washington, 209
Water speed record, 112–13
Weissmuller, Johnny, 171
Wenck, General, 147, 149
Werlin, Jacob, 140–1
Werner, Christian, 38–9
Westminster, Duke of, 7, 51
Whetherich, Rolf, 173–6
White, Graham, 15
Wilhelm II, Kaiser, 5, 17, 18, 21, 26,
  28, 29, 32
Wilhelm II, King of Württemberg, 21,
  34–40
Williamson, Henry, 98–9
Willingdon, Lord, 130, 131
Wilson, Harold, 194, 195, 196–7
Wilson, Field Marshal Sir Henry, 55–7
Wilson, Lady, 57
Wilson, Woodrow, 203–4
Windermere, 112–13
Windsor, Duke of (Edward VIII), 29,
  128
Wolseley, 9, 87, 88
World Championship of Drivers, 117

Zborowski, Count Eliot, 106–7, 108, 109
Zborowski, Count Louis, 107–10
Zerajic, 42
Zim, 68
Zog, King of Albania, 125
Zuylen de Nyevell, Baron de, 102
Zangara, Giuseppe, 214